Advance P

"What a magically refresh welcome and unique voice subjects, her craft—and most importantly, herself."
— Lon Milo DuQuette, author of *Enochian Vision Magick* and *My Life with the Spirits*

"At a time when most books on occult spirituality splash around the shallows or pass down recipes by rote, Thorn Coyle's *Kissing the Limitless* takes the reader on a dizzying and rewarding plunge into the deep places of magic. Thorn's passion, knowledge, and extensive experience of magic inform every page of this significant new work."
— John Michael Greer, author of *The Druid Magic Handbook*

"Lucid, frank, creative, and firm, Thorn Coyle is an engaging guide to the work she charts in *Kissing the Limitless*. Though she draws on a wide range of sources for inspiration, Coyle's work is rooted in a direct, practical concern for discerning and enacting practices that will make life richer, more solidly grounded, and more rewarding."
— Eugene V. Gallagher, Rosemary Park Professor of Religious Studies at Connecticut College and author of *The New Religious Movements Experience in America*

"What Thorn Coyle does in this book is no less than the miraculous. She offers real insights and real exercises that lead to a new form of the Great Work that results in a unification of the modes of the mystic, the magician, the witch, and the shaman. If you are willing to apply the fullness of yourself to what is contained within these pages, you will be transformed."
— Ivo Dominguez, Jr., author and elder in the Assembly of the Sacred Wheel

"Masterful magician and extraordinary witch, Thorn Coyle places the emphasis of magic upon the Great Work, not only for the development of the self, but also for the entire planet. Weaving together many traditional spiritual perspectives with personal insights drawn from her own practice, she guides us through the elements of the world, into the darkness of 'demons' and back into the light of reintegration. *Kissing the Limitless* is both an amazing manual and a much-needed map for those on the path of self-possession."

— Christopher Penczak, author of *The Inner Temple of Witchcraft*

"Rarely do you come across a comprehensive magical text that approaches the subject of personality integration with such directness, clarity, and compassion. Thorn succeeds in not only the call to awaken, but to arise and take possession of life and light. In the final portion of *Kissing the Limitless*, a more mystical and subtle aspect of alchemy unfolds; an identification with unity has taken the place of the sleep of fragmentation."

— J. Aeptha Jennette, Director of Light Haven

"Coyle offers readers a deeper level of magical work at a time when renewed engagement and rediscovered purpose is essential not only to our fulfillment, but to the future."

— Phyllis Curott, Priestess and author of *Book of Shadows, Witch Crafting* and *The Love Spell*

Kissing
the
Limitless

Deep Magic and the Great Work of
Transforming Yourself and the World

T. Thorn Coyle

WEISERBOOKS
San Francisco, CA / Newburyport, MA

First published in 2009 by
Red Wheel/Weiser, LLC
With offices at:
500 Third Street, Suite 230
San Francisco, CA 94107
www.redwheelweiser.com

ISBN: 978-1-57863-435-4
Library of Congress Cataloging-in-Publication Data available upon request.

Cover and interior design by Maija Tollefson
Typeset in Bembo
Cover illustration © Lunagraphica/iStockphoto
Author photo © Paul Nordin

Printed in Canada
TCP
10 9 8 7 6 5 4 3 2 1

Contents

Acknowledgments

I give thanks to all of my students, teachers, friends, and peers, and to every spiritual seeker and magic worker engaged in the Great Work of becoming fully human and fully divine. You all inspire my way. Thank you to everyone at Weiser for your efforts on behalf of this book. Thanks to Valerie Walker and Lillitu Shahar for graphics help, to Ruby and Ellen for being first readers, to Sarah Whedon for research and her 11th-hour indexing help, and to Robert and Jonathan for love and support.

May our work be blessed. May our work be a blessing.

LVX Amor,
T. Thorn Coyle

Introduction

The price of kissing is your life.

—MEVLANA JALALLUDIN RUMI (IN *Open Secret* BY
JOHN MOYNE AND COLEMAN BARKS)

Each human has the potential for full integration: the constant awareness of and union with our emotional, mental, physical, and spiritual
parts. In exploring the Great Work spoken of by ancient alchemists
and magicians, *Kissing the Limitless* provides a contemporary spiritual
map for attaining clear communication with one's divine nature, and
further, opening to a luminous connection with the Infinite Divine.

Taking possession of our souls opens our lives to vibrancy, grace
and power. As students of the Great Work of transformation, we make
magic as we never have before and step fully into our humanity and our
divinity. Be we activists, parents, teachers, or planters of trees for a new
generation, we take our rightful places in the world.

This is a book of deep magic, of high magic, of magic for our hearts
and souls. The potency of this magic rests deeply within us, and the universe supports its unfolding. We step into the flow of Love.

Magic is the marriage of breath, will, and desire. Continuous exploration of these three weds our deepest parts to our highest, leading
us into self-possession. This place of wholeness is one of human health
and integration, which is the necessary step toward enlightenment.
Anyone can have a spiritual epiphany or a flash of deep connection,
but for most of us these will quickly fade. Sustained change, however,
requires a good foundation, and building a foundation requires effort.
With breath, will, *and* desire, all things become possible.

This book helps to guide seekers through the stages of growth and
personal consciousness that will enable us to step into *inclusive* consciousness, a consciousness that encompasses the personal, political, environmental, social, mental, and transpersonal. Inclusive consciousness

enables us to reach the Limitless, also known as the Divine, Goddess, and God Herself. The magic of self-possession is the magic of inclusion.

Self-possession integrates all of our parts with the fullness of our divinity. Reaching the self-possessed stage, rather than simply walking through random states of presence or the lack thereof, requires the examination and commitment of every facet of self. Rumi's price for kissing the fabric of all is that of pledging our whole lives. It is worth the cost.

One man, upon being introduced to these concepts and practices, remarked, "I just woke up for the first time in forty-five years. I didn't even know I was asleep." And therein lies the power of magical practice and the hope for integration. Too often we, like the man above, have been practitioners of a spiritual path for many years and have never tasted the possibility of deep magic or touched the core of the work. We have practiced the form without grasping the essence.

The world needs us to touch the essence of our very souls and, in doing so, take hands with the soul of the world.

This is not a book about politics, social justice, saving the environment, or helping a world in pain, and yet it is deeply so. The concepts in this book do not take the place of kindness or speaking out or refusing to comply with the orders of evil and disconnection. Yet in doing the work in this book, in bringing about the Great Work of alchemical integration, each act of kindness and courage will reverberate that much more loudly through this world and all the realms seen and unseen. In setting ourselves the task of self-possession, our lives will ring true. *That* truth will indeed set us free. Our freedom, our autonomy, will bring about the great revolution and evolution that is possible for every being on this planet.

I am a woman for whom the ways of justice are important. I have worked fiercely for clean water and soil, and to cease the testing of nuclear weapons and the waging of wars. I have fed the hungry, sat with the dying, and listened to the ravings of the mentally ill. I attempted to live my life according to the precepts of love, strength, and honor, though, of course, I often fell short of this. But I never really knew love, power, and honor until I tasted the sweetness of the barely known. Self-possession brought me into myself, and that enabled the eventual merging of that very self into the All. I have since returned home to the place of beauty and integration, balancing severity and mercy in heart and hands. The work continues, and the world is still wounded, but I have seen the gates of eternity and know firmly as I know nothing else: liberty is possible. Liberty is happening right now.

In this book, I will talk a lot about practice, about work, about energy, emotion, ethics, and still more practice. But I want to state quite clearly that the undercurrent to all of this is the fabric of love. It is love that keeps us seeking, and it is love that enfolds us during the journey. Love helps us to commit.

This book is written for all serious spiritual seekers. I myself am a magic worker and a Witch, and these are the backbones of my practice. However, having kissed the Limitless, I see that there are many methods that lead one to truth. Diligence of application is what is necessary. Whatever your path—Shamanism, Sufism, Heathenism, Thelema, Kabbalah, Hermeticism, mystic Christianity, Witchcraft, the Gurdjieff Work, Alchemy, Buddhism—I hope some of the teachings in this book will help you in the Great Work, the work the world needs us to do. Once we have tasted limitless love, limitless light, and limitless power, there is no turning back.

Source and Inspiration

I have been a spiritual seeker my whole life, ever since I was surrounded by light at the age of seven. It was a palpable, mystic experience that at the time I could only call *God*. All these years later, having come and gone from that sense of grace, I am once again surrounded by light, though it is not always so visible, because it has become incorporated more thoroughly into my being. My years of seeking have brought me more clearly into myself and into the firm knowledge that God Herself is right here, as close as my heart.

My path for the last twenty-five years has been enmeshed in neo-Paganism and the Craft. In my search for spiritual truth and integration, I have also taken initiation with the Mevlevi whirling dervishes, studied the mystics of all the great traditions, sat in meditation with Buddhist friends, spent time in the Gurdjieff Work, and made peace with my Catholic upbringing. More recently in my search, I have studied Kabbalah, ceremonial magic, and Thelema. All of this was in the service of trying to get context for the rapid changes my body and soul were undergoing. I had a feeling that other seekers had been through similar experiences, and luckily friends were able to point me to sources that broadened my understanding.

To give an idea of where the work in this book comes from, I can say that the cosmology is inspired by the Feri Tradition, which is my religious base. The exercises, other than soul alignment and the "Cleansing Life Force" rite, (see p. 28) are my own, but an astute reader will likely hear echoes from whatever tradition she has immersed herself in. This is because all seekers come to a similar place if they dig long enough.

For example, a student of mine once said, "It is clear that Thorn is influenced by Israel Regardie." Actually, I came to my reading of Regardie quite late, during a period of trying to make sense of my experiences, only to find that I was reinventing the wheel. He trod the ground well before me, and I happened to have unknowingly reached some of his conclusions all these decades later. Simply stated, magic works, and deep practice gives eventual results. If readers want to pinpoint my greatest influences, they will need to look to Victor Anderson and G. I. Gurdjieff. Throw in a dash of Rumi, some Crowley, Dogen, and Hildegard of Bingen, and you have the beginnings of the soup that has been bubbling within me since my Catholic childhood.

That is how it goes with this work; the only purity is the gold we refine within. Every true student finds teaching all around him. I hope you find something in this book that resonates and is of help, just as I have found help or confirmation in all the authors and books whose quotes pepper this one. The results of the work in the lives of my students all over the world—their questions, comments, and experiences—also inform this book.

I have walked my own path, forging ahead and often blundering from lack of coherent teaching. I sought help from wherever I could get it, even from sources I had rejected years earlier. After the changes occurred within me, I was able to say, "Oh, I guess those old medieval magicians I've ignored all this time were onto *this* thing," and "Right, there are steps that this relatively secular thinker has articulated that feel similar to what happened in me, and hey, maybe they're similar to the teachings of that Sufi mystic too!" Some religions have gone seriously awry, as do all our human systems. But the true seeker can find nourishment anywhere. That is part of our magic.

I have followed the Craft since age sixteen. It is my religion. The Star Goddess moves in my life in ways that inspire me. But I also see her touch everywhere, in anything that smacks of truth and connection to Source. She is the All, after all, so why would my experience of limitlessness not also show up in the rocking of the *rebbe* and the stillness of Zen?

The world needs us to come into our fullness. We live in a time of ripeness and incredible availability of resources. We should use these in the service of the Great Work that awakens our souls. The insights that may come from the book you hold in your hands are best served by diligent application within some formal system. Pick one way to work and stick with it. I have. Then draw inspiration from how others work too. It will help keep us all on the path.

May our lives be born from the beauty of darkness, and shine with the possibility of light.

How to Read This Book

This book is primarily written for the seeker who already has a base of practice, so you can use it in concert with whatever tradition you are currently involved in. If you don't work in a community of practice or some magical system, I recommend seeking one out. For those who live far from a viable community, my earlier book, *Evolutionary Witchcraft,* is designed as a self-training course.

There are many ways to work with this book. First, it can simply be read through to lend insight to whatever phase of the journey we are on. There are "reflections" sprinkled through each chapter that should be of help to both the advanced and beginning practitioner. Each chapter also contains some exercises under "doing the work" that are highly recommended for those newer to the Great Work and for those who might find holes in their current spiritual practice. The index breaks "doing the work" into categories, so you can see which ones you really need to focus on, and which you can let go.

This was a difficult book to write because while I wanted to tailor it for those who were actively seeking self-possession and full integration, during the writing of it, I realized that many more of us are not quite there yet. So I added in some foundational work, in the hope that it would point beginning seekers to other sources and challenge established magic workers to rethink our practice. We can all grow lazy, and sometimes need outside help or even just a different viewpoint. The final chapters of the book may feel beyond some of us who are closer to the beginning of our journey, or even to those of us who have grown lax in our work. That is fine. I know in my own path that reading the stories of those who are well beyond me has been a helpful inspiration. I remembered these men and women when the time was right and revisited those sources.

Actively working this book can take between two and four years. After the initial reading to see where we are going, the work comes in three levels. Our current spiritual practice is level one: our primary work, which is establishing a healthy spiritual foundation. I include some foundational practices in part 1 to help with this phase. The first two parts of the book are level two: our secondary work, which is making certain we are sound in body, mind, emotion, sex, and spirit, and have developed will and ethics. This will keep us going for the long haul. Parts 1 and 2 can be worked over the course of one and a half years or more, depending on how far along our practice already is. Part 3 represents level three: the work that leads us further into connection with our Godhood and opens us to self-possession, also known as the Great Work, or "Knowledge and Conversation with our Holy Guardian Angel." The work of part 3 will take anywhere from six months to four years, again, depending on how much work we have already done, how consistent and deep our practice is, and how integrated our personalities have become.

Here is a guide:

1. Read the book all the way through.
2. Ascertain where your work is:
   a. Are you closer to the beginning of your path, or have you grown rusty? Look in appendix A for "foundational" exercises (see p. 248) and make certain you incorporate them into your practice.
   b. Are you well established in a personal spiritual practice and working a path deeply? Look in the index for "foundational," "deepening," and "rounding out" exercises (see appendix A on p. 248) to see what you may be missing in your current roster, or what may need strengthening.
   c. Were you actively working on self-possession, or "knowledge and conversation," before picking up this book? Look over the above question and, if you are in pretty good shape, dive right into part 3 (see p. 173) of the book after you've read the whole thing. Then look in the Appendix and tackle the "integrating" exercises. If you are missing some of the shadow or demon work, please do not skip those sections of the book. Your work

will proceed with greater certainty if you embrace these parts fully and bring them on board to help with the Work.

3. Set aside time each day to dive into practice.

Each segment of the book is also assigned Deity to help us look at some of the concepts from a deeper religious viewpoint. The first segment is under the hand of the Star Goddess, God Herself. The second works with the Divine Twins as poles both inside and outside of us. The third segment births the Peacock, born of the reintegration of all opposites into a new and beautiful whole. If these deities do not work for you, feel free to use your own matrons or patrons to help you delve into the practices at hand.

PART I

Breath—The Star Goddess

The essence of God is that there is no essence of God, for God is all and nothing, here, now, and forever.

—Reb Yerachmiel ben Yisrael (in *Open Secret* by John Moyne and Coleman Barks)

In the dust of Her feet are the hosts of heaven/and Her star sequined hair/ Is crowned with a coven of six and seven/Blue suns burning there.

—Victor H. Anderson (in his poem "Quakoralina," in *Thorns of the Blood Rose*)

The Star Goddess breathes out and everything rises. God Herself breathes in, and all things contract. Her breath, the breath of the Limitless, infuses and connects every living thing. We can connect with this breath. We can dance the dance of all creation, with her, for we are reflections of her beauty.

God Herself is beyond gender. She is all gender and no gender. She is the great Zero, the limitless, holder of the Cosmic Egg from which all life flows and to which all life returns. I do not think of God Herself as One, because that separates her from all else. Rather, thinking of her as Zero, the circumference that includes everything and the center point around which everything else revolves, is closer to my experienced reality.[1] There is nothing that is not part of the fabric of God Herself. Another name for this fabric is love.

Monotheists almost had it right in speaking of the unity of love, but they did not yet have the number zero, the cipher, the void. By naming something *one*, they were trying to get at its unity. They were not able to realize at the time that naming something *one*, instead of *all*, can be a first separation; a distancing that can turn the All into the other. And therein lies trouble. The One, rather than remaining a unifying force, can become a separate being, and that separation opens a deep wound of alienation, jealousy, and war.

Mystics of all religions and cultures have experienced the truth of the wholeness of God Herself as Zero and All, regardless of the name their religion assigns to this concept of deity. Those who are not mystics have not always felt this unity, and have waged many bloody wars over the separation and disconnection they have felt.

We sometimes fight these wars inside of ourselves, whether we believe in many Gods, no Gods, one God, or a limitless divinity that is All. We can feel separate from God Herself. We can disconnect from the pattern of love. The practices in this book lead us back into connection and the flow of the Limitless. In that flow *we* can become the center to her circumference, and we can learn to include everything. The Limitless is beyond duality, beyond black and white, dark and light, anger and hope, though she is within all of these and expressed through all of these. The Limitless is zero and many, nothing and all.

As individuals, we are whole, a unified being. Yet our parts can act as though they are separate. Our minds and emotions can fight, each insisting that it, and it alone, is "I." This is the lie that causes conflict and dissolution within. However, there are ways to remember that we are her reflections, and reflect the universe in turn. Just as all possibility abides in love, all possibility rests within us.

We must practice presence, bringing our whole lives to bear on our spiritual work. There is nothing beyond this. The Star Goddess is everything. Born of her are the Divine Twins, figures of the duality we parse our emptiness into. Their union brings us the Peacock, the angel that synthesizes disparate parts back into the wholeness reflected in his mother's mirror.

To practice presence, we first draw in breath. We then notice our feet, thighs, shoulders, and the back of our head. We see what is in front of us and feel what is within. We are moving through the world, as we are, encountering the world as it is. Every leaf on each tree practices with us. Every scrap of paper on the sidewalk is another piece of life.

We need to make magic from where we are, not where we should be. We can set ourselves up for failure because we are not honest about who we are right in this moment. Magic is simple. But to get simple takes a lot of practice, and a lot of presence.

Let us breathe in and be present, right now. God Herself abides within and around us. This is reality. Step through the door.

ONE

Discovering Possibility

Beyond anger, beneath fear, past numbness and alienation, there rests within each of us the possibility to be more than we are now. Magic is available. Wholeness is just around the corner. The power of wholeness is the power to change the world.

Our walking through life as internally splintered human beings with compartmentalized lives has compromised human dignity, whole cultures, and the precious biosphere. Humans live in a crisis of our own making, and *living in this way is not necessary.*

These are times when all humans need to be the best beings we can. Every day, a new species goes on the endangered list. Every day, war is waged, or a child starves. None of this is inevitable; it has just grown to seem so because of epidemic states of disconnection and isolation. The time to reconnect is here.

We can become fully present in our lives: present to self, to others, to work, to joy, and to Deity. Our current condition of dissonance, disparity, and scattered self is not a condition that need persist. Simply because it is the common human experience does not mean it is the *only* one. Living a disharmonious existence is not our lot in life. But to shift that, we need to learn to choose something different.

Included in this book is a lot of work on becoming more self-aware, examining our unconscious, looking at thought and emotions, and getting our everyday lives in full working order. One may ask why a book on self-possession—coming into Godhood—contains so many "mundane" exercises.

I have done this for specific reasons. We can buy books or do practices that only focus on awakening or on enlightenment. While I advocate doing these practices and reading these books (and include practices from my own work to this end, later in the book), we must use caution and not *only* do these things. There are too many people who enter this work only partially prepared and walk around spiritual and magical communities with shattered auras or egos puffed up out of proportion to their beings or great "powers" they use to manipulate others. These are often the direct products of the type of work toward self-possession that does not include thorough self-examination, deepening of ethics and the shifting of priorities to bring all the parts of our lives into balance.

A significant shift often does happen within these people, but the complexes they had before awakening become stronger, more tenacious, and much harder to move. Blind spots remain blind spots but are exacerbated by the new power flowing through the person. Until we bring ourselves closer to what priest and teacher Ivo Domínguez, Jr. calls "health," we should be wary of taking on the Great Work. Better yet, we should realize that the Great Work includes body, emotion, mind, practice, our jobs, our families and relationships, and our studies and work in every facet of our lives. Nothing is excluded in the realms of magic and spirituality. Everything is necessary for the task at hand.

A phrase that comes to us via the alchemists of old, the Great Work is literally the turning of base metals into a product of gold. Alchemists do this in a physical laboratory, with alembics and flames. We can use our everyday surroundings as laboratories, forming something of lasting value from the variegated stuff of our lives. This lasting "something" is Gurdjieff's immortal soul and the alchemists' philosopher's stone, the act of becoming fully possessed of our own divinity: autonomous, creative, and living a full life unconstrained by mere convention.

Becoming fully who we are is the greatest work, and the greatest service, we can do for the world, the Gods, and all the realms seen and unseen. All of our other work must stem from this. This process of be-coming wholly who we are and entering the state of full integration that I call the "I am" is sometimes brutal and sometimes meticulous work. Great excavations must happen within, while we simultaneously cultivate detailed attention.

Perceiving the Levels of Magic

. . . the Western ideal is not to escape from the body but to become involved more and more in life, in order to experience it more adequately, and in order to obtain a mastery over it. The ideal is to bring down god-head so that one's manhood being enriched may thereby be assumed into godhead.

—ISRAEL REGARDIE (IN *The Middle Pillar*)

When we first begin our spiritual practice, particularly the practice of magic, we may fall into two tendencies. The first is a strong inclina-tion to believe *everything* and to hope for instantaneous changes in our lives, or that we, by burning a piece of paper, can simply do away with whole swaths of personality. The second tendency is to psychologize everything, working only in the realms of archetype and metaphor. I want to challenge us to move beyond both of these, to deepen our practice, our relationship to Deity and magic, and to come into full possession of our own lives and authority.

If we move beyond basic spell work and the very real self-help quali-ties of magical psychology, we stand the chance of accessing the deeper work on self and the expansion into the work that touches that which lives beyond our skin. Spells and prayers become more real, a form of connected attention, and psychology becomes part of a larger whole.

There is self. And there is unity. Neither can be accessed without the other, not on this plane and within this lifetime. Our whole lives are brought to bear in the magic of the Great Work. Whether we see that as using physical or metaphysical alchemy, whether we are working on energetic levels or on gross material, every aspect of our lives is brought to bear in the work at hand.

In this way, magic changes to a path of integration. As integration slowly occurs, the levels of perception about the self and all the realms seen and unseen will naturally change. We become aware of forces and Gods beyond the archetypes, and of the true power that arises from the development of engaged will rather than the simple good feelings that come from more facile, wish-fulfilling spells. Our wishes become deeper and broader, and our magic opens into spaces we could only imagine before.

The keys to this are found in self-knowledge, soul alignment, and cleansing. Deep self-knowledge always leads to relationship outside of ourselves. Through this work, we begin to sense our place in the world, our purpose, and the reality that the fabric of all holds us, just as we are part of the fabric of all.

Reflection

Look at the path that has led you to this place. What is your wish for your life? Examine your current work. What do you notice about yourself right now? Think five years back. Look at the questions above in the light of your life as it was then. What were your perceptions during that time, and how have they changed?

Do you want further self-knowledge and mastery? Are you willing to attempt the work of integration and autonomy? Do you long for full integration?

Understanding Self-Possession

The knowing of one's self in totality and honesty brings us face to face with the infinite potential within.

—Frater Omen (in "Om Mani Padme Hum: The Buddha and the Holy Guardian Angel" by Hermeticus Nath [Denny Sargent])

When we see a person who seems collected, confident, and stable, we may say that he or she is "self-possessed." That meaning reflects some internal mastery cultivated by the individual. This mastery is a large part of what I mean by self-possessed. I am speaking of an individual who has done the work to know himself, and who has faced himself unflinchingly and learned to love what he sees. This person has integrated many of her parts, and remains essentially the same in any situation or in the midst of any emotion. By self-possession I mean all of this and something more as well.

In various magical and shamanic traditions, people become "possessed" by Gods or Goddesses. Even in Charismatic Christianity there is the concept of being "filled with the Holy Spirit," which is another form of divine possession. What these traditions do *not* stress is that seekers can become both possessed by and possessor of their own divinities, their own full selfhood. In fact, without this self-possession, possession by any other force can be dangerous to mental and physical health at worst, and at least, can sometimes derail a person's quest for spiritual wholeness. Feri Tradition Grandmaster Victor Anderson insisted that we not do possessory work without having clear contact with our own God Soul first.

When given prime of place, the quest for spiritual wholeness leads to self-possession, to full human health and integration, coupled with one's own divine potential. Without self-possession, there is no chance for full and balanced enlightenment to occur. As I have mentioned, flashes of enlightenment or moments of grace may happen, but there is no foundation for them to rest upon, leaving people hungry for things beyond their ken. This is the cause of transcendent thinking: "Things will be better after I lose weight or find a new job or get the right partner or go to heaven." In these scenarios, something always gets left behind. That something is often the seeker herself. *With* self-possession, seekers open themselves to *inclusive consciousness*, a new concept that argues for the embracing of all parts of human existence into the fold of the spiritual quest. When all of life is included, all of life can aid the Great Work of coming to know our own divinity and our life's purpose.

There is nothing that lies outside of this quest. Our magic includes our whole lives and, in time, will come to include the life of everything in the universe, everything held in the fabric of God Herself, the limitless divine.

Remember my definition of magic: the marriage of breath, will, and desire. By exploring these components and applying them to the self, we arrive at a place internally—and in relationship with the world—where the processes of integration will unfold. At that point, the universe steps forward to greet us.

Opening to inclusive consciousness enables us to grow to have fully integrated, magical lives and to have consistent conversation with our own divine natures. This conversation will in turn help us to reach toward spiritual Adepthood and the even larger inclusiveness of this reality, that immanence and transcendence are one. The microcosm *is* the macrocosm. Further work can, in the few who are called on, open a permanent channel to the non-dual, the great All, enabling the magic worker to become the Lover, the bodhisattva, she or he who brings extension back into form, sowing love. But the latter is the subject of yet another book, which perhaps I will write someday.

Self-possession is my hope for all people. I believe that individuals can become more than they are now and that some of us possess a strong enough wish, with enough openness and dedication to see this process through. If you are reading this book, you are likely one of those people.

To do this work with the fullness of our beings, we must be simultaneously voracious and calm, and also filled with enthusiasm, the inspiration of the Gods, for this work is the unfolding of the great mysteries. The mysteries are only hidden to us because we lack practical, applied knowledge. Engaging the work held in all deep spiritual traditions—whether Western Occultism, Witchcraft, Taosim, Sufism, New Thought, or any esoteric expression—will give us a way to touch the mysteries and come closer to understanding.[2]

So much is possible we can scarcely comprehend it. But when we close our eyes, take a deep breath, and *reach* with our whole being, we catch a glimpse, a glimmer, a sense of hope. And then we move through the layers of darkness and light that are ourselves, in order to better touch the All.

God Herself is the building blocks of all creation and the movement of all destruction. We are pieces of these processes, and reflections of workings more vast. If we can first come to know ourselves and then connect out, we will better serve the processes of All. We will come to help all beings, animate and inanimate, visible and obscured.

It is easy to say that the seeker must just stumble upon this stage in the midst of her work. Why? *Because self-possession cannot be planned.* It isn't something a spiritual aspirant can schedule, unlike some other initiatory rites; rather, all the preparation he has done makes the aspirant ripe for the experience. He has laid the ground with meditation. She has primed the cosmic pump by aligning her soul. Zen teacher Baker Roshi once said, "Enlightenment is an accident, but [spiritual] practice makes us accident prone." The same statement can be made for self-possession. No one can tell us how to do it; even Abramelin the Mage couldn't tell us how to say the necessary prayers.[3] We have to figure it out for ourselves. All that can be offered are maps. I offer what was helpful to me, cobbled together from the maps of others and that which I wrote myself along my stumbling way. There are also signposts and insights that have come from the work that followed integration.

I hope these are of help to those still seeking or those who wish to confirm the strength and stability of their own work.

So, while there is no guaranteed outcome, the map provided by this book can strengthen you, open you, and generally prepare you to receive the grace of your own Godhood.

Everything opens to he who is open. Nothing is closed to she who dares.

Possessing Yourself

To know yourself is to know your Lord.

—IBN ARABI

Feri Tradition artist Anaar says simply that our goal is becoming self-possessed,[4] not initiated, not holding power over other people, not commanding forces outside of ourselves. Our goal is to possess ourselves fully in every moment.

Self-possession is the quality of being fully in touch with all of our parts and aware of the relationship those parts have to our own divinity, known as our God Soul, or our Sacred Dove.[5] Since the God Soul is connected to all things, establishing a constant link to it places us in concert with the All-encompassing. Self-possessed, we open fully to an awareness of ourselves as a point of matter, anchoring the endless flow of spirit and energy. In this stage we not only have knowledge of our divine nature, we have active conversation with it.

This can feel as if we are open to a being outside of ourselves who is a helper or guide, which is both true and untrue. The nature of our God Soul is that of being linked to the macrocosm, having access to all space and time, *in the present moment*. This is beyond the awareness of my body and personality parts, which are settled into time and space as discrete units rather than in constant flow. Because this feels beyond the scope of understanding of the rest of my human parts—my instincts, my physical form, my thoughts and opinions, my personality—it can seem that this divine and fully connected nature must be solely distinct from me. Actually, once joined with us, it makes us more *fully* ourselves. All the things called "I" before are shown to be simply component parts of this vital, shining whole of grace and light, matter, form, and formlessness.

In some metaphysical and occult circles, what I call self-possession is known as "Knowledge and Conversation with our Holy Guardian Angel," and because of the macrocosmic quality of this part of our soul, the Angel is also sometimes talked about as an outside entity. However, Victor Anderson used to quip, "'Thou shalt have no other Gods before me,' means you!" He related this to the Sacred Dove, our God Soul, and he was talking obliquely about the state of self-possession and the processes of alignment that lead up to it. Still others call this "finding the Authentic Self," and recognize the importance of its function on the road to enlightenment.[6]

What is the upshot of this? What are we making, with this choice, this practice, and this spiritual life? A full self—not just our disparate personalities or drives, or our physical needs, but all of those, along with the part of us that touches something even larger and includes everything.

Self-possession is integration; we step into our Godhood. With self-possession, we can leave personality behind for something greater, and meet the challenger at the threshold of space and time, entering a place of unity. And from a stage of self-possession, it becomes possible to return back into personality *and maintain that constant connection with the All.* In this way, self-possession is the necessary precursor to a stage, rather than simply a state, of enlightenment and effective magic.

All the mystics write about this in some form or another. From the platform of self-possession, it is possible to touch the fabric of God Herself and not go crazy, not become an egomaniac, and not dissolve into a couch-surfing leech. We can bring the Limitless into everyday reality.

That is what is possible. The integration is a gift unto itself: to be a whole, autonomous person, living from the place of health. The Kabbalah teaches us that health rests in the sphere of Tiphareth, of Beauty.[7] It is the place of the integrated magic worker who has looked at all her parts, come into conversation with them, and done the work necessary for the Sacred Dove to descend. Grace, also known as fortune, descends upon the prepared person who can accept and acclimate to that state. That temporary state then becomes a stage from which further life and growth occurs.

This distinction between states and stages is a helpful one made by Ken Wilber.[8] When I speak of epiphanies that get eaten by life, I speak of a state. When we align all our parts for a moment and then life throws us off course, that alignment is a state. Full self-possession is a stage of alignment. It is a stage, because even though other things come and go inside and around us, the stage is constant. We are aligned with our God Soul and our purpose even when upset or in ecstasy, sorrow, joy, or anger. We always have the perspective of, and conversation with, our divine nature.

The achievement of full possession of one's God Soul—or gaining Knowledge and Conversation with one's Holy Guardian Angel, the descent of the Genius, or connection with the Authentic Self—is a full linkage of all of our parts, and opens the door to true communication with the supernal: with God Herself, the Limitless, and also with other beings unseen.[9]

Once we reach full possession of our God Soul, we have the chance to continue the further integration of all the parts we have previously brought into contact with each other. I advise doing the bulk of this work before achieving self-possession, or you will have a much harder time of it. For example, if one has not begun to set his financial and romantic life in order, the push to do so after possession will grow more severe, sometimes breaking the individual who hasn't done the proper preparation. For some, this feels almost impossible, raising the question of whether self-possession as a stage, rather than a temporary state, actually occurred. Sometimes epiphany that has no foundation set for a permanent connection to form *does* occur, but goes nowhere except to spin the person's life further into disarray. And thus we are thrust back to the ancient advice to know ourselves.

If we have built a foundation of good work; right attitude toward money; and knowledge of our mental, emotional, and physical needs and of our relationship to others, and then we achieve "knowledge and conversation," or full possession of our God Soul, we will be in a good position to expand into our integrated lives and to be of greater help to those around us. We will be able to rightly see what further integrative steps are necessary and have greater reach toward what lies beyond our current scope.

This is a state of greater connection, rather than the space between connection and disconnection most of us swim in, and will therefore give us greater success in all areas of life. Life will expand around us in ways either unforeseen or only previously hinted at. All will become easier. The strength of internal connection and integration brings rightness to all things, lending a broader, more cohesive view of the world and our place therein.

Seeking to Flower

Who is this flower above me? And what is the work of this God? I would know myself in all my parts.

—FERI TRADITION PRAYER

Upon reaching full possession, our place in the world will open up significantly. We will dither less and act more. We will come more fully into our true work and what is sometimes called our True Will, which is the key to the prayer above.

This prayer holds many layers of mystery and passageways to knowledge. The first statement, "Who is this flower above me?" asks first,

"Who is my God Soul or my Holy Guardian Angel? What is my divine nature?" This is the supplicant's question, a seeker's question. This can be asked well before we have formed any permanent connection. It holds our wish to be simultaneously fully ourselves and more whole than we currently are. We can still ask and, through the practice of soul alignment and awareness, form a fleeting connection that grows stronger over time, allowing us to center around our divinity rather than simply around our fears, drives, or appetites.

When the question is asked by one who has achieved self-possession, it is a way of checking in: "Who am I today? What is my relationship with my own divinity?"

In answering the rest of the prayer, ". . .what is the work of this God?" we come into our True Will, our larger work in the world. This is the space where our will is working in accordance with Divine Will. There is no longer any separation between the two.

In wishing to know ourselves fully, we must forget our quest for gain and seek only completion. At a certain point in our development, we no longer even seek to become Mystic, Magister, Sorcerer, or Witch; we seek only our own perfection in the wholeness of our Will, in the joining of light with dark and strength with love. We are varied and gorgeous yet pure of heart. Our aim is this: to know ourselves and to know the world.

Moving Past Preconceptions

The whole aim of magical training is to integrate the personality, so that in all your mundane and supermundane affairs, you will display a balanced and controlled mind.

—W. E. Butler (in *Apprenticed to Magic*)

There is a common cultural assumption that a fully integrated person will always behave like a saint. But if we read accounts, even of those considered to be saints in various cultures, we see quite a different picture being painted. Some of these men and women retained quite a sense of humor. Some enjoyed their wine or bawdy jokes. Still others used the shock of anger as a teaching tool.

Where this idea of a person who is free of all desiring and in a constant state of flat benevolence stems from, I am not certain. Perhaps it goes something like this: "An unchanging state of perfection is not possible, so I cannot achieve it, but surely these saintly types have, and they must be of a different type than I. Surely they don't have to deal with partners, children, cooking dinner, or a cranky boss, or saving the world." Nonetheless, integration, even the further stage of enlightenment, does not mean that our personalities cease to exist, nor does it mean that all problems and pitfalls disappear.

What it does mean is that the self-possessed person is better able to cope with the parts of her personality. He can have a better sense of patience and compassion with self and others. Problems are faced with greater equanimity, and center is returned to far more quickly than before. There is control present, even in upheaval. This stems from a combination of committed practice and grace.

Doing the Work

What in you holds an unattainable image of perfection that you run from or flog yourself for not having? What causes you to give up? Can you look for what emotion might be beneath this? As you do your other practices, take time to notice when these feelings arise.

Find an image that inspires you and use that as a touchstone in your work for the next month. Every time you notice yourself not measuring up, take a breath and try to notice the story beneath the story. Then remember the inspiring image and move on for the moment.

Taking Internal Stock

If that which you seek, you find not within yourself, you will never find it without.

—Doreen Valiente (in "The Charge of the Goddess")

The ancients had their pathways to self-possession and integration. They charted a person's stars or noted signs at significant points in a person's childhood. They looked for innate talents and deep aversions, and helped to train the person in mysteries that were for his or her soul only. They pointed seekers toward the Gods who would best help them, and the symbols and rites that would best forge the link between human and divine form.[10] Some used the magic of sacred geometry to alter the consciousness of individuals and the collective. Others placed creation and the soul onto trees of energy and psychology, and still others mapped whole worlds, seen and unseen, that magical practitioners or shamans might traverse for the good of their own psyches or for the people who turned to them for guidance.

All of this is to say that maps and means have existed for every age. We must find the map that works best for us. For me, that map is a combination of listening to my Gods, balancing my soul, studying ancient texts and systems, and sitting in meditation, attuning my energies to the energies of all the worlds. The most important guide for this work has been the work of self-observation. I have gotten to know myself.

We will do more work with this in the chapters to come, uncovering hidden facets and seeing how many faces we show the world. Right now, we must ask ourselves the first, essential question: "What has set me on this path? Why am I choosing to do this work?"

For some of us, the answer will be that our lives have always been filled with seeking; for still others, we may be here out of fear of living or dying unfulfilled. Some of us are in this place because we have been inspired by the example of another, and some are simply filled with longing that ordinary means can never fill.

Imagining the Real

The ancient Greeks understood that magic began with the imagination. Imagination was a real thing to them, a palpable sense just like any other. Imagination can help make things manifest. Without it, nothing new is created.

Every world is made up of individuals who are part of the whole. In remembering this, we acknowledge that every step into our work is a step in the work of the world. Every breath that fuels the Great Work is a breath that transforms God Herself. We are alive within her, and she is alive in us. Every being relies upon our awakening. Every being rejoices in our work, even those who resist it. Change is inevitable, so we may as well choose the direction we desire.

Reflection

Imagine a world in which everybody has plumbed the depth of his or her soul. Imagine people who are strong and compassionate, thinking for themselves and working with each other. Imagine a world where disagreements occur in order to foster further growth rather than divisiveness. Imagine a time when everyone knows himself fully, accepts who he is, and stands tall. Imagine everyone knowing her work and her will. Take a breath, say a prayer, and ask this of your own self.

Cultivating Practice

Chance favors the prepared mind.

—Louis Pasteur

To walk toward self-possession and mastery requires some measure of discipline. Most of us reading this book already have done work toward this end, or we wouldn't even be expressing interest in the Great

Work. We live in a time where interest in this work is increasing, and necessarily so. Our world is at the tipping point of further violence and decay or widespread growth and renewal. The seriousness with which some spiritual seekers are stepping up is impressive and makes sense. Potential is in the very air that we breathe.

The world of magic in the late twentieth and early twenty-first centuries has been riddled with dilettantes, partiers, and those seeking to escape the shackles of repressive monolithic sects. In the midst of these have always been those who diligently applied themselves to the crafting of the soul through magical means. The same has been true throughout the ages, and those of us who carry the mantle of these recent and ancient ancestors have a task that is made easier by knowing others have made the attempt before us. Many have succeeded. It is my belief that many more shall do so than ever before.

In order to continue the trajectory of this work, we must be serious about our practices, our work, and our methods. There is nothing haphazard here. There will likely always be practitioners who want results without effort, or who are battling internal impulses between the parts that wish to work and the parts that are afraid. This manifests resistance that can sometimes look like laziness and sometimes like belligerence.

Sloppiness and laziness in practice often masquerade as this attitude: "I'm just relying on my intuition. All that structure gets me down and is too mechanical. I don't understand it. It bores me. I don't need tools anyway. No one can tell me what to do."

I am acquainted with a sleight-of-hand magician. Does he learn to pull coins out of the air by simply wishing really hard they would appear? No. He wishes they would appear, and then he takes a physical coin and practices—every day. Several times a day, until the coin appears out of air, he repeats the basic exercise: desire, object, effort, time, appearance, desire. This is also a map for our spiritual work.

Picasso could not have painted *Guernica* without practicing life drawing. The manifest world and its objects and practices are as necessary as the silent wish. There is room for intuition, of course, but there is also room for disciplined commitment. If "God is in the details," we should make the details important. Just because something feels easy doesn't mean it is good; it might be easier because we don't have to put in as much effort or because we don't have to confront parts of ourselves that want to disconnect by glossing over. Conversely, it must be said that just because something feels difficult doesn't mean it is good. What is our tendency? Is it toward the easy out or toward punishment? Either can sound a warning bell that we are acting automatically and not necessarily in our own best interests. And in addition, often for something to feel *really* good, we must have practiced. This is true in playing music, having sex, participating in athletics, cooking, or performing any other skill.

The ancient Greeks were well aware of this. For Iamblichus, ritual success depended on proper preparation of ritual objects, acquiring of theoretical knowledge, the soul's communion with the Gods, and then the union in which the soul "takes on the shape of the Gods" and the awakening in the soul of divine Eros. Here, the formula is similar to used by my illusionist friend: object, theory, rapport, becoming, awakening. We see that Iamblichus started with material object and ended with awakening, gross to fine. The spirit is in the material, for they are the same, but one cannot be bypassed for another. Everything is necessary.

Similarly, the mystic philosopher G. I. Gurdjieff tells us that we must move from two, our duality, into three, our struggle for consciousness, into four, stability or a "permanent line of results in time," into five, relationship with the thinking, feeling, moving, instinctive, and sex centers.[11] Once these are in harmony, the Pentagram is locked within us and we move to six, the Hexagram or Seal of Solomon, as beings independent and complete, not prey to accidental shocks from outside ourselves.[12] In other words, by moving through stages one through six, permanent self-possession occurs.

Do we start at six? No. Is this progression a falsely imposed hierarchy meant to keep some people above others? No. Does equality mean equivalency? No. Can I pluck coins out of the air? No. I haven't practiced. Does that make my friend better than I? Again, no. We are equal in worth but not equivalent in talent and presence. The world would be a boring and less viably healthy place if we were.

God Herself is zero. All. Contemplation of zero helps us, but we cannot bypass the rest of the steps in the path to harmony and wholeness. Therein lies madness. The zero is present in everything, but we cannot assume we have full access to it. For we "have been divided for love's sake."[13] Our becoming one, united internally, is necessary before we join fully with the zero. But still, we start at division, not union, for we are human. A baby figures out "self" by figuring out "something else." A baby discovers "two," and then life continues on in states and stages through childhood, adolescence, and adulthood. Mastery of adulthood takes even more effort.

We must recognize our parts and bring them into concert. We must practice. We must get the necessary objects in place. There is something to be learned in grinding incense and lighting candles. There is something to be learned in breathing properly. There is something to be learned in reading theory. There is something to be learned by picking up a blade and feeling how its shape and function differ from a cup's. All of these teach us clear attention, which brings us more fully into ourselves and gives finer access to the whole world.

In the beginning, we may wish to skip steps because the work feels too difficult and we want to incorporate ease. Once we know more, we may skip steps because we think we know better. We think that our inner voices that tell us we don't need something are wise teachers. Some of these voices are, but some of them are simply faces of resistance, voices trying to keep us from our full power and beauty. We want to skip steps because we are part of a culture of step skipping. We are members of a culture that tells us things *should* be easy now, and we can just buy things to make us look good and feel better. With the exception of a few trades, the model of apprentice, journeyman, and master is almost extinct. We tend to think that we can *all* be masters, or that we all must *not* be masters, in order to establish equality. The lowest common denominator becomes the ruling voice and the guiding impulse.

I want us to work. I want a world filled with bright and powerful people. The inspiration that rises from being in the midst of every person working in his greatest passion and with her finest skill fans an unquenchable flame.

Let us keep our feet firmly on the path and learn to enjoy the journey. We can only learn *in time*. "In time" means in the flow of Nature, in the state of our lives as they are: physical, mental, emotional, intuitive, divine. We *will* learn. Learning requires experience gained from living our lives to their fullest.

CHAPTER TWO

Tapping into Life Power

The world beckons you. Life thrums around you. Can you hear it? Can you feel it? Blood moves through your veins, and saliva washes your mouth. Deep in the earth, insects crawl. Stars explode in space. You are alive. The earth is alive. The cosmos is in an endless dance of life, growth, death, decay, and renewal. This is life power.

Life power is everywhere and is the basis for all of our magic. Life power is in the trees thrusting toward earth and sky. Life power is in the smile shared with a stranger on the street. Life power is the great connector. Life power is sex and breath; sex and breath are everywhere and everything. Tapping into life power will change you, inside and out. Life power, coupled with intention, fuels our magic.

The first steps toward self-possession require getting in touch with life power. This begins with looking at the ways in which we live in illusion, and points us toward ways to look at *what is actually in front of us.* Solace, strength, and a realization of the life power available are derived from a trip through the primal elements of life: air, fire, water, earth, and the spirit that connects us to all.

This seeker's path takes us through the steps necessary to open to the flow of awareness, creativity, and success. What has this to do with magic? Without tapping into life power, magic remains limited in its effectiveness. *With* life power and a trained will, there is nothing we cannot do with our magic and our lives. We will be able to step more firmly on the path toward our destiny, our life's work, our greater service, and our soul's longing.

Those of us fortunate enough to have already worked toward this can cultivate still *more* presence, and a stronger and still more flexible center. At every stage in our practice, we can do work that is both more subtle and more strong. Every time something integrates inside of us, we are ready to approach another layer. Whether beginning seekers or master practitioners well on the path, we all have work to do each day. This work requires further integration with—and presence to—all our parts and with the universe. And for those few who have both, the work continues still, in service to the Great Work in all beings. Each day a choice must be made: how will we serve the limitless flow? How will we remain open? How can we best engage?

The first step is always to ascertain what life brings us this very day. The first breath upon waking draws us closer to that day's work.

Returning to the Flow

Seek not that the things which happen should happen as you wish; but wish the things which happen to be as they are, and you will have a tranquil flow of life.

—Epictetus (in *A Manual for Living*)

Without the full range of life power, there are large swings through depression, anger, resentment, and apathy. Nothing is good enough, including ourselves. Life has no luster and is only filled with a competition we are doomed to lose. Even experiences of joy can be pursued in ways that become brittle and addictive. When life power is twisted by old hurts or a sense that we are not worthy, it takes a lot of work to clear ourselves and come back into the flow. The flow is always present, but we can become cut off from it. This divine flow is God Herself, and stepping into the divine flow is opening up to life power.

This chapter includes both theory and practice. If you are an advanced magic worker, you may have your own versions of some of the exercises here, though you may wish to try my versions to see which works best for you. For the newer practitioner, please do all of the exercises in this chapter without fail, as you will need them for our subsequent work. Everything in this book, including some energy techniques later on, builds upon this chapter.

The first aid to all facets of practice is getting clean. Cleansing is core to spiritual work, and this, too, must flow into all areas of our lives. Can our thoughts become clear? Can we be clean in emotional expression? Can our homes, our bodies, and our lives be clean?

People we most often admire, people of integrity, are usually the "cleanest" people we know. They are not overly muddied by uninvestigated wounds or desires. They know themselves in all their parts.

Cleansing Life Force

Instantaneous change is rarely possible and not advisable. If we have spent years building up complexes, illnesses, thought forms, and emotional habits, we cannot expect them to vanish overnight. What helps is to slightly shift these energies in order to call back the life power that they have been holding, whether it is buried or tied in knots. Once shifted, we begin to have access to that life power once more.

I want to stress that this process is not about getting rid of parts of the self we do not like. Rather, this process of cleansing begins to bring those parts back into conversation with other facets of self that may feel healthier or stronger. By freeing up the life force held dormant or twisted in old wounds or habits, we come to better know all facets of our personalities: dreams, fears, and desires.

This cleansing act not only calls back life power but also opens that which was in darkness up to light. Things may need to stay in the darkness for some time. There is power in darkness: the power of gestation, deep dreaming, and the sweetness of night. However, sometimes darkness obscures our vision, making it difficult to see some of our very important parts. And sometimes darkness is a messy closet into which we shove things we can't quite get rid, of but don't know how to use anymore. It is time to open up the closet door and begin the excavation. It is time to bring some things into the energy and flow of light.

The process I will outline below can be done simply, as shown, or in a more complex manner.[14] It requires the supposition that we have a multifaceted soul and that one part stores life power, one part is able to set intention, and another part is divine. This act will bring these parts of our soul into communication. For more information on the parts of the soul, please consult appendix B (see p. 250).[15]

All cultures and religious systems understand the importance of spiritual and psychic cleansing. The rite that follows is similar in nature to the "Lesser Banishing Ritual of the Pentagram" used by Ceremonial Magicians and the saltwater cleansing used by many Witches. It is also akin to Christian baptism, although obviously it can be done far more often, or to Hindus washing in the Ganges, or Jews ritually washing their hands before meals or going to the ritual bath when greater cleansing feels necessary.

Spiritual cleansings require intention. One thing that sets the following rite apart is that this act requires the concentrated use of breath as the carrier of life power. It not only will cleanse our energy fields, like the other spiritual techniques mentioned, it will also begin to unbind and clear deep-seated complexes, illness, and pain, and can be done on a regular basis. This rite has even been successful in healing people from long-standing drug addiction. It is the process of unknotting energy and praying to our own divine natures for healing. Another factor that distinguishes this rite from other forms of cleansing is that we are not getting rid of anything. The unbound and cleansed energies are intentionally re-consumed, reconsecrated within our bodies so as to be of further use to us. Life power should never be wasted.

Doing the Work

This exercise is foundational and can be done daily or, at the very least, weekly.

First, you will need a small glass of water. You may use a sacred chalice if you have one, or any ordinary glass will do. Set the glass in front of you so it is within easy reach of your hands.

Still and center yourself. Clap three times to get the attention of your God Soul. Slow your breathing down and begin taking deep breaths.[16] Let it be your intention that every breath you take in carries life power with it. Begin to circulate this through your body. As you feel your physical body begin to fill with life and breath, imagine that you can push it out into the energy body that surrounds your skin, known as your etheric body. *As you do this, think of that within you that needs healing, forgiveness, or unbinding.[17]*

Hold your hands over the glass of water. Let this life force that is flowing into and circulating through your body begin to flow down your arms and into your hands. From there, let it flow into the water. Keep breathing in life power. Keep breathing it out through your hands and into the water. In your mind's eye, "see" the water begin to hold a charge of life power. Feel that which is bound up in you begin to loosen, lending energy to the water. The water grows lighter and brighter with this life connection. Call upon God Herself to lend more energy to the process. When the water is luminous with life power, drink it down, imagining the luminous water flowing all the way through your body, bringing life and healing into every cell.

Once you feel this, tilt your head back and breathe up a prayer for your healing into your God Soul. The life power that was bound up now flows more freely. Feel whole, centered, aligned, alive, and clean.

Gauging the Real

We are more than we know.

—H. D.(in the poem "The Dancer," in *H. D.: Collected Poems, 1912-1944*)

Rather than becoming alienated from the earth, we can find the sacred everywhere. Magic comes to life in the space between what exists and what is possible. We can cultivate a balance between seeing ourselves as we are and the world as it is, and accepting this, and also know that we and the world can become further aligned, stronger, and more in tune with the sacred.

This balance may seem tricky because we are not taught to hold these tensions during our childhoods, by our cultures or by our spiritual systems. Most spiritual systems either ask us to simply accept things as they are, unchanging, or to seek to transcend the stuff of our lives. Neither supports a holistic view that all is necessary: the compost, the earth, the water, the sun, and the flowers and fruit they produce.

We are beings of multiplicity and unity, or at least, this possibility dwells with us. Think of the Star Goddess (see p. 2) from the meditation beginning this section of the book. God Herself is the great Zero, the fabric of all, and in that, she is also everything. We, too, can know this for ourselves. This is the process of "re-membering," or putting our parts back together.[18]

Oftentimes, what keeps us from realizing and fully cultivating our multiplicity and potential unity is that we *think* we are unified, but actually, one part or another is running the show. Through exploration of our many parts and diligent practice in connecting with our divine natures, over time we stand a good chance of becoming permanently unified. Our many parts do not go away; rather, they come into open conversation with one another. This is preferable to their usual state of skulking around behind each other's backs, using sabotage and subterfuge to get their way or just hoping the other parts won't notice what they desire.

We often have a picture of our lives that is not accurate. The first step to clean, effective magic and tapping into life power is assessing our lives. Each spiritual seeker and magic worker sooner or later has to face the oracle that tells us to know ourselves. Without that component, our work is lost. We ask a lot of questions and think many things about our conditions, but do we really look at our lives inside and out? Do we see? Do we know?

This is a lifetime's work, of course, and wherever we are on our spiritual journey, we can always take further steps in knowing and understanding our parts. After that comes acceptance and, hopefully, love.

Doing the Work

This exercise requires a notebook and an open attitude. Take one month to assess your life as it is, right now. Observe yourself. Take notes. These should cover several categories. You may continue with your other work and reading this book while you do this practice. Eventually this work can be integrated with all of our other practices and our daily lives, becoming second nature.

1. *What are my thought patterns?*
2. *What is my predominant way of feeling?*
3. *What do I eat?*
4. *How do I sleep?*
5. *What sort of exercise do I get?*
6. *How is my sex life?*
7. *What do I do at work? Do I enjoy it? Is it satisfying?*
8. *How do I spend my leisure time?*
9. *Do I have a spiritual practice? What is it? How often did I engage with it this month?*

These categories help us to know ourselves from the surface on down. We will need to do further work to know ourselves on a deeper level. Beginning with the basic patterns of our lives helps us to better uncover what motivates us. We need to know the what before we can come to know the why.

Calling the Vital Flow

Life, sex, magic, and creation are all around us. It is easy to lose track of this in the midst of contemporary life. Through the work of "Gauging the Real," we begin to see the patterns that disconnect us from the vital flow. We notice what makes us feel tired, apathetic, frustrated, or worn down. Sometimes these are internal processes that have begun to feel like emotional or mental traps. Other obstacles are external activities or relationships that no longer interest or serve us. While the internal factors are deeply important, they can also take much longer to shift; we have to wait until the juice is gone before attempting to give them over. The juice is life force and connection, made apparent by the presence of longing, anger, sorrow, or any other strong emotion. Because of this, we will begin looking at some of the things on our list that feel external, knowing that the inner and outer necessarily affect one another but that our exterior factors can be easier to let go of when the time has truly come.

Conversely, we can look at what feeds us and notice what makes us feel energized, happy, and alive. We can also ascertain how much time we actually spend on things we like and what we do not do that we might like to try. One of the powers of the Sphinx is the power to dare.[19] Daring opens up still more energy that we can then feed into other facets of our lives.

Everything we do can help us tap into life power: washing dishes, gardening, working at a computer, making love, walking the dog, building a house, or reading. All we have to do is remember that we are part of the flow and that the elements of life are all around us.

Doing the Work

Look at your life again. Is there any external thing you wish you were not doing? Make a list of up to ten things that drain you. Pick one thing to magically and physically cull from your life: an activity, physical objects, tired relationships, things you thought you "should" do. Make certain that you are really done with this rather than just dislike it. What will you need to do to make this shift? Do the "Cleansing Life Force" exercise (see p. 28) to help you free up some energy around this. Set a timetable to make the shift. Do a ritual around it. Then step back and begin the process of dropping this from your life.

Wrapping in the Elements

That which is Below corresponds to that which is Above, and that which is Above corresponds to that which is Below, to accomplish the miracle of the One Thing.

—HERMES TRISMEGISTUS (IN THE *Emerald Tablet*)

Vital flow is not just held within, of course. "As above, so below" can also be stated, "as within, so without." The microcosm and the macrocosm are engaged in divine reflection. Just as we are embodied, have systems of blood flow and digestion, firing synapses, and some form of spirit, so all of these exist outside of us. We can touch what lies beyond our skin and learn to call the vital flow. We are not isolated creatures but live within a vibrant world and vast universe of realms seen and unseen.

We will visit each of the classical elements that the ancient philosophers considered to be the building blocks of all life. To know them is to know ourselves. All of the elements are both the things themselves *and* what we say they represent. We will work with both facets.[20] Getting in touch with the elements in and around us helps us enter into a state of constant awareness of life power. The more open to life power the seeker is, the easier her life will become.

Reflection

Air

First there is breath and wind. Inhale. Exhale. Feel the breath as it fills your lungs. Go outside. What is the air like right now? Is it cold? Still? Moving? How does your breath relate to air? Look up at the sky. Is it black? Blue? Brown? Is it clear or hazy? Is there pollution you can see? How is your own clarity reflected in the sky?

Mental clarity is one of the things magic workers associate with air. If the outside affects the inside and vice versa, how is your mind affected by days that are smoggy and nights that are warm? How does your mind work when the air is relatively clean? Does high wind affect you? Are you contributing to clarity of air and mind, or are you throwing pollutants into the sky and muddling up your own brain as well?

Fire

Look at a candle's flame and notice how the fire dances around the wick and melts the wax. Feel the sun on your skin, letting it warm you. That huge explosion of light and heat in the sky is necessary for all life on earth. As we know, it can also be a dangerous friend.

What warms you? Fire is a literal expression of fuel, giving off energy and heat. Every cell in your body gives off an electrical charge, sending signals to other cells, which then respond in kind. Nerves, brain cells, blood—all of these produce electricity as a communicator of information. Electricity is energy, and energy is also how you communicate to others. Are you withdrawn, excited, animated, depressed, angry, in love?

Look at fire in your life. What feeds your energy, and how does energy connect you to others? What light do you emit?

Water

Fill a glass with water and drink deeply, until it is gone. How does that make you feel? Look at a pond, a lake, an ocean, a birdbath. What do these show you? Our bodies are filled with liquid just like that glass or that ocean. It is in our cells, in our spit, in our eyes, in our sex, in our brains—water, water, everywhere. Water is said to carry emotion, for emotions are like the changing of the tide.

Think of the world's water supply and how the water in your body connects you to it. People all over the world are fighting for clean, affordable, accessible drinking water. Are you privileged enough to have easy access? Climate change is causing ice shelves to melt and oceans to rise. Are changing weather patterns affecting your outlook?

What is your relationship to water? Do you drink enough of it? Do you luxuriate in bathing in it? Are you in touch with your emotional states?

Earth

Earth is in you and around you. Every step you take is on the earth. You are carried by your flesh, muscles, and bones. These are all earth. We humans tend to think we are separate from earth and from the natural world, forgetting in our hubris that we are the natural world, along with mountains, rocks, animals, plants, and insects. It is this separation that causes such problems and devastation to the wild places, to the topsoil on factory farms, and to our personal physical health.

How does earth manifest in your life? Do you have a solid yet flexible relationship to your body, to home, to work, to money, to soil itself? What food do you eat? Listen to your muscles, and see the muscles in the earth. Notice your spine, and look upon the spine of a tree or an animal. What makes you feel most healthy and connected? Celebrate the earth by celebrating that which lives in you. Then pick up some garbage or save a tree.

Rebuilding Our Foundation

In examining our lives, we will likely notice patterns. Often we will find links between our sex lives and exercise, for example. Or we may come to notice that our thought patterns affect how we feel about work. Bringing this information to the surface is the first step toward becoming an integrated and whole human being. It will also help us later in our practice, when we begin to examine our desires. Until we can look at what is, we cannot form a true image of what may be. Our desires will be in conflict.

The information we gathered in "Gauging the Real" becomes the basis for building a new foundation for our practice, our spirituality, and our lives. Magician and esoteric Christian W. E. Butler said, "When we come into the occult movement and begin our occult work, the first thing we have to do is to get rid of the rubbish built into our temple. We have to remake our foundations. That means we have to work on it while we are still living in it."[21] For many of us, that is the most difficult part. Some of us are good at tearing things down, and others at building things up. Not many of us are good at holding the tension of the old, the current, and the possible simultaneously. Our work at every phase, whether we are experienced practitioners or bare beginners, lies in the confluence of these. We have to look at the old plaster and broken glass, find the lines of the foundation as it stands, and decide what needs to be excavated completely and what just needs to be shored up. We also have to examine all the things we've moved into the building just recently. What do we do with those during the reconstruction? We need *something* usable. We can't just do without a kitchen, because we don't know how many years eating out would be required, or what the expense may be. Along with building the foundation from the ground up, we also need to gauge whether or not it will support the walls we want to build and are in the process of building. Flimsy walls don't need such a strong foundation. If we have grandiose plans or desires, we need to dig even more deeply.

Finding Your Center Point

What are the Gods on the altars of your mind?

—ORION FOXWOOD (AUTHOR OF *The Faery Teachings*)

Mystic philosopher G. I. Gurdjieff enjoined us to find our center of gravity. He wasn't only talking about our physical center but, rather, was intimating that *there is something in us around which we center.* Our lives are given course by this center, whether we know it or not. Whether we feel thwarted or successful, it is helpful to figure out what is centrally important to us. We need to look at what we spend the most time thinking of or obsessing over. We need to look at how we spend the bulk of our days, not only externally but, more importantly, *internally.* We may not be in our ideal job situation, but are we free in other ways? The potential for freedom lies within, perhaps sleeping, but a strong enough desire can awaken it.

That desiring cannot merely take the form of wishing, though wishing can help our path. That desiring cannot take the form of blaming others or blaming general "life conditions" for our plight. Our internal life *can* be our own. Once we have mastery of that, our external life will also change. The world tries to tell us this is impossible. The mainstream, or what I call the over-culture, wants to keep us dissatisfied so we will buy more products to try to fill the yawning need inside. Let us take a breath together and step back from that culture for a moment. The secret to our magic, which the mainstream culture does not realize, is that it is more real than all their products put together.

The over-culture has a profound hold over our psyches that is hard to gauge when we are in the middle of it all. Think of the things we could do with our time if we were free of the hold of the corporate media. I once saw a beautiful "art car" that had been painstakingly painted and inlaid with mosaic in fabulous patterns. There was a small area near the back panel, a message to its admirers. It stated simply, "I did this in the amount of time you spent watching television." I laughed in delight at this, because I could just imagine the repeated question, "When in the world do you find the time to be creative?" The artist had a simple answer: a modified media fast that freed up untold hours of life power to his or her disposal.

How we spend our time shows what we think we love, what we are devoted to, or what we worship. Be still, and come to know that *you* are God. You may not be connected to that yet, but it is all there in potential.

Releasing Worry

Worry gives a small thing a big shadow.

—Swedish proverb

One sign that something is awry or constricted in our lives is noticing that we worry. Worry gives us a false sense that we are controlling a situation over which we really have little or no control. When we cannot be effective, worry can help our emotions feel that we are *doing* something, even though we are not really.

Along with giving little things big shadows, worry can also raise our cholesterol levels and blood pressure, give us a rash or a headache, and generally make life more miserable than it needs to be. Worry causes our fight-or-flight responses to go into overdrive. It can make us feel important, as though something were really going on in our lives and as though we might spring into effective action at any moment.

Mostly we don't. Mostly, we just worry to no end. We waste our energy: it fountains out around us as we dither over things that are none of our business or over which we have no control at all. If worry is not leading us to action, to an engagement of will, then it is best to look at the processes of worry, and figure out why we worry so much and whether or not we can cultivate an alternative.

I am not one to preach about getting rid of negative emotions. I don't find this to be a helpful attitude, and agree that thinking we can excise large swaths of self is a good route to denial, delusion, and a cutting off of sources of life force. But I also feel that chronic worrying saps our energy and is something that we should look at if that is our tendency. What is worry trying to tell us? What need is it trying to fill? What is it masking? What can we actually affect?

The more open to life power we are, the easier life becomes. When we begin to close down because of worry, this constricts life power, making any task or obstacle that much more difficult to face. If we can open to our work, to life, and to the task at hand, ease will come.

Constriction of life power is caused by uncertainty, tension, and fear. Take a breath: do I really need to worry about this right now? If the answer is yes, what can I do about it? If the answer is no, can I attempt to let it go? Magic requires waiting until the proper moment and then acting with full engagement. Choice and will are of the essence in fully accessing life power. Worry impedes freedom of choice and acting from will. When one begins to close down because of worry, this constricts life power, making any task or obstacle that much more difficult to face. If one can but open to her work, to life and to the task at hand, there will ease.

Those who are effective magicians and effective in their lives tend not to constrict around the flow-of-life power. Rather than waste energy dithering, worrying, or blaming, they either act or decide not to act, both of which conserve life power and use it in such ways as give access to still more.

Worry, like all constriction, keeps us small and often causes us to constrict others. We curse each other with smallness. We curse each other with fear. We curse each other with lack of beauty. We curse each other with indecision. Why? Because we ourselves do not want things to change, and we're threatened when someone near us changes. So we curse. We try to keep small. We try to force others to constrict.

We can break the curse that binds us! We can call down the Promethean fires in service of our own liberation. The energy freed up from our worrying can be placed in the service of integration, possession, boldness, freedom, and daring.

Doing the Work

Below are nine steps toward changing a pattern of chronic worrying:

1. *Identify the issue of worry.*
2. *Take a deep breath.*
3. *Ask yourself whether or not this is something you actually need to worry about.*
4. *Ask yourself if there is any alternative to worrying.*
5. *Try to make one small change in the pattern of worrying.*
6. *Meditate.*
7. *Clean your house.*
8. *Get some physical exercise.*
9. *Get ready for an influx of energy and joy.*

Praying Our Lives

The Star Goddess can help us begin this work toward full integration every moment of every day. All it takes is a breath of remembrance of self. With each breath in, we breathe in life; each exhalation breathes out connection to all living things. There is no part of our lives that is not part of the sacred. "Re-member."

Reflection

Do the "Cleansing Life Force" exercise (see p. 28), light a black or indigo candle, and say the following prayer or one in your own words.[22]

"Star Goddess, Limitless fabric of All, flow into my life, let me be open to that flow. May I step wisely and well, love with joy and passion; may I recognize you in everything I encounter. May each breath bring me back into myself, into you."

All is limitless. Even the specific.

THREE

Awakening the Vital Breath

Life is breath. Life is sex. Vitality enters through skin, lungs, air, and heat. Enter breath and energy. Imagine a great wind blowing across your face as you stand in front of a hot fire, snapping sparks into the disturbed air. This is primal energy, the life of stars, sun, and earth, the life our ancestors gathered around and taught to nurture.

In awakening our breath, we awaken our relationship to all that lives. Conscious breathing leads to conscious presence. In this chapter we will look at breath itself, and at all that feeds and blocks our energy.

Risking for Our Lives

You are the first in God's divine image. You are sex. You are that which gives birth to all else.

—Victor Anderson

Creative flow is the energy that Prometheus risked the wrath of Zeus to bring to humans. Accessing this fully requires a willingness to risk, a willingness to pay for the privilege of it, and the ability to share. The payment need not come from external suffering; it can come in the form of showing up to work every day, to learn to pay attention, and to walk in gratitude for the gift of the inspiring fire.

On one hand, energy is a gift freely available to us by virtue of our being alive. On the other hand, many of us only open to a small portion of what is flowing all around us, and fewer still have active intercourse with a life energy that fills every inch of us: soul, mind, body, emotion. This is the Promethean spark that formed life force. This is the fire that we risk safety to obtain, that we nurture and tend as part of the Great Work spoken of by the alchemists of old. The base metals of our lives are turned to spiritual gold.

Reflection

What in you is frightened to move forward if you can't have the perfect outcome or cannot see all the permutations ahead? Can you harness the desire within you to move anyway? Or can you face the fear and ask it what it really wants? Take a breath, center, and find a way. Oftentimes the next step is a willingness to remain present to who you are right now, regardless of who you may become.

Looking for Longevity

To me life is a great force, a great energy, and through experience we begin to realize [that] there are ways of keeping that energy alive. One way is to accept the difficulties of life, just face them as they come, treat it all as an adventure.

—Ruth H. Cooke (in *The Uses of Life: A Conversation with Ruth H. Cooke and Jacob Needleman*)

There are many ways to approach spiritual work. Some paths advocate retreat from the world at large, and others encourage us to simply say particular prayers and leave the heavy lifting to the experts. Some religious or spiritual systems are simple and others elaborate, but all form their own energy and culture. The society we live in often conflicts with these spiritual cultures. Currently, this over-culture is one of instant payoff and immediate reward. The fact that the rewards are not long lasting doesn't matter. Shortsightedness and lack of sustainability are the subtext of our times, but we need not fall prey to those voices and messages.

Anyone who truly wishes for an active spiritual life has to turn a deaf ear to the clamor of advertising and instead listen to the voice within. The voice within, known in kabbalistic traditions as the "voice of sheer silence" or the "still, small voice," is our initial guide into the Great Work.[23] In fact, nothing will open without it. This ability to be present will increase over time, but we all begin at various places of distraction and attention, attention being a combination of sense and thought. The main thing to remember is that no one else's journey is our own. We cannot even know where we will end up.

Does the spiritual quest require us to deny the world? No. As a matter of fact, spiritual work requires full engagement in life. The way of magic is not that of renunciation. The fodder for our work is the stuff of life itself. Since life is sacred and matter is not fallen from some "better" place, we have only to look around us to begin. Things that need give way will do so when it becomes natural. There might come periods of more intensive practice, where going to movies or parties might feel like a distraction. In those times, we will redouble our efforts, only to emerge into a new phase, in which we can take up those activities again. Brief interludes of retreat are advisable. We may also achieve heights of spiritual epiphany or catharsis, but we should always come back down the mountain. Be it Nietzsche's Zarathustra or Jesus in the Gospel of Luke, great teachers all know that going back down the mountain to continue the work is important. As the Buddhists tell us, "Chop wood, carry water."

Our work requires inner struggle, but that inner struggle is reflected in, and gathers fuel from, our relationships, in misunderstandings large and small, in sharing deep joy, or in flashing hot with love or anger. All of these teach us something new if we let them. The work is in the listening, the opening, and the attempts to trust. Sometimes the work is in holding on and sometimes in letting go.

The Great Work requires us to practice and to be attentive to our lives in all their parts. Harnessing breath and life power requires both openness and diligence. This doesn't "just happen" by some minor miracle because we have the *idea* that we would like to become good magic workers and true seekers. Practice is to be done daily. Some days the effort feels deeply satisfying, and others, as if we are bashing our heads against the wall. It is too easy to feel we are getting nowhere simply because things don't necessarily feel good. We need to look at our expectations of how we think things ought to be, as well. This is all part of our work.

Our practice is with what is, and gathering information from that is the heart of our work. Sometimes we are in what is called the "open-hearted state," and sometimes not. We are not striving for anything right now but more information about the self. If moments of peace, quiet, bliss, or openness come, that is great, more information, but not our goal. Our goal is to keep showing up to ourselves and to our Gods every day.

We are to be "delivered from lust of result," not attached to the outcome of our work and our desire.[24] That is often difficult! We are trained toward achieving results rather than letting our processes unfold. What that does is actually keep us from the information we need. We only skim the layers in order to get to where we are going as quickly as possible. But if we let whatever arises arise, we can actually learn much more and therefore have a lot more to bring to bear when other changes naturally begin to occur. We don't want to crystallize too early in a state not well prepared to handle new influx of energy and power.[25] This is what can happen when we try to be precocious or achieve certain states of insight or action without going through the many layers of personality and time first. We risk growing a crust around ourselves too soon in our development, hardening around old taboos, patterns, habits, and ways of being. This makes us brittle rather than strong.

Am I saying we are to have no goals at all? No. But we need to be clever about choosing our goals and not getting caught up in what their exact manifestation might look or feel like. We change in every moment, and so does the trajectory we are following. As soon as we step forward, things around us change. In being present to our lives, we can remain present to the work at hand and to the subtle shifts in process and the realignment needed to move forward without becoming brittle and stuck in some old idea.

Remaining present in our lives, loves, magic, and work is not only a true way to build will and being but also an antidote to our propensity for sleep. So much around us wishes to rock us into complacency and keep us from full awareness. Part of our job is to notice this, and part is to awaken that in us that can.

Replacing the Rote with Intention

Habit: A shackle for the free.

—AMBROSE BIERCE (IN *The Devil's Dictionary*)

Often old, ingrained, habitual emotional or mental response is the direct cause of a lack of kindness toward self or others. If space is made, kindness can enter and ease the irritation. We can feel and respond to all of our emotional states, but we don't have to be wholly taken over and controlled by them. Some of us like to feed states of frustration, cynicism, outrage, or impatience. Getting to know those states and working with them, rather than allowing them to run the show, can yield surprising results and still more information to fuel our efforts at presence, attention, and transformation of soul.

Sometimes active interaction with rote behavior can increase irritation for a time. We may go through phases of not suffering fools gladly. But this interaction also serves to increase the strength of our will and presence, which will feel like a pretty good payoff over time. Sometimes, in order to starve habits that do not serve our magical will, we need to put better habits into place. Rather than falling back upon rote activities, we can seek out activity that feeds us, regardless of the level of difficulty. We can replace a second cup of morning tea with ten minutes of yoga. We can take a breath and think before maliciously gossiping about an annoying coworker. We can choose keys to bring us back into a state of attention rather than a state of daydreaming. We can discover what is truly important to us and see how our lives reflect this. We can repattern our brains to want to choose new things. That is magic.

Serving the Work

A calling is a deep sense that your very being is implicated in what you do. You feel that you fit into the scheme of things when you do this particular work.

—THOMAS MOORE (IN A *Life at Work: The Joy of Discovering What You Were Born to Do*)

Coming to consciousness when our whole culture is designed to lull us back into sleep is difficult and takes time. We must recommit each day to serving the work of our own God Soul and finding our will. Having a connection with God Herself, we can also ask each day to be of service in general. That requires wakefulness and attention. My habits, fears, and demons often wish to keep me from this work, but I want to bring my whole life to bear on this work of serving the All and opening the Great Work in the world. Each of us can do this.

Service is an awkward word in our culture and in certain magical circles. It has received a bad rap by some because of many examples of people who wish to be selfless and subsume themselves, working from a place of suffering and martyrdom rather than generosity and joy. Service does not have to be so. Service is not servitude. It is the simple acknowledgement of being part of a whole larger than we can usually see.[26]

Developing ourselves to the best of our abilities can bring us into fuller service as we discover the work we are born to do. The work that deeply satisfies us also satisfies the larger body we are part of, the body of the Limitless, which includes the earth, culture, and all who are engaged in an active spiritual quest. Working in service ends up serving our work. The more we do, the more things open to us. The more we hoard, the more difficult life becomes, and fewer doors open to inspiration, instruction, and success. The way of the purely selfish becomes a way that requires everything to be done through effort alone. Remarkable things can be accomplished through sheer force by some of these practitioners, but more remarkable to me is the work done by those who are more generous, and wish to work for something larger than just their own personal gain.

We require a strong balance between the healthy selfishness that enables us to attune to our needs and get our own work done without getting caught up in the work of others, and the sharing of skill, attention, and knowledge accrued that can be a blessing upon the work of others. Selfishness and service can support each other. The more we carve out time for the real interests of our work, the more energy we have to help others. Added into this equation is the fact that the more work we do on self, the better the effects we have on those around us, even without making extra effort. In my own life I find that the more adept I become, the gladder I am to share with the world, whether in simple or more esoteric ways.

Once we enter the Way, the Way opens to us. In order to do deeper spiritual work and to be of the greatest service, we must find what truly feeds us and gravitate toward that. Service for service's sake helps none.

The "work of this God," our inner God, always nourishes our soul and gives us vitality.[27] The work that serves us is the work that serves the world. There comes a point when the lack of separation between them will become clear, though it can take awhile, sometimes years, to ascertain. When we reach this place of alignment, joy and power dance to the rhythm of our hearts. There is no turning back once we have reached the state of integration. Those who do, become menaces to themselves and others, so we may as well learn to serve.

Feeding Ourselves

To be sensual, I think, is to respect and rejoice in the force of life, of life itself, and to be *present* in all that one does, from the effort of loving to the breaking of bread.

—JAMES BALDWIN (IN *The Fire Next Time*)

In order to serve the Great Work of self-possession in ourselves, it is helpful to discover what nourishes us over time, what helps us feel stronger and cared for, and gives us some amount of satisfaction or joy.

Sometimes, to figure this out, we must clear things from our lives for a time. This is like an allergy test for life, where one cuts out whole classes of things and adds things back slowly. Of course, we cannot do this with everything, or we would cease to be able to pay the rent, but I recommend experimenting with this. Years ago, I found I was getting ill too often and started cutting things out of my life, sometimes to the consternation of those around me, who had grown to expect certain participation from me. Simultaneously, I made adjustments to my diet. The combination of the two showed me clearly that things I used to like to do had become obligations that drained me, and that I had begun eating more things that didn't nourish me, as a consequence. These days, if I start to notice I'm getting ill, it is much easier to make adjustments, because I did so much of that work earlier, setting a pattern for overall health and well-being. I now can work well, but only if I am also being well fed in the process. As a consequence, former compulsive eating habits have dropped away, because life itself actually feeds me and makes me happy.

So, service need not mean sacrifice. Service must also serve the self. And the cycles continue.

The Life of the Breath

Breath is the bridge which connects life to consciousness, which unites your body to your thoughts.
—THICH NHAT HANH

The life of the breath is the life of humans, animals, and plants. Breath feeds all of these and is, in turn, fed by these. There is no escaping the miracle of air. More than simply a specific form of atmosphere, it is the very stuff that enables us to live in the forms that we do. The taking in and processing of the products of air is the first relationship we have. It is a relationship we have that shows we are individuals no longer reliant on our mothers for oxygen, yet simultaneously shows our interdependence on all other living things. Without them, the atmosphere would falter and we would cease to live as human beings on this planet Earth. Without the give and take from minerals, plants, and mammals, the atmosphere would change again, perhaps become inhospitable to the very things that help to keep it constant. We are part of the web that both sustains and feeds on life. This is breath. This is air.

All life, all magic, and all spiritual work begins with the breath. Breath is acknowledged as sacred in many world traditions.[28] Spirit is said to travel on the breath, and divine presence is often seen as the wind. Lovers share breath in the midst of kissing, a sign that their lives intermingle. Breath seeds one lover into the other. Breath is the great connector. Stand outside on any day or any night, and breathe. Try to imagine that this breath you give off and take in is shared with everything around you that feels alive. Imagine this, and then know that it is true. Breathe in life. Breathe out connection.

The whole universe breathes, expanding and contracting around us. God Herself is breathing in us, around us, through us. We share in her by sharing breath. The more conscious we can become of this, the more we open to life itself, in all of its beauty, ugliness, and possibility. When we close to breath, we close to life.

Reflection

How often are you in the midst of tension, wanting to run away or make something else go away? You will find that your breathing is shallow and constricted, and you are therefore trying to literally close off from life. Pause. Open. Relax even one small bit and allow more breath to flow. Life will enter with it.

Courting the Deep Inhalation

In essence, one who knows how to breathe properly has a healthy mind.

—GERALD DEL CAMPO (IN *New Aeon Magick: Thelema without Tears*)

Air is the conduit for life and all connection. We breathe together, conspiring. We breathe with the Gods, inspired. We create, we rest, we play, and we work, all on the rhythm of our breath. Each time we inhale, we breathe in life. Each time we exhale, we breathe out connection. All living things share in the power of air.

We are trained out of proper breathing by tension, fear, and disconnection from our physical bodies. To breathe properly, we must get in touch with our bodies. Whether you are an intellectual, an athlete, a homebody, or an avid outdoors lover, awareness of the physical is paramount to living fully. To be in touch with Nature, we can begin by looking at our physical selves.

Body awareness is our starting place, but we can then attempt subtle shifts in body consciousness and movement. We are not trying to force anything here but will attempt to introduce our bodies into a state of fuller awareness, relaxation, and breathing. Whenever we sense the beginnings of internal or external tensions that do not feel good, we can connect with slow, deep breathing. Connecting with life through breath keeps us from disconnecting from the situation at hand. The more present we are in our lives, the more present our lives become to us. Spirit flows on breath, and life flows with it.

Doing the Work

Read the following through and then attempt to follow the instructions. You may close your eyes at first, if it helps you to focus on sensation, but then I recommend opening your eyes so that you can "normalize" the practice and take it into everyday life.

Notice your body right now. Where is it tense? Notice if parts are warm or cold. Notice if you feel energized or sleepy. Now take in as deep a breath as you possibly can. Hold it. Notice what happens when you hold your breath. Exhale. Notice how you feel now. Now you are ready for the next step.

Slow your breathing down. Ask to connect with air and spirit. Feel the muscles of your lower abdomen expand as you inhale. Exhale and let them contract. Now inhale again, feeling your abdomen expand and then letting the air rise up to open your rib cage. As you exhale, allow your shoulders to relax further. Let your awareness begin in your belly on the inhalation and shift to your shoulder blades as you breathe out.

Allow yourself to breathe consciously like this for two minutes.

Learning to Center

My students think I don't lose my center. That is not so; I simply recognize it sooner, and get back faster.

—Morihei Ueshiba (also known as O'Sensei, the founder of Aikido)

We all have a center, whether or not we are aware of it, or are actively in touch with it. People we see who seem always capable and sometimes even unflappable are likely strongly connected to their centers. Many things can develop this center: sitting practice, dance class, martial arts, or yoga. Finding and cultivating our center is part of the powers of the Magician: to know, to will, to dare, and to keep silent. Our center is based upon the strength of the last one, silence. Our center is a point of quiet stillness.

In learning to center, some people grow frustrated because they get thrown off balance. "I put in all of this practice to stay centered, and I *still* grew frazzled during that meeting at work!" This is beside the point. Our work is not to remain completely calm and smooth at all times. Our work is to be able to return to our center as quickly as possible in the midst of upheaval. Our work can include being centered and joyous, centered and angry, centered and sorrowful.

Learning to center enables us to access breath and stillness, *and* develop our will over time. As we will discover in the next part of this book, will is the key to a strong spiritual life. If we practice centering in the morning before starting our workday, we will begin to have access to it all day long and simultaneously develop our will. Will is the ability to follow through on our commitments in ordinary life. Greater Will is the ability to follow through and manifest our life's purpose.

Emotions play a large role in our thought processes. We get used to feeling a certain way physically and having an emotional response, and then our thoughts loop from there, as though they had arisen of their own accord. These thoughts then link to our physical and emotional state, wearing a deep groove in our psyches, and often spiraling us deeper in or farther out: into anger, joy, sadness, futility, ambition, or whatever our patterns may be.

Some of these states were implanted in childhood through old family stories. Perhaps they were even passed in our blood. In coming to know them, slight shifts will naturally occur over time. Courting centeredness and stillness is a great help in establishing emotional and mental equilibrium.

The following is an easy yet potent technique for centering and returning to center. Once we have practiced it, we can apply to any situation we may encounter.

Doing the Work

This is another exercise that will become integrated into all of our other practices over time. Practice it daily, and you are sure to sense powerful results.

Take a deep breath. Drop your attention down to your belly, to that space between your navel and your pelvic bowl. Imagine that you have a still point there. Send a breath down into that stillness, and imagine it opening slightly. Tell yourself that this still point is always with you, no matter what chaos swirls about inside you or outside of you. You can always breathe and connect to this stillness.

Standing in Stillness

The world lives inside us, and we live inside the world. The only steps that will take us where we want to be are the steps into stillness and silent observation. All movement arises from stillness, and all integration comes from some form of observation. A life lived without consciousness is a life run by random chance, pain, or folly. The life lived in search for and in service of consciousness is one lived toward integrated enlightenment. With practice, the core of stillness become palpable, and radiates out at every moment, bringing consciousness to joy, sorrow, sex, love, anger, and grief.

If we choose a conscious life, we are choosing a life of effort. We can also carry the knowledge that this life of conscious effort brings the chance of integrity and well-being. All the systems in this book come from magic, but my aim is beyond that, to the great magic of the self, unified within and with all that is. We can become fully realized, masters, adepts, Gods on earth.

In order to reach this, we have to practice, and the primary practice, as many teachers tell us, is the cultivation of stillness and presence to the parts of self and soul.

The practice of stillness is important in will development, centering, and in becoming more resilient.

Courting stillness helps us to eventually reach a place where a triggering state, such as exhaustion, may not bring up the old thought processes we tend to associate with them. Every master in any tradition will carry a core of stillness that is palpable, even in the midst of play, active work, or strong emotion.

Our ability to access stillness will ripple out into all parts of life. This is a potent step toward self-possession and mastery. Though people can gain some measure of power without it, they will never be true masters of their Craft.

Doing the Work

Another practice that can be done daily, the following builds on the previous exercise. It takes the centering meditation and moves with it. This tests and strengthens our ability to actually use this technique in any situation.

Close your eyes and breathe into stillness. Feel the stillness expand slightly. Drop your attention into that space deep in your core. Then open your eyes and find that stillness once more. Breathe. Allow yourself to move from that center. Walk from this center.

Once you have done this, sit down. Sit for five minutes, focusing on this still space. Regulate your breathing and become as quiet as possible. For right now, we will not try to observe thought or emotion, we can do that later, now our task is to simply settle into our still point and breathe. Keep returning to this space. If thoughts or emotions arise, let them, but keep breathing.

Once you have done this, rise again. Go about whatever tasks you may have before you. See how long you can keep returning to this center today.

Do this again tomorrow.

Aligning the Soul

Just as we have different body parts that need to work in harmony, and personality parts that need to do the same, so does our soul have components that need to come into harmony. Most traditions have techniques that help with this, but they are often not stressed explicitly. Celtic-based traditions balance the three cauldrons, Theosophists work with the three fires, and ceremonial-based traditions do the Middle Pillar meditation. Heathens can meditate on the *eihwaz*, or world tree rune.[29] My practice unites the parts of the soul with breath. (Please see appendix B for further explanation of the parts of the soul, p. 250). We, the vital human, become the world tree, bringing all the realms together.

Some traditions posit that one is born with an "immortal soul." Others state that the human must grow or earn that soul in stages. I believe that both theories point to a similar truth: each of us has a part connected to the macrocosm, to the Limitless, but few of us are in touch with it in any satisfying form. For most of us, the connection is vestigial, and for others, possibly broken. Many people will catch the occasional glimpse of the eternal, fewer still will have any regular contact with this part at all, and still fewer will become fully connected to this part, living as whole persons, guided by their own divinity and connected to the divine that rests beyond their humanity.

To become fully human and fully divine—this is our aim. The breathing process below is used to balance and align the components of our soul. Another foundational practice, soul alignment should be done daily, regardless of how advanced our practice is.

Doing the Work

Take a deep breath. Fill yourself from the soles of your feet to the crown of your head. This is a breath for your physical body.

Take another breath. Feel it pushing just beyond the edges of your physical form. This is a breath for your Sticky One, the etheric body that stores the energy you need. It is instinct, animal, and child.

Take a third breath. Feel it filling your aura, the egg of energy that surrounds you. This is a breath for your Shining Body, which communicates with the world. It is human; it listens, thinks, feels, and speaks.

Take a fourth breath. Let it fill all of your parts, opening your crown chakra to communicate with your divine nature. This is a breath for your Sacred Dove, the God Soul that hovers above you. A halo intersecting your auric egg and your etheric body, it kisses the top of your head.

Repeat these sacred breaths until you feel so full of life force that you tingle. Then, on the exhalation of your fourth breath, tilt your head back and breathe up in a powerful, whooshing breath that feeds your God Soul. Feel the parts of your soul align within you. They might snap into place with a rush, filling you with a sexual charge. Stand tall and in balance, heart open, ready to greet the world. Your God Soul knows what to do.[30]

Vital Energy

Life flows on breath, maintaining our vital energy centers. We also take in and maintained energy through food, exercise, sex, and rest. I often ask my students to take an inventory of these, to ascertain whether or not the above activities are feeding them well. It is too easy to eat bad food or get barely enough exercise, and certainly many of us do not get enough good rest. If we look once more at the writing from "Gauging the Real," (see p. 29) we will notice further patterns. Perhaps there is more work to be done on some of the basic categories. Some people find keeping a daily food and exercise diary helpful in accurately assessing patterns. Other people grow careful about where they shop, others maintain home gardens, and some read labels of ingredients to check for toxins that might impede their well-being. We can learn to moderate our intake of false forms of energy that rob our vitality. For example, replacing or cutting back on caffeine and products that contain high-fructose corn syrup can only help our overall health.[31]

Another gauge of vitality and the availability of energy is our emotional state. If we are often tired or depressed, or feel anxious or angry all the time, more than likely we have issues with energy flow.[32]

The more embodied, healthy, and vital we are, the better able we are to be present. Lack of health diminishes our ability to act fully in our lives. Exercise raises serotonin levels and stills the mind. Good food gives sustaining energy. We know all of this, but sometimes our lives conspire to keep us from acting on that knowledge.

Another factor to maintaining vitality is to have fun. Too often between work, family, and other engagements, we can only spend time in a stupor when not actively taking care of responsibilities. We would be well served to remember that fun is part of spiritual practice, because it is part of human and animal life: dance, swim, play, make art, do whatever happily engages you.

We can get to know those moments when we are less in control of our energy. Is it when we are overwhelmed by strong emotion? During a blood-sugar crash? When we're impatient? The more aware we are of how energy runs in our lives, the more likely we are to replenish rather than lose ourselves.

Sensing Vital Flow

One fairly easy way to train our energy sensitivity is by using a pendulum. If you are an advanced practitioner, you likely tried this technique years ago, and I encourage you to dust off your pendulums again to see how things are flowing now. People newer to the magical arts may have never used a pendulum at all. One thing that is good about them is they are easy and inexpensive to make. All you need is a short length of light chain, some heavy string, or dental floss. I like to use about a foot's worth, so there is enough to loop around my index finger a couple of times, leaving me with a six-to-eight-inch length of cord. After this, you will need a weight. Small fishing weights are good, or a pendent with an oval or pointed bottom works well. Saints' medals are favorites of mine because they are really cheap. Sometimes a favorite necklace can do the trick, but the rounder the pendant is, the more difficult it will be to sense energy. Metaphysical shops often carry specially designed pendulums.

Some of us may need to try this many times to get the hang of it. Other people will have an easier time of it. The pendulum might swing back and forth, side to side, or in a clockwise or counterclockwise circle. Once you are able to sense energy with the pendulum, internally ask it, "What is your yes?" Once this is established, ask, "What is your no?" You can then use it to ask simple divinatory questions, and use that as further practice for your energy-sensing work.

For further energy-sensing techniques, I recommend studying *qigong* or *tai chi*, or the chakra systems, or doing some work with the

Celtic "three cauldrons."[33] All of these will aid your ability to apprehend and move energy. Simply turning your attention to energy flow during weight lifting, dance class, or your evening walk will also help. You can tune in to breath, and then notice how your heart pumps and how the temperature of your skin changes. All of these are good indications that energy is moving through you.

Doing the Work

Practice by first imagining energy running through your body. Start with breathing deeply and fully, and imagine that on each breath your body gets fuller and fuller with life. Do this until you can feel the energy bumping up against your skin. Then hold the pendulum in your dominant hand, looping it over your index finger, and holding the string or chain in place with your thumb. Raise your other hand, holding it palm up about an inch below the pendulum. Make certain the pendulum is still. Then imagine energy fountaining up out of your hand toward the pendulum. See if any movement happens.

Keep working at it. Re-center yourself, and still the pendulum. Lift your non-dominant hand again, letting it slightly cup itself naturally, rather than forcing it to open all the way. Breathe in life energy. Imagine breath exiting your body through your nose and also through the palm of your hand. Imagine that breath flowing out of you as pure energy, as heat or light or sound. Let it grow more vital and vibrant, fountaining up. Keep the rest of your body as relaxed as possible. Watch the pendulum.

As we become more adept at sensing energy through a specific technique like using a pendulum, we increase our ability to sense energy in more facets of our lives, on a daily basis.

Opening to Sex

You are the first in God's divine image. You are sex. You are that which gives birth to all else.

—Victor H. Anderson

One night, while standing outside of a dance club, I jokingly remarked to a friend, "I'm a very religious person, you know." He replied, "I know. And your religion is all about sex!" Yes, indeed.

It's all about life force, all about connection, all about expression, all about love, all about creativity; all about sex in its many permutations—pleasure, heartfelt communion, breathing with trees, accessing power, tapping into energetic flow, awakening the spine, kissing, arousal, laughter, tears, meditation, yoga, sweating under sheets, praying, walking tall, sitting on rocks, dancing, and cultivating compassion. There is genital sex and nongenital sex. There is fierce frenzy and there is flow, but there should always be connection. God Herself caught her own reflection in the black bowl of space and fell in love. All else flows from that place of love and lust that sparked creation. It permeates our work, play, rest, reflection, and endeavor.

The wheel of life turns upon the hub of sex, love, and spirit. But what *is* sex? I have talked about sex as the connective life power that runs through everything as both source and connection. This is deeply, profoundly true. We need to remember that sex is *also* genital pleasure, and connection with our own bodies and the bodies of others. This can include physical, mental, emotional, and energetic connection.

People are often skewed one way or another: either we want to focus on sexuality as genital pleasure to the exclusion of all else, or we wish to only focus on sex as life power in a more "spiritual" sense. But our relationship to actual physical sex is a good gauge for our relationship with other parts of self. In "Gauging the Real," (see p. 29) our sex life was one thing we looked at. I want to explore this further, because life energy and sex are such important components of magical work, as well as good human health and integration overall.

If we do not have a strong connection to our sex lives—by which here I mean sensual pleasure and genital sex—other aspects of our lives are likely to become out of balance. This does not mean that we have to have any sexual partner outside of ourselves. What it means is that if we are not willing and able to be open to pleasure, we can end up being in denial about certain emotional states or mental assumptions. Lack of physical sex and sensual pleasure also makes running energy cleanly and clearly far more difficult. All of this is a hindrance to spiritual and magical work.

If we are having no sex, scant sex, or dissatisfying sex, or if we are grasping at sex to fill a yawning void rather than for the enjoyment of the act and the sharing therein, there is a part of us that is out of touch with the divine flow. Again, sex can be self-sex. Learning how to properly access and run our sex energy by and for ourselves will help every aspect of our lives, opening us to greater power, generosity, and certainty. If we are having satisfying sex with ourselves, we are stepping toward the divine flow. If we are not happy with our sex life, or are so shut down from it that we hardly give it a second thought, now is the time to look at our energy, our connection to God Herself and to all living things.

Many of the great magic workers of the twentieth century knew this, and perhaps ended up stressing active sex too much so that still others have recoiled in response. But they were onto something. Sex and sex magic are incredibly powerful, potent processes. If we have ambivalence or strong constriction around our sex lives, we would do well to examine this now. We can do this through therapy, magical workings, journal keeping, or experimentation. We can also find entry points that feel safe, such as dance, massage, or any sort of movement that will open the body and emotions to sensual energy.

I recommend doing "Cleansing Life Force" in chapter two (see p. 28) to help us into a more balanced state around sex and life energy. Many of the emotional and mental complexes that we end up dealing with in the course of this work are rooted in sex, vitality, and our physical openness or constriction. The cleansing will help ease us toward an open place that is not a devouring or projective state. Replacing being shut down with being voracious may be necessary for a short time, as a natural swing of the pendulum between extremes, but over time what we wish to cultivate is a strong and healthy sexual expression, free from addiction or fear yet full of juice and joy.

Over time, we will learn our natural patterns of need, want, and desire, which will likely include both sex activity and non-activity. The following exercise is designed to help us get in touch with life energy as it moves through our sexual centers.

Doing the Work

Begin with breathing and imagining. Imagine taking a deep breath in through your genital area or perineum. Do this for a few repetitions. Next, physically "squeeze" the perineum or vagina while drawing in breath. Feel the energy rise up from your genitals through the center of your body, until it reaches your skull. Pause here for a moment, then release the muscles as you exhale. Upon exhalation, for now imagine the energy floating "out" through your whole being, to connect once again with the world around you. Breathe in and squeeze your perineum or vagina as you imagine the breath and energy rising in you. When your inhalation reaches its apex and you "feel" it in the crown of your skull, exhale again, releasing the muscles and allowing the breath and energy to connect you out again.[34]

This exercise serves three purposes: first, it activates the breath center and sex center simultaneously, galvanizing pure energetic presence within us. Second, it shows us that we can run sex energy up and down, for ourselves, rather than always running it *at* someone else or suppressing it. Third, it reinforces the fact that breath connects us within as well as with all living things outside of us. This firmly places us in the cosmos, on the continuum of life.

The great wheel turns. What is our relationship to sex in all its forms? Can we take it out of the box and let it shine?

FOUR

Accessing the Stable Planes

Stand firmly upon the ground. Feel how it supports and pulls you. Feel the skeleton holding up your muscles. Feel how earth can be soft and hard, yielding yet firm. Things grow from this stability, this nursery, this home. The chaotic riot of wildflowers is firmly rooted here. Without the constancy of earth, the flowers would not grow.

A life that lacks basic stability is a life that cannot progress and risks regression. Spiritual seekers must set their houses in order. If a person has trouble holding down a job, he will have even greater trouble seeking spiritual success. Spiritual experiences for this person may become panaceas, or methods of escape. If a person has trouble being in relationship with others, she will not have any greater success being in relationship to Gods or spirits, and will need to work even harder to come into a valuable relationship with herself.

Sometimes the spiritual path can help a person to "bootstrap" himself into a better working situation or into stronger, more intimate relationships, but there must be work done in the manifest, everyday world as well as in front of the altar.

In order to integrate the parts of our soul and fully touch our divinity, we must include each area of our lives. We get the picture: our whole life must come to the spiritual quest for the spiritual quest to take us anywhere. Otherwise, we simply feed the same patterns we've laid down in the past, and try to raise emotions that feel new but are really the same, just wearing a variety of masks. Nothing there speaks truth. The only truth lies beneath our ability to see ourselves for what we are: humans trapped in an endless, solipsistic cycle of our own making, rather than humans actively engaged in a practice that places us in the larger cycles of life.

A person once asked me, when I was speaking of distractions in life, "Isn't everything part of the work?" My answer is no; we must *choose* to bring everything to the work. Unconsciousness does not denote choice. I can go to a nightclub and be conscious of running and sharing energy while on the dance floor. I can remember to take a breath when annoyance rises while waiting, yet again, in an airport. The annoyance, rather than getting squashed or expressed, becomes more energy to fuel my inner work. The energy of the dance floor fuels joy and sex, rather than overwhelming or depleting me, or taking me out of myself. We can be present, wherever we are and whatever we are doing.

To become conscious, we must bring the varied parts of our personalities to bear on the disparate parts of our lives. We will look at our lives in light of practice, home and relationships, physical health, mental and emotional health, work and money, and our place in the natural world.[35] I call these catagories the planes of stability. All of these form a cube of earth, an altar upon which we stand and from which we can expand more fully into our lives and our larger purpose. Seeking our larger purpose or attempting the Great Work without attending to all of these angles of life will destabilize us. Unhappy is she who ignores herself in attempting to see the world.

In the midst of all of this, we must develop that in us that *is* connected, the part that we can name "I." Because of this, our inventory begins with a look at our spiritual practice and then moves to home and relationships, physical health, mental and emotional health, money and work, and Nature. Each plane of stability will have two exercises or reflections to help our exploration.

Sitting with Spirit

My task is self-observation.

—Jacob Needleman (in *Seven Aspects of Self-Observation* by
Irv Givot)

The basis for all of our work starts with spirit. A person living in the midst of the most difficult conditions of poverty or war can find a way to connect, even if that connection takes the form of one simple prayer each day. Here we look at the condition of our own lives and notice how much time we devote to spiritual development. Do we focus on this every other month, once a month, once a week, once a day, or throughout the day? Our goal is to be in the flow of spiritual practice and able to engage several times daily, until we reach the state in which we are constantly engaged. In esoteric circles, this state is often known as Adepthood. However, this level of work does not just "happen."

Practice is the spine of our skeleton. This is why I caution people to not say, "Well, my practice is just integrated throughout the day." For most people, this is an impossible task. They may occasionally re-member to breathe with consciousness, or may send up a quick prayer, or they may use a grounding technique off and on. These are all good and helpful things, but they are not what I call "foundational practice." While it is true that these people may use skills from their magical toolbox in their lives, without dedicated practice these skills can erode over time and the energy flow becomes more erratic.

All deep spiritual traditions require daily, foundational practice, and for good reason. Foundational practice is activity that "resets" our spirit bodies every morning and brings us back into relationship before be-ginning our day, so that we can start as a whole being to the best of our abilities. If we start a day scattered, we will remain scattered, even in our attempts to bring spirit into our work. Foundational practice enables more of our self to be present throughout the day. Without it, our personality is the only one running the show, reacting to stimuli, pushed buttons, attractions, and repulsions. This is not the route to effective magic. With the aid of consistent practice, personality comes into greater balance with the rest of our parts, enabling it to act in concert with intellect, emotion, and the part of us that holds divinity. In *this* state, our magic flows with a strong and easy current. Grace is easy, once the preparation has been done.

For those who don't yet have a foundational, daily practice, I recommend choosing one thing to start with that you can commit to doing at least five days per week. Start with five minutes. Then work up to twenty minutes of whatever it is: yoga, sitting meditation, or energy work. Do the soul alignment or centering techniques in the previous chapter (see pp. 55 and 52) I will start us out with a simple focusing technique that is a variation on something magical practitioners have been using for years. This will ease us into whatever foundational practice we decide to work with for the next few months. I recommend doing the following for two weeks, then adding on meditation, energy work, or whatever we choose as our morning practice. Meditation, though it can be a struggle at first, it is the single most helpful spiritual practice I have ever found.[36] Every effective teacher I have encountered has practiced some form of it.

Basic practices keep us in touch with the current of magic that called us to this path in the first place. Engaging with them also serves to keep us honest. Self-delusion grows more difficult to maintain when we are sitting with ourselves every day.

Doing the Work

Write out a "practice contract" with yourself. Make certain that you start with small steps so you aren't set up for defeat. Draw it up for one month's time. Once the month is up, expand the practice and write a new contract. Keep going until you have a full, functional, sustainable practice to carry the rest of your life's work. By this time, the contract should be internalized, because your soul will recognize the help given.

Remember, if you ever fall off, you can always get back on again, beginning with five minutes at a time.

Seeking Still Vision

This technique is a basic one but, if done over time, aids in will development, psychic openness, steady meditation, and magical attention. Seekers who engage with this as serious work and set about doing it every day will, over time, form a stronger presence in the world, becoming more effective in all of their work. All we need is a candle and a place to sit in good posture. Remember the breathing techniques we learned in chapter two (see p. 24).

The experienced practitioner who hasn't tried this for years may wish to. Sometimes our simplest, earliest work will yield surprising fruit when the tree is revisited. This work not only focuses attention and cultivates stillness but also activates our psychic centers over time.

Doing the Work

Light a candle, using this prayer: "Bring the hidden to light. Bless my work."

Sit comfortably with your back straight, either on a chair or cushion. Make sure your knees are slightly above your pelvis, so as not to put extra strain on your back muscles. Slow your breathing down and focus on the flame of the candle.

Let your vision narrow until the flame is all you see. Breathe slowly and gaze upon the flame for five minutes. Be open to the experience. Don't try to control it. Just breathe and gaze. To close, when you snuff the candle, say, "May the diligent work of all be blessed." This statement is a reminder that we do not work in isolation and that our work on self can also serve the world.

You may find it helpful to keep a daily work journal to chart any changes you may notice in your practice or throughout your day once practice has begun. For example, "Today, I noticed a slight tingling in my third eye while doing my breathing." Or "Today, I had trouble settling into the practice." This will help you toward the work of self-observation and show the effects magical practice has upon your daily life.

Looking for Home

After connecting to our spiritual life, our gaze needs to turn toward home. Both our physical and emotional homes are key. Within the rubric of home, I also include all intimate relationships. We need not live with another person for him or her to act as a stabilizing (or destabilizing) influence on our lives. Think of home as that which contributes to our ability to act in the world because we have a place to return to.

Magic workers, and Pagans in particular, tend to like *stuff*. Since the manifest world is sacred, our things often remind us of beauty and spirituality in solid form. This can lead to lovely spaces, filled with art, books, and music. However, it can also lead to big messes. An overly cluttered, dirty home is a home of trapped energy and frustrated desire. If this state is true, we may wish to enlist help in setting our physical houses in order.

From the physical home, we move to the less tangible but no less real. We look at the people we have made a home of. These relationships are often shaped by our younger years. Our childhoods were what they were, and we live with the joys, strengths, weaknesses, and other consequences. This does not mean that the forces that shaped our young lives wholly control us. If we need some short-term therapy to deal with the fallout from childhood, we ought to seek it out. If we are happy with our childhoods but feel stuck in other ways, we may consider doing the same.

Reflection

To inventory "home," we will start with our physical space. First of all, is it a stable situation that you don't have to worry about week to week or month to month? Second, do you like the space itself? Does it reflect the parts of you that make you feel comfortable and happy in your life? Is it fairly clean and orderly, so you don't have to root through clutter to find things you need or to find a place in which to rest comfortably? Is it so overly neat that you are afraid to rest?

Look at your intimate relationships. Do you have anyone with whom to share the deeper parts of your life, be it a close friend, family member, or lover? How honest are you able to be with yourself and this person or these people? Are the things you keep private things that, in a healthy relationship, might be better off shared to enable greater depth of connection? Do you share too much, not leaving any breathing room in your relationships? Do your friendships feel well balanced, with each person contributing and receiving support? What is your connection to sex? Do you have a healthy, vital sex life—alone or partnered— and a good connection to life force? Do you live so firmly in your own world that you don't connect with others at all? Is it hard for you to break out of your shell of shyness or superiority in order to actually relate to someone? Or are you the opposite? Do you fall out of yourself and onto or into someone else's life? Would you rather take care of someone else than tend to yourself?

The first step to fuller relationships is this sort of self-knowledge. Without it, no change can occur.

Manifesting Home

There comes a time when we need to look closely at our home and relationship patterns, and actively choose what we want. All acts of magic are acts of choice. Better to choose consciously than continue to let the unconscious choose us.

The previous reflection asked us to look at how things are. This exercise is to help us begin to map how things can be. Unless we have some sense of what we want, it is hard to make choices that help us work toward that. Sometimes, the beginning stages of manifestation will include things we know we want and other things that currently seem right but will, in retrospect, prove to be off the mark. That is fine. What is important is that we begin somewhere.

When I was attempting to manifest the relationships and living situations that I knew I wanted deep down, I included things that would later prove to be untenable. But as I didn't have a broader vision of what was possible at that moment, I knew I needed to begin where I was. As our self-awareness grows, our desire comes more into balance with what is truly healthy and possible. Sometimes we think too big, and sometimes we limit our scope.

The very act of putting my spell for joyous home and partnership out into the world began to shift things inside of me. Those changes, while not always easy and not without difficult fallout, ended up walking me into the home and relationships I truly wanted. Along the way, I had to struggle with my internal voices and old patterns that told me it was too scary, that I couldn't possibly have or deserve these things. I let those voices remain, *but I moved forward anyway*. My life is now full of true joy and the sort of challenges that help me to grow without tearing me apart.

My favorite, simple spell work around manifestation is to still myself, align my soul, and then write out my desire in red ink. I sometimes do this with paper and pen, or sometimes simply use the red ink font on my computer. I recommend doing a few drafts in regular ink to make certain you have the spell as right as you can make it. If you are a person who works better with tangible objects, design a spell bag, or talismanic bracelet.[37]

If your home and relationships feel stable and good, as if they feed you, instead of doing the following exercise, I recommend picking one thing to do that would make them even better. And on top of that, you can give thanks to the Gods and intimate friends for good fortune, and recognize your own good work in building a satisfying home.

Doing the Work

Begin by writing down everything you think you want in a friend, physical home, or lover. What would your ideal home be like? What would it feel like inside, or what might some of the physical hallmarks be? What do you want in a good friendship or love relationship? What is important to you? Honesty? Passion? Openness? A willingness to engage with the difficult stuff of life?

Write the answers to as many questions as seem to apply. This can take the form of a list or free-form paragraphs. Once you are done, go back over your writing to see if these are things you really want or things you think you should want. I recommend that you divorce this spell from specific people or places. You want to be as specific in qualities as possible, but also leave room for the universe and your own shifting psyche to work.

Once you have this pared down to your satisfaction, let it sit for a few days. Then, time it to the traditional phase of the waxing-to-full moon, asking the natural world to help lend this spell power. When the time feels right to you, do a cleansing and some centering meditation. Then write or type the spell out in red ink. The next step is very important. Put the spell away for one to three months. Do not look at it during that time.

Making a pact to put the spell away is very important, because it gives the magic time to settle and gives all of our parts time and space to make what changes are necessary on subconscious, conscious, intellectual, physical, and emotional levels. If we look at the spell in three months, we will likely find some things already manifesting and others perhaps needing to change, because *we* have changed. Remember, once we move, the universe moves too. After this, we can alter the spell at any time. When the spell feels "done," we can bury or burn the paper it was on, thanking the gathered energies for doing their work.

This spell work is not passive. We put a lot of effort into the making of it and the execution of it, yet we also opened up to movement outside of ourselves. We put forth intention and work, and the world stepped up to help us.

Committing to Health

Glory to the body, which wants and has and will be satisfied! Glory to the body, imperfect, earthy, aspiring, revolving wondrous flesh!

—ANNA DALLARDIN AND JAMES BUTLER

Embodiment is a key component to a spiritual path based around inclusive consciousness. Transcendence of the body is neither desirable nor practical. The more firmly rooted in our bodies we are, the more vibrant our spiritual practice can become. Good physical health encourages good mental, emotional, and psychic health. Exercise improves our ability to develop our will, to calm our mind, and to focus our attention. Magic workers are not very effective if they get no exercise. This is as important as daily spiritual practice to our Great Work.

I am talking about being as healthy as our bodies allow us to be. We can be in a wheelchair and be healthy, or we can be ambulatory and be a physical wreck. I am speaking here of making our best attempts, within our own physical strengths and limitations, to be engaged with our physicality.

We are embodied. We need to be embodied. Our spiritual practices do not attempt to deny the body. So why not engage the body to its fullest and allow it to aid us in our work? It is a simple proposition, really. Here is an example from my own life: After two months of only getting my usual moderate exercise of walking a lot, I went back to the self-defense class I was taking at the time. I had been off, partially because of the vagaries of my travel schedule but mostly to let the tendonitis in my left arm have a rest. After two days back at the class, with a particularly vigorous session one evening, the next morning's prayer and meditation session felt radically different. My body was far more still, centered, and present, settling in without any problem into the meditation posture. And my mind was sharp, clear, awake, and still. I've been doing sitting practice for so long that my body and mind are well accustomed to settling in, but even so, I felt a difference.

The sleepy or untrained mind spews out constant chatter. The mind will *always* generate thoughts, but the rate of generation varies according to the person's disposition, mental state, and—germane to this conversation—physical state. When the body is well exercised, it is contented and feels better, and is therefore better able to be still. When the mind is in a stilled body, it can be better attuned.

We all know that exercise gives the brain more oxygen, enabling it to function at a greater capacity, but how many of us put this knowledge into practice? If we want to be effective, we are better off getting some sort of exercise. We are better off eating well. We must connect with our bodies, not just our minds or emotions. The body is the basis of the soul.

Reflection

How do you feel about your body? What is the first thought or emotion that enters you when you think of your body? Thankfulness? Dismay? Surprise? Note that. What does that say about your relationship to your body?

What kind of exercise do you get? Is it regular or sporadic? Do you partake in the best sort of movement and work that you body is capable of? Do you have a list of excuses for not getting whatever amount of exercise is possible for your particular body type, weight, and state of health?

Celebrating the Body

We need to come into right relationship with our bodies, to not pretend they are not there, to not constantly be in battle with them, to learn to treat them with respect for all they give us, and to learn to treat them well. What does it take to commit to our bodies? Our hearts pump and our lungs fill. Even if our legs or arms don't work so well, our skin feels and our tongue tastes. What can we give thanks for? In what way can we glory in our physical selves?

Celebration of the physical, and our connection with holy Nature, starts with learning to love even one part of ourselves. Meanwhile, let's stop reading magazines or watching television ads that enforce insecurities so we will buy more that we do not need or send ourselves into a spiral of self-loathing that involves more physical abuse of our chosen variety. We can get some support to quit smoking, cut back on caffeine, get more good exercise, or eat better food. We can also get some support on working through the deep emotional and mental habits that threaten to drag us back toward hatred, disconnection, and abuse. All of this will help us toward greater autonomy. The more autonomous we are, the better able we are to step into our divinity and possess ourselves as full beings.

Doing the Work

Give thanks to your beating heart. Give thanks to your lungs that cycle air through you. Aren't their functions amazing? Give thanks to your nose, your skin, your tongue, your ears, your eyes.

Today—whether you are fat, thin, or in between; whether you are a smoker, athlete, or couch potato; ambulatory or not—do something nice for your body. Go for a walk or join a local pool. Eat something that tastes good and nourishes the body. Make love. Take a bubble bath or a nap. Do just one thing—one. And tomorrow, add one more thing, so you are doing two things a day that honor your body. Do two things a day for one month. Then see if you can add one more thing.[38]

Seeking Within

The next plane of stability supports our mental and emotional health and well-being. We will spend more time with these in subsequent chapters but will do a quick assessment now.

Looking at our place in the world, we often forget that the point that everything responds to is the same—ourselves. Until we come into better relationship within, we cannot expect to relate well outside. A strong sense of self in the world is important to magical work and spiritual health. This may seem counter to what we've been taught in some of the other major religions: that the self impedes our connection to anything spiritual. This is not true. Having a strong sense of self is not synonymous with being egotistical.

The self in this case is more accurately called the "personality." Our actual self is the composite of all of our parts, working in a unified whole, from our core essence. It takes a lot of work to manifest that self. In magical and Pagan traditions, self is cultivated and personality does not need to be "given up," but it best serves our whole being when we are aware of its many facets. Our mental and emotional bodies are part of this whole, and the better we know their patterns, the closer we come to wholeness.[39]

Our mental and emotional well-being are linked. When one is out of balance, the other often follows suit. Some diagnostic methods include looking at things like worry or distancing. These are both emotional manifestations, but they often first show up in our awareness as mental states.

We are not attempting to eradicate anything here. Our practice is simply observing and coming into greater awareness of ourselves.

This will hopefully bring us into a state of self-understanding, which is a powerful place to work from, opening us to compassion and true change.

Reflection

Are you spending any time with yourself, or do you feel you have too much time on your own? Do you feel happy, angry, depressed, stuck, or flowing? Do you spend much time in worry or in avoidance? What is your pattern?

Finding Balance

If our thoughts or emotions feel either too entrenched or too flighty, now is the time to examine this. We can easily fall into both mental and emotional habits, and these can come to control us so thoroughly that we fail to even notice we are being controlled.

Reflection

Do you ever have a thought that surprises you? When was the last time this happened? Today, yesterday, last week? Did you notice it very strongly, examine it, or suppress it? These thoughts might have their roots in fear, hope, something we were taught as children, some wish we have for ourselves, love, wistfulness, anger, or some terror of the future. If you can remember one of these thoughts, try to examine it a little. What do you think its roots are?

Enspiriting Matter

Money is no substitute for spirit. Lasting happiness cannot be bought or sold; it comes out of the heart rather than the pocket.

—BOB BROWN (IN *Memo for a Saner World*)

Money and work are separate entities, yet I link them on one stabilizing plane because of how they tend to function in our culture and our lives. Our relationship to one will often give insight into our relationship with the other.

We can do work that does not pay and receive money for not doing much at all. Sometimes the work we love pays in cash and sometimes in other forms of energy. Mystics and spiritual seekers often have a problematic view of, and relationship to, money. To avoid abuse, some occult systems simply prohibit the exchange of money for any kind of teaching or psychic work rather than discuss the possible pitfalls of charging or not charging money.

This must come into balance over time. Money must neither be scorned and avoided nor chased after indiscriminately. Money is part of how we live today, and the seeker must establish a relationship with it as with everything else.

We would do well to examine our attitudes toward work and money, both. Work without money can be admirable if it truly strengthens and expands the scope of expression within the individual. However, we can also learn to do work that brings in a decent amount of income over time. The older one gets, the more important this becomes, because *one must be able to shoulder one's share of life's responsibilities* in order to continue one's spiritual life.

We cannot hope to progress in a balanced manner unless we have brought this aspect of life closer to balance. We may do spiritual work and exploration, but in order to be an integrated being, and a truly spiritual being, we must also set our houses in order. Maslow's hierarchy of needs must be properly in place in order to engage in a deep spiritual practice. The two lower tiers of his pyramid—basic physiological needs such as food, water, sleep, and sex; and then physical security, employment, and health—must be met in order to free us up to work on expanding our emotional, mental, and spiritual well-being. Therefore, avoiding looking at our relationship to work and money will not help us in the long run.[40]

I am a great advocate of "fourth way" systems.[41] Rather than being reclusive practitioners, we can engage in what is known in Indian thought as "householder yoga," which is the spiritual practice of ordinary people engaged fully in ordinary life. This enables us to be very effective: we can be physically and spiritually strong, living life in all of its joy and struggle, giving help to those who need it.

The time of transcendence of the physical is over. This era calls for us to celebrate the physical, the mental, the body, the mind, the heart, and the spirit. All are unified. God Herself flows through everything. And that includes work and money.

The seeker needs a job that feeds her, pays his rent, and keeps her from spiraling too much into stress and worry about such things. Despite examples to the contrary, there was a stricture against studying Kabbalah until one was forty, with one's children raised and having one's life together.[42] We live in a very different world now, but the underlying principle at work in that stricture is still of help to us: our basic needs must be met, and we must become physically integrated before further spiritual integration can occur. The natural mystic will have to struggle with this, but it will be of help in the long run.

Setting our houses in order does not mean that we stop all spiritual work, ritual, and meditation during the process. Indeed, I began the study of magic when I was in my middle-teen years, long before I achieved equilibrium financially. But even so, I always paid my rent, even if that meant eating ramen noodles for weeks on end. Even when I lived in voluntary poverty in a community that ran the soup kitchen I still volunteer at, my basic needs of housing and food were met, and my work was done in exchange for this.

I occasionally hear stories of couch-surfing high priestesses or teachers of magic who were consistently at war with money, home, relationships, and work, often blaming outside forces for their problems. We all go through phases when we need help, and this is fine. However—we know the however—in order to be in any sort of sustained spiritual leadership, one really ought to have her life in order. If money and work are both a constant struggle, something in our magic needs to shift.

Our relationship with work and money is like any other relationship, and should be approached with an open mind, open heart, and open hands. We can stop rejecting and we can stop hoarding. We can come into alignment with ourselves and our world. We are divine but must uncover and *dis*cover that fact by dealing well with every facet of our human lives. Simultaneously, we can work for a world in which there is greater economic justice.

The following exercise will help us open to a healthy relationship with work and money. We will be using the tool of automatic writing, beloved of Victorian spiritualists in America and Britain, who used the technique to contact spirit beings. Writing coaches use it today to help people break through the mental censor.[43] I use it as a call to deeper thoughts and deeper parts of my own self. The rules are simple, time yourself and, once you've begun, don't let the pen stop moving. Don't cross out or correct. You will need a notebook or journal and a fast writing pen.

Doing the Work

Make sure you have a fresh page of paper in front of you. Unlined is best, but if all you have is lined, give yourself permission right now to write outside the lines if it becomes necessary. Set your timer for five minutes. Take a deep breath. Now begin to write, "Money is …," and fill in whatever comes to mind. Keep doing this over and over: "Money is … Money is …" Use the same formula until your writing changes on its own into a free-form flow about your thoughts and feelings for money.

Once you are done, look back over what you have written. Are there old attitudes here that keep you from what you want currently? It is time to examine these. Do the "Cleansing Life Force" exercise (see p. 28) to begin the work of cleansing and shifting the life force around money.

Opening to Right Livelihood

There's a happiness or a joy in having a career or having work that you can do. And if you haven't found it, it's really a crucial part of spiritual practice to look for it. It doesn't mean it's going to be some big special thing.

—Jack Kornfield (in "Eightfold Path for the Householder")

"Right livelihood" is a catchphrase for spiritual people. Part of the eightfold path of Buddhism, it is the quest of many an internal seeker. When people speak of the concept of right livelihood, often there is a tone of wistfulness about their use of the phrase. They are unhappy with their jobs and long to do work that is more fulfilling and better aligned with their politics or spiritual beliefs. Those latter two are admirable goals to work toward, but right livelihood begins right where we are. Right livelihood is working in balance. The first thing most of us need to look at is our attitude toward our jobs. If our job feels meaningless, we can nevertheless affect the people around us. In fact we *do* affect the people around us, and that alone gives meaning to our daily work.

In the long run, what we are matters more than what we do. Our substance will manifest itself in many different ways. Our being may present itself in male, female, or other form. It may present as one who sits in the street for social justice; who types letters for lawyers; who builds houses; who dances; who works equations; who tends gardens; who seems angry, sad, joyful, calm, or scattered.

If our being changes over time, it will affect the quality of our doing.

The following is an example of practical magic. We are setting the intention to affect our workplace, and by doing so, we engage our wills and move energy to effect change in the world around us. That latter is a classic definition of magic, one too often forgotten, because we often fail to remember that magic can actually work in the manifest realms!

This is one thing the ancient Pagans or medieval alchemists knew that we have lost: magic works when we place ourselves in the midst of the flow of life and bring all we are to bear on the task in front of ourselves. Both components are of equal necessity. The practice of full presence rather than escape helps us into magical power. From this place, we can better share power and have further affects on our lives.

Once we have begun our work to bring ourselves into alignment with our workplace and realize we can have right livelihood as a dishwasher, bureaucrat, singer, carpenter, or forest activist, we can then see if our life path is leading us elsewhere. The energy will open up to us, and we will likely learn more about magic, ourselves, and what we truly want.

Doing the Work

Is the way you are right now more of help or more of a hindrance to self and others? What would aid your development toward being of greater help?

Look around at your workplace and at your job itself. What sort of tasks do you engage with? What is your labor like? How often do you deal with others? Start with this simple assessment. After one week of this, find one thing you can alter to have a positive effect in your workplace. Perhaps this means being kind to the security guard in your office building, inquiring after his or her health, or thinking kindly of your supervisor and trying to imagine the kind of stress she or he is under. Or perhaps this will be something such as researching nonchemical ways to fertilize the plants you work with or sources for bamboo chopsticks to replace the teak ones your restaurant hands out. Or perhaps it means asking for a raise or to be put on a project more interesting to you, or asking to take a class to increase your skill level.

Find this one thing and commit to it for one month. Then see what happens.

You are Nature

The Earth is the cradle of our existence.

—BOB BROWN (IN *Memo for a Saner World*)

Spiritual wholeness and full possession of our humanity requires the recognition that we contribute to the biosphere. Contemporary Paganism considers Nature to be holy, because the sacred is not just *in* all, but all is the sacred. Even those of us who live in cities live in Nature, because our particular animal builds cities. This said, whether we live in a rural area or an urban or suburban place, finding our connection to and relationship with trees, sky, water, sun, rocks, earth, rain, and wind is very important. Our lives and bodies are filled with the classical elements of earth, air, fire, water, and spirit, as well as some of those elements from the larger periodic table!

I am an urban creature, fed by people of different cultures living in close proximity, fed by bookshops and restaurants, dance clubs and art. I love the wild, and also love green spaces cultivated by humans. The suburbs feel dead to me, too isolating and disconnected, whereas I can be in fuller relationship in a city or in a wild, or even rural, space. I have friends who feel otherwise.

In highly developed countries, many people have little contact with the world outside of office buildings. Those who work outside—on farms, in gardens, on construction sites, in forests, or on water—are in a better position to remember that the human is also animal and needs animal things. Those of us who work indoors most of the time, or who work strictly with our minds, have to put extra effort and time toward being in right relationship with Nature.

We are not separate from the natural world. In these times of intense climate change, it is incumbent upon us to do our best to be in right relationship to our environments. We also need to find ways to chart new cycles of life and live lives that reflect the world around us, as it is.

Reflection

What is your experience? What feeds you and reminds you of your animal nature? Is it visiting a rocky coastline? Gardening? Roaming alleys filled with crazy art?

Take five minutes away from reading and step outside. How much of what you see is human made or cultivated growing things? How far do you have to go to find a wild space? What do you feel a kinship to and resonance with? What happens to your body, mind, and emotions when you look at plant life or animals?

What commitments can you make to the overall health of the natural world? Are you driving less? Reusing or mending things? Growing your own food? Agitating for local recycling or stopping mountaintop removal?

Lastly, how often are you getting to green spaces, oceans, or deserts?

Listening to Your Animal

The earth remembers us, and the places where we grew up or have lived a long time recognize our patterns, just as we recognize the patterns of those places. Upon entering a new place, I always strive to introduce myself to the energies there. If there is time, I spend long moments in meditation, sending out tendrils of my life force into the land and sky, getting a better feel for the space and the beings that reside there, and noticing what is different from my home. This introduction also gives me a sort of *permission* to be there, and my time there is more joyously spent.

We are part animal, part human, and part divine, and the moment we forget the possibility of any one of those, we are lost.

Reflection

Listen now to your animal soul, the part most closely connected to your body and your instincts, the part that runs and rests and plays and even engages in work for the sheer physical satisfaction of it.[44]

The animal in you longs for something. What is it? Some of its needs probably came up in your work around body and physical health. Listen to your instincts and try to make time to let your animal self free. Do you want to howl and drum on a hilltop during the full moon? Do you want to snuggle under blankets when it feels cold? Do you want to run on a beach or rise at dawn? Give your animal a gift: of time, of pleasure, of challenge, or of comfort. Connect with your own wild self.

If you could be wild for one hour or one day, what would that feel like; what would that look like? What does your animal soul call for? Can you give it this?

The Planes of Stability support our work, our magic, and our will. Without them, we shall fall. In good working order, they give rise to all the magic we can hold. Practice, home, body, mind, work, and Nature all support the structure of the Great Work.

PART 2

Will—The Divine Twins

The Divine Twins dance together. They meet in love and in conflict. They meet in hope and in fear. They meet in brightness and in shadow. They are us, and we are them, constantly moving, shifting from stillness into form and movement into emptiness. It is in this space of paradox and resolution that will is formed. The tension between the Twins makes all things possible. Without will, nothing in us is possible. With will, anything may rise.

The concept of Divine Twins is important in many cultures. The Norse work with Freyr and Freya, some Voudoun practitioners work closely with the Manassah, and Egypt has the tradition of many twins, siblings who activate different polarities together. Feri Tradition Craft works with the Twins as bird and snake, earth and air, bright and shadow. They are all that is within us, mirroring, reflecting, and then embracing.

The poles are all inside us, and outside of us, and there are no poles at all. The concept of duality can help us figure out what is going on in a proximate sense: are things hot or cold, do I feel good or bad? The reality is, there is likely a lot more going on than simply these two. Nonetheless, the Twins appear, one after another, thesis followed by antithesis, forming a synthesis together that, over time, becomes a new thesis.[45] The Twins dance and love in paradox and the reality that change is the constant in creation. Born from the love and lust of God Herself, they are the spiraling of all creation: day chases night and earth kisses sky, and all is born then of their love. Brothers and opposites, they struggle themselves back into love.[46] Their love forms the radiant Peacock, a new being made from the reforming of the separated All-that-is.

Courting Divine Opposition

I am divided for love's sake, for the chance of union.

—NUIT (IN *Book of the Law*, BROUGHT FORTH BY ALEISTER CROWLEY)

We can call upon the powers of the Divine Twins to help us with this work of integration. Since they embody all opposition, yet still come together in love and the rush of life force that is lust and sex, we can use their story as an example for ourselves. When the struggle between what we like in ourselves bumps too hard against what we loathe, we can think of the disparate Twins, locked in divine embrace, on the verge of forming some new and radiant creature. For those of us who work the paths of Kabbalah, the Twins are seen as the two Pillars, with the new creature, the Peacock, being the Middle Pillar itself. All three are necessary for a life of embodied mysticism. One twin will never vanquish the other, but the energy raised from their opposition will propel us into fullness and possibility. We look at ourselves and ask what compels us and why. In gaining knowledge of ourselves, of our conflicting drives and desires, we retain the life force necessary for the great change that will surely come. Over time, we will cease to be controlled by either pole, and become master of both. We will feel, observe, sense, and gain more energy and power.

How do we do this? Every time an old thought arises that startles us, we can say, "What is the name of this twin and what part of self might I match it with?" Every time something strikes us as lovely or thoughtful or strong, we can say the same. This practice trains us to look for parts of self from every facet of fear and desire, liking and disliking, showing us that all are parts of self: personality, mind, body, spirit, emotion. Nothing needs to be given pride of place and nothing needs to be left behind.

This takes some patience and development of skill. Our tendencies are to focus more on "strengths" or "weaknesses" depending upon our predominant personality type.[47] Some days, when we are unable to embrace our parts, we must simply bear them. Bearing our parts rather than burying them is a strong first step toward self-mastery. Thinking upon our facets as doorways to the eventual realization of divinity can allow us continuous access to full life energy. Denial tends to cut off the flow of sex and love, leaving us feeling weak and less capable of dealing with much at all. Constriction of life power can look like running away or like forcefully staying put and "soldiering on." Both can be used as masks to cover our perceived weaknesses.

The realization that this sort of "strength" is actually a "weakness" in and of itself is another key to the mystery of the Divine Twins. We can learn to court our parts, coaxing them into the light through acceptance. This does not have to look like love right away. In early stages, simple tolerance is enough. Greater flexibility will come through the practice of many years. Just as a beginning yoga student has to keep showing up and stretching despite stiffness, pain, and difficulty, so can we show up to our whole selves.

Showing up today, no matter how yesterday went, is one of the best will developers we can cultivate. Can we look at ourselves today? Can we bear what we perceive? Are we dedicated enough to this work to cultivate an unflinching presence of deep compassion? All of this helps us become strong.

I often use dark and light, love and fear, connection and disconnection, or other seeming "poles" to describe the world and our experience of it. But then I quickly move into the marriage and embrace of these as a way to try to express that all are needed. Even this is false, of course, or only touches the tip of reality in the universe, because along with dark and light, there are dawn and dusk, shadow that blinds and brilliance that blinds, shadow that reveals and brilliance that reveals, and shades of gray and pearl and rosy pink and yellow and purple and blue. Life and the universe are both multivalent and multiplicitous, and a reflection of the disparity that union brings together into communication and communion. What is reflected is not either-or but everything-and. So are we.

What will these Twins form, given space, given time, given a place in our lives? They will give us wholeness and the surprise of a being born of love, beauty, and integration. They will form a synthesis that becomes a new thesis, and so the work continues.

Reflection

When you begin this work, meditate on the Divine Twins. How are their love, risk, and power akin to your own? What is it that makes you unique? No one but you has the particular patterns of mind and emotion that you have. No one has the mix of weak and strong, beautiful, talented, ugly, fierce, and shy. Name your twins, as many pairs as you can discern. Write them on a sheet of paper and place them on your altar. Or write them in a journal and vow to look at them each day this week. When you do this work, feel free to add to the list.

Moving Within and Beyond Duality

The expression of Life
through the application of Love
builds our mythological & real bridge
where the twins may meet
the chasm is crossed

— FRATER VOX COR (FROM HIS POEM, "PRAYER OF THE GREAT WORK")

Labels of duality are sometimes helpful in ferreting out categories within which to look at myself. But I need to not get stuck there. I need to keep moving. Or opening out in deep stillness. (I did it again! Up popped dualistic poles of movement and stillness!) Things are many. And when we re-member, things are unified into the All. This unity is not monolithic. It is the reality of connection and immanence and "we are all in this together." It is like organisms coming together to form a body, with the hand still different from the eye. All are necessary. And what is the difference?

Differences are helpful to me. They point me more clearly to that which can draw us together. Distinguishing is helpful, but in the name of understanding, not eradication. The eye sees that which the hand does not. The hand senses things outside the purview of the eye. My eyes do not feel the energy flowing off my love's body, but my hand does. There is perception. There is depth. There is possibility as long as we keep learning in the process and enter the flow.

From All are two, and out of two, love makes three. Or one. Or many. Or once again, All. Step further into the mystery and the magic.

FIVE

Tapping the Unconscious

Welcome to the place of the moon, sometimes shining and full, other times appearing as dark to our eyes. The moon is luminous, shining, enigmatic, and gorgeous. It bathes us in a brilliance born of darkness and reflection. The moon captures us, as one of the most beautiful and bright things we can gaze upon with the naked human eye. What rests in darkness, whispering, and what seeks luminosity? Feel the tides pulled by the moon. Feel the tugging at your soul.

The subconscious holds many things: buried memory, ancestral pathways, social cues, and inchoate longing. It is often considered to be the blueprint behind our physical machine, the hidden place where we are wired and put together. We are going to unscrew some of the plates of our psyches and peer within. One way to begin this work is to dive into our dreams.

Entering the sphere of dreams acknowledges our ability to look into all of our hidden spaces. Dreams hold worries, fears, desires, frustrations, connections, doubts, and wishes. Dreams can, over time, become powerful teachers.

Self-possession occurs when even the subconscious is brought to bear on our Great Work. The Adept accesses every realm, above and below, within and without. The work of this chapter is a precursor to further work with "demons" and "allies," and leads us one more step toward wholeness and integrated power.

Seeing Hidden Faces

Profiles and shadows are the quarter moon's progeny.

—Ron de Maris (from his poem, "Phases of the Moon")

Picture the moon in the sky. Is the first image that comes to mind a full moon? Or is it gibbous, with its little belly thrusting out into the night? Is it the slender crescent riding the darkness like the milky smile of a child? Our relationship to the moon and to darkness can say a lot about our comfort with the uncharted realms. Even the type of moon we imagine can give insight into our psyches.

I keep track of the moods of the moon, as it affects the mood of my city, my particular neighborhood, and myself. It is my key to unlock the hidden doors. The unconscious pulls upon our lives like the moon pulls upon water. Dreams and divination help us plumb these depths, exploring uncharted territory.

In occult terms, the unconscious is also seen as the personal astral realm. The personal astral is that place we visit in our imagination, dreams, and various magical workings. This is seen as connected to a larger astral realm, which is akin to Jung's "collective unconscious." This is the space where dreams are built and ideas have their first glimmerings before entering into solid thoughts or planned designs.

The moon itself has dark and light faces yet is one entity. This is a precursor to the dualistic mysteries that lie further on the path. The moon clearly shows us that dualism itself does not really exist, though things have that appearance in life. The face we show to the world and the face we look at in pensive or unguarded moments are the same. What brings them together? Ourselves.

In various mythologies there are many Gods and Goddesses who have more than one face. These are often the Goddesses of the crossroads, the Gods we call upon in times of transition both in life and death. These Gods, with their two or three faces, are the ones who can show us the way. They open the gates, and we enter. Can you enter yourself? Become the Opener of the Way.[48]

Doing the Work

Think of yourself now. What faces do you show to the world, and which are hidden away? Can you still see yourself as one being, even while carrying these faces? What will it take for you to become one being in functionality rather than simply a loose association of personality parts?

What in you seems to be at odds? How are these parts really the same substance?

Draw pictures of your many faces, using symbols that represent your facets. You may also do this as a collage project, going through magazines and calendars, finding the right images to express these parts of self. Does a larger pattern emerge over time, when you look at these various symbols in relationship to each other?

Reading the Moon

In esoteric circles, another power held by the moon is that of divination. Because divinatory tools are used to bring information up from the depths of the psyche, they are seen as being under the province of the moon. The moon shines in the darkness, and divination is said to access our psychic selves and has been used to chart parts of our lives that we may have trouble looking at consciously. The moon also controls the tides, and this has come to include the hidden currents of our souls, our hearts, our dreams, and our desires.

Divination only reads the past, present, and future as our relationship to them stands in this moment. If the smallest thing changes in our attitude or action, so does our relationship to all three things. Divination is not a reading of fate set in stone; rather it is a way to uncover parts of self and to tune our psychic senses to realities we may not "read" with our rational mind. The irrational is at play here, so we may as well relax and enjoy it. We may also remain skeptical, and simply use this process as another form of self-discovery by gauging our reactions to the symbols at hand.

Below is a three-phase moon reading. Pick one phase to work with now, or if it feels right, lay them all out and look at the relationships within each reading, as well as each phase with the other. The illustration shows the reading in its entirety. If you wish to only read for the dark moon, for example, simply lay out those four cards in the same pattern shown in the illustration, leaving out the cards for the crescents and full moon. [see illustration i]

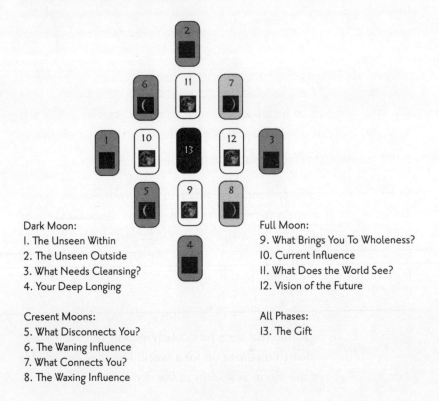

Dark Moon:
1. The Unseen Within
2. The Unseen Outside
3. What Needs Cleansing?
4. Your Deep Longing

Cresent Moons:
5. What Disconnects You?
6. The Waning Influence
7. What Connects You?
8. The Waxing Influence

Full Moon:
9. What Brings You To Wholeness?
10. Current Influence
11. What Does the World See?
12. Vision of the Future

All Phases:
13. The Gift

Illustration i: Reading the Moon

When the moon is dark, it is traditionally a time to rest, or to examine those things that seldom come to light. For this, we will read the unseen forces, things buried in the past or the subconscious that are nonetheless affecting our lives. The dark moon is also a good time to cleanse, to wash the crust off some old wounds and begin the task of healing.

The crescent moons, both waxing and waning, are symbols of liminality. The crescent marks a threshold between dark and light. It shows things coming in, moving from darkness, or things giving way, moving back into rest and shadow. This is a time to look at the ways in which we connect or wish to, and the ways in which we disconnect or wish to. What are we calling into our lives, and what are we letting go? The crescent moon in either phase can symbolize this movement. What is possible?

The full moon shows us all that has become apparent. It is all of our faces, present and accounted for. The full moon also shines a light on what we need to be whole, on what our gifts are, and gives a full view of what this wholeness makes available to us. Possibility becomes a shining reality here, instead of just a glimmer of hope.

As with all divinatory readings, the cards may read what is, what is to be, or what needs to change in order to manifest what we desire. Sometimes the answers may puzzle or surprise us. For example, our gift card may seem like a burden. Perhaps the burden is what needs to be dealt with before the gift can manifest. Or perhaps the burden is an important teacher to us, if only we pause long enough to learn from it. That in itself can be a gift. It is helpful to be flexible in how we read the cards. We can sit with them, write them down, and look at them again. I like to pick one that feels particularly potent or troublesome and set it on my altar to meditate on for a week. The message unfolds under the light of the moon as it shifts in the sky.

Naming the Nameless

In order to let go of something, you must first know what it is.

—NISARGADATTA (FROM *I Am That: Talks with Sri Nisargadatta*)

What is so hidden that we cannot even allow ourselves to name it? There are parts of us that have likely been hidden for years. Those closest to us might recognize these parts even if we do not. Others may just respond blindly, their own hidden parts reacting to ours, until it seems as though years of baggage are attempting to have relationships. We've seen it happen: his mother is talking with her ex-husband, and neither person is actually seeing or hearing the one standing in front of him or her. This doesn't usually work out so well for the parties involved. It takes a great deal of self-scrutiny to not be completely controlled by our hidden parts, and to recognize our baggage when it makes an appearance on the doorsteps of our workplaces or relationships at home.

One way to assess the power of old patterns is to look to our liminal states. Remember the Gods of the crossroads, the Openers of the Way? They are here, as well, in the threshold times between sleeping and waking, waking and sleeping. These are the little transitions that happen every day. If we attempt to be present and aware during these times, we can catch glimpses of parts of self we are barely aware of, or sometimes see things we are totally unconscious of or have been holding at bay.

I like to trace the patterns formed by my first waking thought each day. Is it one of confusion, dread, joy, love, or gratitude? These all point to something very important and will likely show up in larger patterns throughout the day. One of those patterns is the chatter in our brains when we are barely paying attention. The thoughts that creep in when we are otherwise occupied end up occupying *us*, often for long periods of time.

There are our waking patterns and our busy-in-the-day patterns. We can come to greater skill in noticing these. Examination of thoughts gives us much information about ourselves. For example, if I find the thought "I just need to figure out—" arising unbidden from the depths of my subconscious, I take note. Rather than attempting to actually "figure anything out" I try to stay with the moment. In pausing and breathing in that space, sometimes a greater awareness opens. Often, I am staring at a juncture, a shift in my life, and sometimes my emotions perceive that juncture as a chasm, hence the sudden wish to figure something out rather than face the unknown. The figuring out impulse is an attempt to take control, to be active, to *do*. Sometimes the doing is in the *being*, and right here, teaching and learning can occur.

Reflection

What is your first thought upon waking? Often the first thought is the same every morning. This gives us insight into what forms our thoughts and emotions for the remainder of the day. It also gives us some knowledge into our underlying nature.

Listen to the tenor of the conversations or arguments you have in your head. You may wish to note these throughout the day. The pattern that forms will point to some emotional activity arising from your subconscious. It might be an old wound, triumph, or concern speaking, or may point to some other, buried activity.

When a recurring thought arises in you, take a breath. Try to be still, and really feel and sense what is happening within and around you in that moment. What teaching is available to you? If you slow down, does anything shift? Make space for these thoughts. In doing so, you make space for your whole self.

Tracking the Hidden Mood

We cannot force our emotions to conform to an "ideal" state. Our relationship to our emotions does change over time, but trying to force them into a new shape before they are ready will thwart self-knowledge and our spiritual work. When we have reached a certain point in our spiritual development, things may proceed mostly on an even keel. We can enjoy increased levels of success or happiness, or at least have a handle on the ordinary complexes we wrestle with on a regular basis.

But then something happens. We are acting, thinking, or feeling out of the ordinary, even though circumstances are not so very strange. We have triggered an old wound or deep pattern, walking into a situation that seemed innocuous but ended up making us feel sad, angry, out of our depth, exposed, or any number of emotions. We can take our pick, for this will feel different for each person.

When we find ourselves in such a space, we may be quite bewildered, and for good reason: we are acting out of the ordinary, because we've been triggered into something we can barely recognize anymore, something that may have little bearing on the current situation. What do we do now?

We breathe. We listen. We feel. We try to express what we need in the moment, ideally. And then we listen one layer deeper. What really happened? Was it a case of extra pressure in the workplace? Was it a case of "he said, she said"? Was I just tired, hungry, horny, or intoxicated? In the proximate case, the state may have started anywhere, but its actual origins are stranger still, further removed from context than even an ordinary pattern of response. What has really been triggered here?

For me, this might be a fear of abandonment that causes me irritation at another as a form of shoving them away first. For you, it might be the anticipation of being blamed for some egregious behavior when you are simply having a bad day. There are old patterns at work. Once we have identified this, what do we do?

Doing the Work

Give yourself some still space away from the situation that is feeling bothersome. Sit with your spine erect, back strong, and chest relaxed and open. If it helps you, light a candle or some incense. You may also wish to have a journal handy, if writing is a tool that works for you. Having tarot cards or runes available may also be of help.

Once you feel settled, let your breathing slow down. Drop your attention into your belly, dive into yourself, and breathe some more. Then ask this emotional state, "Where are you coming from?" Breathe. Listen. What lessons can you learn from this emotion? You may wish to write in your journal at this juncture.

Answers may arise here, or you may need to return later to seek more answers. If you have received an answer, continue by asking, "What do you need right now?"

Breathe. Listen. You may wish to pull a card or rune to get further clarity on your answer.

Once your time feels "up," thank this part of yourself, whether you feel you have gotten helpful information or not. It has done the best it can right now. It has given you the information you are ready for. If you want further answers, try to listen some more for pointers in ordinary life, and then repeat this ceremony again in one month's time. The rest of your work, of course, continues.

Entering the slightly altered state brought about by a meditative stance and the lighting of candles and incense often helps us to access the deeper parts of self. This form of naming is potent and will be of great help over time. Perhaps our tendencies to be triggered by the same sorts of situations will not change, but the next time we encounter them, we will know what we face and be better prepared to get what those parts of self need in the moment. It may also save our relationships from extra wear or tear, not that arguments or upsets will always be avoided, but they will be engaged with deeper understanding. That is powerful magic in and of itself.

Waking the Sleeping Soul

So long as a man sleeps profoundly and is wholly immersed in dreams he cannot even think about the fact that he is asleep.

—G. I. Gurdjieff (from *In Search of the Miraculous: Fragments of an Unknown Teaching* by P. D. Ouspensky)

Waking up is the core of self-possession and the basis of the Great Work of all magical practitioners and, truly, any spiritual seeker. It is the first step toward union with Godhood, selfhood, and autonomy. We sleep the sleep of the comfortable. We sleep the sleep of the afraid. We sleep the sleep of the complacent, the wounded, the blustering, the hiding, or the ones who demand space. We think we act as one person, but really, we are so little unified that we hardly know who we are from one moment to the next. This remains true until we really sink into the work. And until we sink into the work, those who *are* more unified can seem threatening to us. They disturb our delicate balance, for they show us what is possible.

One cannot possess oneself fully until one wakes up. This is hard work, painful work, grueling work, and, in the end, joyous work.

We must find that within us which sleeps. We must also find that which watches and listens, and that which does or does not think, feel, or act. We have the possibility of walking, dancing, and living in unity, but not while our disparate parts control us: this one minute, and that the next.

Our sleeping selves form whole communities, cultures, governments, and societies, but all it takes for the balance to shift is for one person to awaken. Our work is to be that person, to wake up and become whole.

Waking can occur in many ways. A friend or teacher might say something that feels like cold water being thrown in our faces. I remember when, years ago, a teacher of mine commented, "That must be very difficult for such an angry person." This shocked me into still-ness. I had never thought of myself as an angry person, but the truth of his statement ran all the way through me. I saw how my life was set up to mask and control my anger, never quite letting it out, hiding it from others, and not giving it expression. All the while, because I never saw it with my conscious self, it was controlling me.

It took much more time after that to learn to work with my anger instead of against it, and wouldn't you know, slowly anger abated. This doesn't mean that I don't ever get angry, but that I no longer have a constant, subliminal current of anger running through me. Instead, there is peace, joy, pensiveness, and sometimes—sometimes—anger.

We will take further steps toward walking with our sleeping parts later. For now, just the knowledge that things in us *can* awaken is enough. If we can open to a shock that may come, instead of locking the information away as too threatening, we have taken a huge first step toward our liberation.

Charting Our Dreams

Dreams, and the soul, are not interested in us being perfect. But they want us to put out a reasonable effort.

—ANNE HILL[49]

Other facets of our subconscious appear in dreams. Dreams are power-ful tools for deepening our spiritual understanding. Just as the thoughts we have upon waking or when we are not paying attention are sign-posts to the unconscious, so are dreams. What occupies our minds and emotions in the time we spend asleep? There are dreams that help pro-cess the day's emotions, thoughts, and activities, and there are dreams that harbor deep desires. Dreams can become our guides.

Learning to listen to dreams can be even more complex than learn-ing to listen to our thoughts and emotions. Dreams are rife with symbols and layers of meaning. One thing may seem straightforward but point to something more opaque. Another thing may just seem crazy but, when taken at face value, might cause a laugh or grimace of recognition, the "why didn't I think of that before?" response. By committing our consciousness to remembering nighttime images in the morning, the unconscious will begin to filter up into the waking world.

The more spiritual work one does, the more likely that one will call up teaching dreams or even prophetic dreams. If we are experiencing either of these two types of dreaming, it is probably a sign that we are getting ready to enter a new phase in spiritual development, or that our souls or our Gods are calling upon us to do a specific piece of work.

Doing the Work

Keep a dream journal by your bed each night for one month. Say this before turning out your light: "I wish to remember my dreams, that they may teach me the mystery of the unconscious realms." Each time you awaken, commit to writing down as much as you can remember, whether or not it seems important.

Begin to make note of any symbols or images that recur. Ask your Gods for help in opening to the messages of your dreams.

If teaching dreams arise, do some waking work with your dreams. Ask what they are trying to tell you. Do ritual with the symbols from your dreams, or pull cards for further information. Find our what emotions the dreams bring up. What thoughts do they give you? What direction are they pointing you in? Is it a direction you desire or fear or both? Travel into your dreams on the astral plane during meditation, or have a trusted friend guide you back into your dream if you feel unable to do so on your own. Your friend can then take notes for you.

What are you being told by your dreams? How does this affect your life? How does your unconscious space overlap with a larger subconscious, a zeitgeist? In what ways is the astral realm trying to communicate through you and ask you to bring ideas into fuller manifestation?

Listen to your dreams. They will tell you.

Asking for Teaching

Just as it is possible to remember dreams more clearly by keeping a journal near the bed and putting a key into our subconscious minds to remember, we can also ask for our dreams to teach us. Teaching dreams come during times of great spiritual or emotional depth, change, or upheaval. To call these dreams to us, expanding daily practice is helpful. Scheduling sessions of sitting meditation for both morning and evening, for example, and being diligent about making offerings to our Gods or ancestors are both helpful conduits for opening the subconscious.[50]

Then, we can ask our Gods or ancestors to speak to us through our dreams. We can also set aside some time at the end of our meditation or prayer sessions to just listen. Once we are still enough, information can start to flow through. A deep meditative state can be similar to a deep dream state. The mind is relaxed from conscious thinking, and the subconscious is more open to what may come from deeper sources, whether inside or "outside" of the self.

Learn to listen to your Gods. Know that you cannot teach yourself everything. The more open we are to learning from the world, our subconscious, our rational mind, our body, other people, and Nature, the more lessons will arrive that will be of help to us, and the better able we will be to notice and learn from them.

Another thing we can do in the course of this work is to write a letter to our ancestors to ask for help understanding some of our patterns. What can they teach us about their stories that might shed light on our own? What were their attitudes or experiences? Even if we don't know exactly who our ancestors were, we can find that within us that carries them forward. Be they ancestors of blood or of spirit, they can both gift us and "curse" us with their legacy.

For example, over the last decade I've done a lot work regarding my attitudes toward success, work, and money. I finally reached a stage where I felt pretty clean about it all but was still encountering pockets of resistance. These did not feel like "mine," and I finally noted that they must come from my ancestors. My working-class ancestors were very nervous about my being in the public eye, my head above the crowd, so to speak, besides which, I had no steady "normal" job or practical way to make an income. How was I supposed to take care of myself? I wrote them a letter asking them what they wanted to say to me and what they wished to teach me. I also wrote a note of reassurance to them, telling them that I was OK, and wasn't going to be pilloried for being recognizable and living an unconventional life.

Doing the Work

Below is a simple four-card (or rune) reading to gather more information:

1. *Where am I going with my work?*
2. *What do my ancestors want?*
3. *What holds me back?*
4. *What supports me?*

Seeking the Forbidden

Fear is the cheapest room in the house.
I would like to see you living in better conditions.
   —Hafiz (from *The Gift*)

There are things that hide because they are in our subconscious. There are things we are blind to, that no amount of friends' arguing otherwise will bring to light. There are also things we have purposefully submerged. These float around the edges of our awareness, and we keep beating them back under the water, deeper and deeper. But something always causes them to rise again. That something is often desire, a secret longing, a wish so strong it brings tears to our eyes if ever we allow ourselves to remember it is there.

Perhaps we were frightened at a young age. Or maybe we were made to feel ashamed by peers or family. We may have never known that some things were even "allowed." Our responses to any of these hidden languages control us as surely as the unconscious or fully conscious. We have put parts of ourselves in a box on a shelf, or made another facet toe an invisible line. This hurts us and shapes us, just like those in the old Greek story who were made to fit the Procrustean bed. If they were too small, Procrustes stretched them. If they were too large, he chopped off arms or feet until they fit the parameters he had set. In our lives, Procrustes may have looked like family or culture at first, but he rapidly became ourselves. *We* conformed to lives that did not fit. It is up to us to make our lives fit who we are, instead.[51]

At this point, who we are includes whatever years we spent attempting to shape our lives to fit some other ideal, or hiding parts of ourselves in order to feel more acceptable. All of our parts are acceptable. All of our parts are worthy of love. Even the parts that have injured others must be drawn back into the fold. Only through accepting their reality can we heal, forgive, and become whole. It is wholeness we are seeking, and God Herself stitches each piece back into the fabric of love.

We fear rejection or vitriol or being ignored. And sometimes what we are really afraid of is getting what we want and being more fully ourselves.

Some shamanic cultures have a process they call "recapitulation" in which they move through their lives, examining and releasing old stories. The following exercise is a way to begin to open up to things that may have controlled us without our awareness. We are not trying to "fix" anything here, but the simple process of acknowledging these ossified taboos inside of us that we are still acting from or reacting against is in itself powerful magic.

Doing the Work

For this next exercise you will need five note cards, five thank-you cards, and a pen.

What is taboo in your culture, family, or group of friends? What do you secretly desire? Sometimes this information comes to you while you are sleeping, other times in daydreams. What feels taboo often just requires an internal shift in us and a willingness to take a risk. So we need to look at what that shift might be. The first step is acknowledging the submerged desire. The second is examining the emotions that keep it at bay. Third is looking at why the risk itself is scary.

On each separate note card, write down one thing that was forbidden in your family of origin. Take as much time as you need to do this exercise. Carry the cards in your pocket or purse and think about family taboos every day. When you remember one, write it on its own card.

This process helps to uncover the deep psyche of our family or the people we were raised around. Really work at it until you come up with five taboos, whether they were never spoken of, or spoken of only as proscriptions or in family gossip.

One by one, look at those cards. For each, try to build forward into your current life. How did the taboo affect you as a child? As a teen? As a young adult? As you are today? Just notice.

Now figure out what you might like to say to the taboo. Write that out on the other side of the card.

Once you have done this work for all five taboos, seal each in an envelope within a thank-you card. In thanking the taboo, you are recognizing that it has had a hand in shaping who you are today. You may wish to write a note inside the card, perhaps saying more than you already have on the topic. Perhaps you wish to thank the taboo for being a teacher to you, but acknowledge that you also have other teachers now.

Address the envelopes to yourself. Stamp them. Give them to a trusted friend to mail for you at various intervals beginning in one month. If you don't have such a friend, mail them yourself. They will arrive over the course of the next six months. When you receive the card, open it up. Read what you wrote and then sit down in a quiet space with the card. Dive into yourself as you breathe quietly. Examine what your current relationship is with this taboo. Has anything shifted, or do things feel the same? Again, you may ask your Gods for help if you feel the need.

Tracing Complexity

We need to become ourselves—what we really are in this life and in all lives—and not become enmeshed with our complexes.
—VICTOR H. ANDERSON

Complexes are psychological, emotional, or psychic systems that knot us up, twist our intention and life force, and manipulate our lives in ways that often cause ill health, whether physical, mental, or emotional. Run by complexes, we are not effective magic workers. As a matter of fact, many of the problems seen in spiritual circles come from people gaining power that then gets twisted through their complexes and comes out awry, resulting in power struggles, backbiting, or actually serious abuses. These are then perversions of clean life power.

To do our work well, we must be clean. To do our work well, we must learn to recognize our complexes. All of the work done in this chapter can be used in service of this end. Complexes show up in dreams, in thwarted desires, in tracking our hidden moods or looking at our cultural taboos. Complexes hide within all of these. Until we acknowledge our complexes, we will never possess our whole self.

Reflection

Say a prayer to know yourself in all your parts, even your most convoluted ones. Set your intention to plumb the depths of self-knowledge and to gaze at whatever rises to the surface. Then do the cleansing from chapter two (see p. 28). Afterward, sit in silence and notice how you feel. What arose during the cleansing? What arises after? Ask God Herself for help in blessing the things that surfaced. Imagine them slowly unknotting themselves, releasing some of the hold they have on you. Breathe in deeply, and as you exhale, expand to include these too.

Opening Imagination

The quality of the imagination is to flow and not to freeze.

—RALPH WALDO EMERSON

The moon and the subconscious are places where ideas can form. What grows in the place of unreason? Remember when you were a child. You could have wild thoughts all day long. Most children make up songs or stories, draw outlandish pictures, or build elaborate worlds. Some do this out of sheer joy, others to escape difficult situations.

We are taught out of wild imagining. We are taught to be reasonable, not a bad thing, and to put away dreams and flights of fancy. Magic workers need both reason and fancy. We need minds that are both sharp and supple in order to be open to what the universe has to offer us, instead of just what we think is most reasonably available. Magic workers must be open to paradox and synchronicity.

Sometimes an old self-image has burrowed so deeply into our identities that, even though we may have changed radically, we find it boxing us in and delimiting our possibilities. We can open to dialogue with these old pieces of self that we carry. Sometimes we may find that they are ready to let go. Once their grip has loosened, we can better open to the power of our imaginative minds.

If we celebrate the unconscious, it will celebrate with us.

Doing the Work

If you could live fully and to the limits of your imagination, what would that look and feel like? What in you resists this, and what is the story resistance tells? Who would you be without this resistance? How have the limits you've placed on yourself defined you?

Gather some finger paints, crayons, a pen and some paper, or collage materials. Write, draw, or paint whatever crazy thing comes into your head. What would you most like to see or experience or taste or live? Write or draw that out. Do you wish to go to Mars, meet an angel, float through the air with ease, become a superhero? Write or draw that too.

Once you have given yourself time to do this exercise, get yourself a glass of water and drink it down. Then put away whatever you created for three days. After three days, pull it out and look at it. What symbols occur? What does it tell you about your desire? What does it show you about the power of imagination?

If you find a symbol or word that still speaks to you in the piece you created, use that to start a fresh piece. Repeat the process above. By doing this over time, you may begin to hone in on something that can be grounded in ordinary, reasonable space and time. What is that thing? What is the first step to its manifestation?

Six

Honing the Will

Enter the forge, a place of heat, smoke, fire, and darkness. There is the fire, coals glowing brightly to support the dancing flames. Here is the quench, filled with cool water. Can you see your reflection? The anvil and hammer are ready to form the metals into a useful shape: a tool, a wheel, a sword. Do you feel the possibility of strength within? The bellows waits until it is needed to fan the flames with a burst of air. Fill your lungs and feel yourself filling with life itself. Look around you.

We have the ability for mastery, to use these tools and form a unified self from our own raw materials. We have desires and aspirations, weaknesses and fears. Hiding among all of these is our potential. Do we have the will to apply the tools at hand? Are we willing to change not our component parts but the strength of their relationships to each other?

The forge is another place of alchemical transformation. The realm where our power and endurance are tested, it challenges our willingness to be soft and melting as well as firm and unyielding. The dance of the forging process is that of knowing when one state is more necessary than another. To do this work, we must prepare to be both forger and forged. Can we submit to the testing of our metal? Our will and our work give us shape. Without will, we are too readily shaped by everything outside of us. In willingly entering the place of heat and darkness, we walk forward into our lives and become true.

The processes of recognizing, choosing, and then softening are very important to our life's work. If we cannot gaze upon the parts that control us in unhelpful ways, we cannot learn to shift the energies that coil around them. These energies are life force, bound by habit and patterns of long standing. Recognizing our tendencies is the first step toward holding the power of gnosis. Gnosis is brought through fire and light. First we recognize, then we engage our will and choose. After these two phases are complete, we make our tendency sacred by placing it within the holy fire. The holy fire then softens the pattern, readying that energy to be re-formed.

The next step after softening is beginning to craft a more useful form. This takes time. We can hammer, pound, and shape, but we will have to return the substance to the fire to soften some more, then cool it a bit in the healing waters, then hammer and shape again. This is a process of trial and error. The more skilled we are at self-observation and magic, the more precise this will be. If you are a newer practitioner or a teacher helping a newer practitioner, greater patience, time, and effort may be required. For those long experienced, this work can become quite subtle and refined, the taps from the hammer more certain and less brutish. But in any case, the lessons must be learned.

Reflection

Take a deep breath. Imagine yourself standing in the middle of the forge that is your life. See the fire, water, and anvil. Feel yourself as you are right now, not who you have been or who you would like to become, but who you are, right at this moment. Are you happy? Frightened? In love? Lonely? Satisfied? Seeking? What is your work like? What sorts of relationships do you have? What environment do you live in? What are you willing to sacrifice to this process of melting and re-forming, right now, today? Pick one thing. Start small. There is plenty of time to deal with all of the aspects of your life, so just pick one small thing you are willing to let soften. What have you been holding onto that you might be willing to see change?

Now give that thing physical form. Is it a lump of metal? Is it a coin, a silver teapot, a sickle, or a hoe? Gaze upon this, and name what it is metaphysically:

"My inability to speak clearly to my partner." "My habit of self-deprecation." "My impatience at taking any criticism." What is this for you? Take another deep breath, pick up the bellows, and breathe some fresh air onto the flames. Now take your object and place it in the fire. See it melting down, softening and changing shape. Let it be your intention that this softening process will begin to shift your relationship to this aspect of yourself. Feel yourself soften a little bit inside, as you watch the melting process. Once the object is soft, imagine picking up the tongs and lifting the softened metal out, placing it gently upon the anvil.

Are you ready to pick up the hammer? What shape would you like to represent the change that is beginning inside? Imagine turning that shape upon the anvil. Let each blow be filled with the power of your intention.

Testing Our Metal

Every incarnate being forges its own destiny by its deeds, feelings, and thoughts.

   —MOUNI SADHU (FROM *Theurgy: The Art of Effective Worship*)

Tests and hardships are rarely pleasant. But often, they cause us to be more actively involved in our lives than we might be otherwise. This is why sports such as rock climbing are popular: people thrive on being challenged. Giving up too soon is often simply the by-product of a childhood where we were told, "You can't do that; you aren't (fill in the blank) enough" or when we were made to feel bad about attempting something and failing the first time. Some of us never went back to pick up the task. Lying down when a challenge arises can lead to depressed states. Humans need friction, for it is what helps us to grow. The green shoot must crack the shell and burrow up through earth before the flower has a chance to grow.

Think about the metal-smith, working and sweating, laboring in the heat to create a useful form from disparate elements. The smith needs both intuition and skilled precision. Every tool is different, every batch of metal is different, and each day the fire burns in a slightly different way. Each day, the smith is different. One day, she may be well rested and strong; another day, he might be preoccupied, so his mallet swings are less accurate or firm. This is the way of life. We must always account for difference, and learn to face each day and each situation anew. In developing our relationship with ourselves and the sacred elements that make up our lives, we develop the ability to respond accurately and openly to everything we encounter.

As magical practitioners, developing ourselves also develops our will and connection to all the things of life: the elemental forces, deity, and a sense of our own place in the world. When we combine the above, we are suddenly able to act rather than be manipulated. We become able to make decisions from our own sense of ethics and our connection to each situation at hand, no longer needing to rely on moral tropes that may or may not be applicable. We see a need, and move to fill it. We choose to act or not to act, to speak or not to speak. All of a sudden, we are moving through life as sovereign agents, as divine beings, and as people who can think for ourselves.

Once we can think and act from our own strong sense of place, we no longer need a moral rubber stamp to tell us right from wrong. We are connected. We know. And if sometimes we are off and make a mistake, well, we are strong enough to have risked ourselves and strong enough to accept the consequences of our actions. The forging process makes us strong. The forging process makes us true. We must be willing to bear it. It is not always easy—actually, it is mostly not easy—but the rewards of being autonomous, upright, and ethical are great. Life is richer for our struggle. And once we have been through our own struggles, our compassion for the struggling of others only increases, lending more joy, beauty, and love to the world.

Reflection

Have you ever risen to a challenge? How did you feel during and after this? Were you enthusiastic, impassioned, or raring to go? Or did it all just feel like too much? Did you end up seesawing between these two states? What made the difference?

What is your biggest challenge right now? How are you dealing with it? Are you facing it, engaging with it, or avoiding it?

Defining Will

Put your principles into practice—now. Stop the excuses and the procrastination . . . Decide to be extraordinary and do what you need to do—now.

—EPICTETUS (FROM *A Manual for Living*)

Every moment of every day, we have a choice. Epictetus was born into slavery yet was not a slave within himself. What are we slaves to? Can we cease our slavish behavior? Yes. All it takes is one deep breath and remembering; we can act other than this: we can stop complaining; we can be more fully who we are. All of these acts and small decisions help to build will, which is the core ingredient to our magical work. It is also the core of successful artists, businesspeople, scientists, and athletes. Most often, anyone who has achieved success beyond the ordinary bounds of having basic food and shelter has developed his or her will.

Will is willingness. Will is the action of our intention. It is the coupling of a goal with discipline and skill. Will without skill is ineffective. Skill without will has little aim.

We must make explicit the difference between an open, strong will and constricted use of force. Will is not *machismo*. Force is used in the absence of true power, which is a power from within that lends the ability to act in the world. Internal power is a welling up of strength that knows itself and needs no one else to define it, nor does it need to fight over scraps, because it has enough. If it does not have enough, it knows the steps needed to get what is necessary or desirable. All the political infighting that goes on in human groups denotes a real lack of power. Those who hold power wield it wisely. Those who wield force are not good leaders.

Sometimes, because developing will requires discipline and commitment, we enter into a punitive relationship with ourselves. In general, this is not helpful. By use of force and punishment, we can train ourselves to perform amazing feats, but to what end? The result is a person who is used to force, and becomes brittle and lacking in compassion for self and others. Compassion, not pity, is a true sign of power held well. Compassion means the ability to see others as they really are, rather than trying to fix them or fight them. A punitive nature does not foster any deep empathy and can train us into a hardness that will break others and ourselves given enough time.

We develop will by making a commitment and fostering discipline. At the root of discipline is the word *disciple*, "one who takes on the teaching." Everything we commit to should be a teaching for us. We can become disciples of our lives.

There is no concept of punishment here; rather, we are showing up for ourselves and our work, and we are building muscles, slowly and over time, just as we would in a gym, lifting weights. We don't start out lifting two hundred pounds; rather, we add weight slowly as our muscles develop.

There is satisfaction in stretching beyond our immediate comfort levels to work on a long-term goal. However, the punitive aspects of discipline often enter in when we bite off more than we can chew by setting ourselves up with grand projects whose execution is way beyond us. If we instead just figure out what the next step is, we can take that step and move forward until we gain enough momentum to find some ease and joy in the project.

Doing the Work

Pick one thing to do each day and stick with it. If you say you will practice figure drawing on Tuesday evenings, then do that every week. If you decide to do a ritual once a month, pick a date and stick with it. Choose to not eat sugar today, and don't. Choose to meditate in the morning and just do it, even if you would rather sleep in. What sort of struggle arises in you around this? How will you deal with that? The conflict of the Divine Twins within you is vital, as it creates fuel for the work.

Look over your practice contract from (see p. 67) and see if you have been upholding that.

Struggling to Connect

All excuses are lies.

—JANE HEAP (FROM *Notes*)

Everyone struggles to work. Practice requires a continuous sense of coming home to a self we may or may not wish to talk with today. Will development calls for a fine balance between dedicated action and the awareness that a person also needs to have fun and some days off.

Sometimes we find ourselves in patterns of avoidance. We clean the refrigerator or play video games. We are in a state of resistance. The parts of ourselves that fear—change, success, sticking out, finding out something new about ourselves—conspire to resist the activity that will bring about the changes. We don't meditate. We don't take that class we've been wanting to. Our altars grow dusty and our jogging shoes are buried at the bottom of the closet. So we say we are lazy or procrastinators. What we really are is afraid. Or some parts of ourselves are, the parts that want to keep to the status quo, even if it makes us miserable in it. In these cases, I start by renaming what is happening as resistance and then try to look at the manifestations and what they are trying to tell me.

At one point during the writing of this book, I stalled out. My usual tricks and schedule I had set were not working. Needing to prime the pump, I set myself the task of writing every day, seven days a week. Even when I did not want to write at all, writing happened. Even if all I got out was one hundred words, I did it, though my daily goal was much higher. The next day, I would make up for it by writing at the top of the scale. As a result, I was able to exceed my weekly quotas, and writing became pleasurable again. I broke through the resistance by being both firm and kind to myself.

All practice is the same. Take sitting practice, for example. We can do five minutes if twenty feels like too much. We set our intention, show up, and this develops our will. Sometimes true discipline and compassion is asking ourselves again, "What do I really want?" and listening for the deeper answer. If what I want is spiritual discipline, if what I want is to write a book, if what I want is to be healthy—no matter what the answer is—then I have to make sure I'm making the choices that support that desire.

Discipline is not punitive. It can be the greatest act of self-love there is.

Know thyself. Know thy will, and keep returning. Life is the great return.

Freeing the Self

The commitment to our becoming centers us and provides a compass for the journey. It gives clear purpose and a feeling that we can stand tall. We can walk firmly on the earth with an erect spine, an open heart, and proud bearing. I wish for no more hunched shoulders and for heads to only bow when one is called to do so by awe and love rather than in deprecation. "Submit your life force to nothing and no one," says Feri tradition. Access life force and move from that place. Breathe it in, letting it infuse thought, action, and emotion. Life force is connection; all things breathe, and together we conspire.

What are we conspiring? We are conspiring for our freedom, a freedom based on power from within and power shared, a freedom based on integrity, depth, and joy. This is a conspiracy of breath, will, and laughter; of commitment, discipline, and desire. Once freedom is attained, the work continues, choices become clearer, and the pathway opens up. We have the chance for greater and greater integration.

We can look to others for support, but we cannot look to others to make our decisions for us. We must prepare ourselves to assess each situation and our place in it as accurately as possible. We will sometimes make mistakes. The walk toward self-possession requires risk for us to learn. We learn by acting rightly and by acting wrongly, but we will not be able to blame anyone else. Our actions are our own, not disconnected from those of others but not rising from them either. This is not about group-mandated morality. This is about personal choice.

How do we exercise personal choice if we don't work to develop our will and to look deeply into our own patterns, habits, and belief systems? We don't. This is obvious, but how many people do we know who are simply carried along by life, relying upon the opinions of television commentators or their friends at school, work, coven, lodge, or the local bar? How many people do we know who continue to engage in behaviors that are harmful to themselves because of emotional difficulty or addiction?

We can be free. We don't need to be slaves to our insecurities, our fears, or our laziness that masks more fears. We can be human: alive, awake, and potent. Vitality becomes the magical elixir that we drink in daily. When we are living fully potent lives, the world around us changes to reflect that. As we become stronger, healthier, and more integrated, so does the world. We are required to cocreate with the Gods. All time and space are here and now. We are alive, if only we would choose to recognize it.

Satisfying the Soul

Sometimes in the service of developing will, we have to ask what about our work satisfies us. Dissatisfaction often comes from lack of engagement. Some of us disengage as a form of protection from less than ideal circumstances. Others of us disengage because we have grown used to hampering our full reach. The world might change if we figured that out. For us then, the question becomes, what does satisfy?

For me satisfaction is the product of consciousness, will, breath, and creativity.

Brute force and mechanical activity do not build will. It is conscious effort that builds will. And consciousness and will bring creativity into any task. Why? Creativity is engaged activity. I can learn something and spark anything, as long as I am engaged, fully present. One facet of my engagement is the awareness of my breathing. In conscious breathing, as I inhale, I take in life power, and upon exhalation, I connect with all living beings. I can bring this conscious breath, my will, and creativity to martial arts class, writing, washing dishes, teaching, making the bed, or taking a walk.

All we have to do is remember—and choose. And know that the energy of this work can flow out to be of help to all.[52]

This is not much to ask, really, but it changes everything by allowing us to be fully here now, not with our minds racing in some phantom conversation or rehashing an old emotion. It is always our task to be present. If we are bored, impatient, or exhausted, we can still make effort. This builds energy. Energy is the fuel for the great alchemical transformation.

Gurdjieff talked about making "conscious efforts." These are pushes toward full presence with whatever activity we are engaged in, knowing that we are making an effort and not just going through a task in a rote manner. He also spoke of "super efforts," which are the same as the above, only the tasks being asked of us are beyond the pale.[53] The conditions are far too harsh or difficult, we don't like the people we are working with, it is raining, or we have been up since six and it is now past midnight. Super efforts are those occasional bursts of conscious work that open us up to brand new energy, taking us beyond what we ever thought possible. Psychic, emotional, or mental breakthroughs often happen during these periods, because fresh information enters into spaces that might otherwise be caught sleeping. If we are trying to escape the discomfort of our situation, the new energy will not arise. By sinking further into the situation at hand, anything becomes possible. We can call upon the Divine Twins to help us with this and pray, "May my wish to work come together with this extreme duress. May the two parts kiss within me." The product of that kiss will be the Peacock, the alchemical shift that reveals itself in fresh insight and more readily available life power. Perfection and rightness appear that would never have been manufactured had the difficulty not been borne.

We can apply these concepts to our own work by setting ourselves tasks of full presence, knowing that these will provide us with new information and help our will development. If we are sitting in a class or at a party that holds little interest, what is our task? We can work on posture and listen attentively. We can tell ourselves we wish to learn one thing, and then reach for it. We can attempt to see where a conversation *might* go and attempt to steer it so skillfully that no one notices. These are regular conscious efforts. If we are laying tile, we try to set each tile as precisely as possible, not wholly letting rhythm take over but perhaps setting each final corner with a breath. The opportunities for engagement are always present. If we use these opportunities to their fullest, we can truly rest when it is time to rest, for we know that our efforts were never half done.

After practicing conscious effort for some time, if super effort becomes required, we will have far greater ability to work beyond our usual capacity than otherwise. In making a solid effort every day, when need arises we are better able to shoulder what is necessary and to learn from it as well. Mechanical pushes are of little help. Only conscious pushes can build will in ways that are helpful to our project of coming into self-possession.

The active seeker is never bored.

Feeding Our Will

To be thus strong enough to refrain or consent at will argues a consummate and indomitable soul.

—MARCUS AURELIUS (FROM *Meditations*)

In learning to move from will and desire, in developing both, we establish a firm core. Living from this core itself frees us to choose our own thoughts and actions. Until that time comes, we are prey to the morals and ideals of those outside of us. Others dictate our behavior, or we fall back on rote morality in order to make our decisions. This does not allow for ease of action or for individual choice. It does not make presence truly available. Without will, practice, and our own ethical sense, we tend to fall back on some idea that may or may not apply to the situation at hand. In such cases, there is only reaction; we are not free to choose and therefore not free to act.

Without will, nothing happens of our own volition; we can only react to things that happen to us. Learning to act from our own wishes, desires, and sense of responsibility is paramount to our practice. Not doing so is an abdication of responsibility. It is a refusal to step forward and take our place. Simultaneously, sometimes we need to set clear boundaries in order to assert will. We must say "no" to patterns that undermine us and sometimes to friends who want our lives to be easier in the short term, not understanding our strong wish to live for our larger aims.

There are two types of will. The first is one we have talked about already, that we learn to develop like muscles. It is saying, "I am going to sit in the morning" or "I am going to dance class," and then doing so, whether or not I feel like it. This sacrifices my small desire of the moment for a larger life's desire.

Exercising will in these ways makes us stronger overall, and enables us to meet our commitments and to grow spiritually. Without a developed will, we have no access to true choices, being instead pulled willy-nilly by every outside force, large or small.

The other type of will—sometimes known as True Will, or the work of this God—is our connection to a larger life's purpose. This is knowing somewhere in ourselves that we are called to be healers, and going to medical school or studying massage no matter what it takes. When we get an inkling of this, we can begin to shape our lives according to this purpose. Developing our smaller will serves our larger Will.[54] As a matter of fact, without will, Will is impossible.

When we give ordinary tasks the added push of consciousness by turning them into will developers, our work becomes stronger. No longer do we just beat ourselves up, saying, "Oh, I missed dance class *again*! I'll never get back into shape and may as well just give up trying." We can say instead, "In this moment, I missed an opportunity to work on strengthening my will, but new moments are always arising. I will try to be more diligent." Changing our attitudes in this way also makes our actions sacred. We aren't just trying to get fit in order to be more socially acceptable but because we are attempting to connect ourselves to what we really want. This connection can become an acknowledgment that the immanent divine flows through all things.

Developing will requires consciousness, and further development of consciousness requires engaged will. To be a warrior, a healer, an effective person, we need presence.

It is my will that I be present while I write. It is part of my Will that I write. It took exercising the muscles of my will to make my Will manifest in my life. I have always written, sometimes only when inspired, sometimes snatching moments here and there throughout the week, sometimes disciplined and sometimes haphazard. But there was always a return to this, for it is my Will. This return eventually was bolstered by my spiritual practices that required conscious presence. All of a sudden, not writing when I said I would was no longer something to beat myself up about because of a thought that I *should* be writing. Rather, my commitment to writing blossomed into a wish to expand as a full, vital human being because I wanted to commit to myself.

Once I began working in this way, my commitment to writing flowed more naturally and easily—and I began to have greater successes with it. The struggle did not disappear, but it became an ally rather than an obstacle, and the energy I used to expend combating myself was now made available for the work itself. That felt like the greatest success. All of a sudden, my work was deeply satisfying. And my will was strong and ready to couple with my desire.

Desiring Fullness

Be intent on action, not on the fruits of action.

—THE BHAGAVAD-GITA[55]

Magical people live for engagement. A powerful practitioner lives life to the hilt, knowing that as spiritual beings, we must be physical beings. To connect with the sacred, all we have to do is open the door, greet another person, plant some flowers, watch ants at work, or build something. In other words, we interact. Engagement requires activity, and activity hooks into the continuous flow of life's energy. Life's energy is the fuel for our desires. Even those practitioners who have everything they want can still strive for more of that, and to learn and better themselves and the world. Life is perfect, but perfection involves change.

No matter what stage we are in, we must always seek out teaching. If we could live fully, to the limits of our imaginations, what might that look like? Likely, something in us longs for this, and something in us resists it. The Divine Twins form within us once again. We will work more intensively with desire in chapter ten, but looking at it in relationship to resistance will be helpful before we continue on.

We have talked about resistance taking the form of laziness or avoidance. Sometimes resistance is even less noticeable than that. This is a clue that it arises from an old self-image that has buried itself so deeply into our identities that even though we have gone through radical changes, we may find this appearing still, popping up to restrict the flow of our burgeoning life force. Old parts of self can establish internal contracts with us in order to keep us safe, which often means keeping us small.

Oftentimes we believe that wanting something for ourselves is wrong. We also end up not claiming, and therefore not taking responsibility for, our talents and abilities. In not doing so, we keep ourselves small. This sort of smallness can impede life force. I say "this sort of smallness" because there are moments when we all need to rest, to be held, to let someone help us. It is good to know our capacity to be big and our need to feel cared for. What in us needs care and what needs to let go?

When an old identity is still pulling our emotional strings, the subconscious is engaged along with a whole host of emotions that inform and empower the identity shell. I call it a shell because it is not our current identity or one we likely want to live in. This part of self is animated by the energy we fed it for the years when it was still a viable and functional part of self. Now that it is no longer fully functional yet still *functioning*, it becomes easy to not even notice its presence—until it hits us all of a sudden, constricting us. Then we need to look a little deeper and ask, "What is really occurring in this moment?"

Anything can help us to learn if we choose to make it part of our work. Throw away nothing, but attempt to bring all parts into working alignment and health.

Doing the Work

In journal or trance work, you may have discovered that either a part of you from an earlier phase of your life or perhaps even your ancestors swimming in your blood have bargained with your subconscious. Talk to that old part. Look at what it has to teach you, then thank it for its work and care. Show it all the ways in which life has changed since that part took charge.

Name this old part and teach it something the rest of you knows right now. Negotiate a relinquishing of the reigns of control.

SEVEN

Living in Greater Strength

Before we move into the place of beauty and integration, let us pause for a moment. At this threshold we can reassess the work we have done so far, and gauge where we are to go. This is the place to recommit and to further develop virtue and skill. Look around. This is the place where your power resides. All you are and all you have been stands with you now. What does that feel like? What are your allies here? Take a breath, close your eyes, and listen.

You have been. You are. You will be.

This is the place within us where we can look at our resistance and decide to move forward despite our fears. This is the place within from which ethics arise: we know we are in relationship with all things, and can act accordingly. The very awareness of relationship brings about the possibility of being in the right relationship, which is ethics in action.

Self-possession is the product of our work on integration. Can we be true to ourselves and to our unfolding? The first requirement is commitment. A commitment—to self, practice, and our word—flows into honor, truth, and strength. All of these come together to form a true base of compassion.

Considering Ethics

Don't you think
we all should study Etiquette
before we study Magic?

    —LEONARD COHEN (FROM *Stranger Music*)

For the sake of ease, and because the dictionary doesn't make much of a distinction between ethics and morals, I will make my own. My tradition is based on ethics. We follow no rede. Instead, the practices of presence and self-scrutiny are called for. When these two are left out, our magic goes awry.

The Divine flows through all things, a connective thread in the pulse of life force. This is immanence. Immanent divinity means that all is sacred. However, I can forget that. I can disconnect myself from the Divine flow, forgetting that I myself am divine and that you are too. As soon as disconnection enters, the web of immanence is rent. This is the moral basis for my magical ethics. There is no outside morality, imposed by law, book, or culture. In each moment, we can connect and remember, "Ah, the Divine flows here!"

An exterior, imposed morality can impede an ethics borne of connection, for if I am simply thinking of what is against the rules—right or wrong, as previously stated—I can sometimes act in ways that are harmful to others or myself, without having strictly broken any moral code. However, as soon as I connect to another, to the situation at hand, as soon as I open my eyes and heart to the divinity inherent there, I can make a true choice. I speak and act from connection, and that is what is right, and that, though it may hurt, generally will not cause harm. There is no way to know this ahead of time. This sort of ethics requires presence, awareness, self-examination, and a commitment to steady spiritual practice. In other words, it demands total self-responsibility. I cannot look to some outside authority to make my decisions for me, nor can I assign any outside blame.

Ethics arise from within. In refining our moral compass, we find our direction. We cannot wait for someone else to tell us what to do, because our vision arises from our living. Our action arises from our vision. We are present, on the earth and in our lives, choosing. Always choosing.

We cannot wait until our lives are better in order to begin this work. Once our basic needs are being met—and hopefully even before this point—we can take the stance of centered will and begin to decide things for ourselves. The longer we wait, the more difficult it becomes to act according to our deeper truths and desires, and the more difficulty we have becoming integrated souls.

People who are moving further into their power often lack grace. I know, because I saw that in myself and my peers, and see it now in some of my students. There is a reactionary crashing about that often happens before we acclimate to our new abilities. Rather than acting from a clear place within, we simply set ourselves up against other powers. The poet Rilke wrote eloquently about the ways of learning that form a master rather than simply another dilettante or follower: we humans learn "by being defeated, decisively, by constantly greater beings."[56] In ceasing our need to win and prove ourselves at every turn, in seeking instead to live in a way that feels right, we stand to learn more than is even imaginable.

Cultivating ethics helps us learn to seek what is best for ourselves and others, instead of being set off by simple dislikes, partial information, or our perceptions of hierarchical structures, be they just or unjust. If we are seeking level ground, we need not always tilt at every windmill. We get to decide what *we* actually want instead of letting others dictate terms for us.

The more we have a basis for ethical behavior, the easier our transition into integration will become. Practitioners who wait until after they have achieved self-possession to think about ethics or make their own decisions will have a much tougher time of it. Not only will they be dealing with an influx of knowledge and energy, but they will also have to acclimate to a new way of living in the world. When called upon to act autonomously, the seeker can become overwhelmed and may not always end up acting his or her best. I have seen brittle natures solidify after this phase of integration. Over time we end up with people who are really good at manifesting certain aspects of their wills and at teaching others to do the same, but they are not well rounded, harmonious, or whole. Sometimes they spiral into worse patterns, assuming they are correct because they have a new vision of the world. There are no checks or balances, and these practitioners often end up without peers, let alone superiors, to continue their studies with. This is dangerous to them and to anyone who tries to work with them.

The more we build our ability to be ethical, the stronger we will be when further integration comes. Grace will balance with power, and we stand a fair chance of becoming wise.

Sharing Power

One always commits oneself before fully knowing what one is committing to. There is no such thing as a commitment that is made only after all the evidence is in. Commitment is based not on facts but on desire—and the root meaning of desire is to follow a star.

—PATRICK HENRY (IN *Benedict's Dharma: Buddhists Reflect on the Rule of Saint Benedict*)

What is sharing power? It is the process of acting from our internal authority and showing others how to do the same. It is allowing space for others to act within the sphere of their own experiences. It does not mean giving over something that we truly have in order for others to feel more comfortable. Sharing of power allows for us all to be skilled in different venues and areas, and to speak of this and to learn from each other. I want to learn from someone who has developed her or his skills. I want to lead with people who have internal authority. I want to live among people who do not conflate equivalency with equality.

Internal authority needs to be developed in most of us. We are not raised in a culture that teaches this, and we sometimes use the *concept* of internal authority as a placeholder for true internal authority. Claiming internal authority requires commitment, work on self, and a taking on of responsibility. It is not just attempting to take away someone else's authority so I can feel more comfortable. When people become peers, there is a natural give and take, a flow, not a giving over or a taking away.

Over the years, I have taken on responsibility as a priestess and teacher. It is something I've had to ease or sometimes blunder into. I made mistakes when I didn't realize how powerful that responsibility was, when I was first learning to lead.

Fully accepting responsibility can be hard, because it is a refusal to be small. It is saying, "Yes, I have power" in a world where it might be easier to abdicate power, turning our life force over to another. That "yes" is strong magic. Accepting responsibility says, "There is enough in the world for us all. We can all be big, we can all be beautiful, and we can all be strong and talented." How do we get to the place where those words ring true instead of sounding like cheap platitudes? That takes some effort and awareness.

We live in times of great energy and possibility, ripe for the creation of new thoughts and new systems as the old ones begin to crumble around us. For those of us doing the Great Work, this becomes the time to step further into responsibility, really examining our accountability and opening further to kindness. We know who we are. We *all* need to be accountable if power is truly to be shared. One who has accomplished the work of self-possession has so much more to offer others than those who have not. We may as well prepare ourselves for this.

Doing the Work

Light a candle. Take a deep breath, from the soles of your feet to the crown of your head. Fill your aura with breath, with life force. Take a breath into your heart, feeling it gently open. Ask now that your heart be cleansed. On each breath, fill with kindness. On each breath, let yourself become more and more clear and clean. Ask for forgiveness if you need it. Ask for help if you need it.

Now take another deep breath. Ask for courage. Imagine a circle in front of you on the floor. That circle is responsibility. When you are ready, take a breath and step into that circle. It may feel hard or oppressive at first. Take another breath and let the circle expand. Let your capacity to take responsibility increase as the circle expands. Don't close up around the energy; breathe into it instead. You are able. Let your aura grow and pulse with life.

If you wish, you may say this prayer: "May I be open to love. May I be healed. May I walk the road that lies ahead of me, following its curves and listening to its ways. May I take courage and step forth into responsibility, accountability, and true kindness. May I find my work, and may my work be of help to me, to my community, and to the Gods."

Step back out of the circle of responsibility, knowing that you carry with you exactly the amount you are able to handle at this time. As you continue this work, each time you step into the circle, the stronger you will be and the more your capacity to do your work will increase. Be loving with yourself. This magic takes time.

After you have stepped back out, feel the new sense of responsibility in your body and straighten up into it. See the circle in front of you dissipate, sinking into the earth as a blessing. Put one hand on your heart and one hand on your belly. Breathe.

The Pentacle of Autonomy

Evil does not naturally dwell in the world, in events, or in people. Evil is a by-product of forgetfulness, laziness, or distraction: it arises when we lose sight of our true aim in life.

—EPICTETUS (IN *A Manual for Living*)

One aim of the Great Work is autonomy. Autonomy is a hallmark of the self-possessed human. When we have developed autonomy of spirit, we live from the pentad of commitment, honor, truth, strength, and compassion. These become the base for our ethics, our magic, and our lives.[57] These five qualities are necessary to live full, adult, human lives. When they are integrated, we become engaged with ourselves, our communities, and with the culture around us. Once integrated, we are makers and actors in the world rather than simply reactors. This is also the work that enables the bodhisattva to return and help others from a place of power rather than pity.

I often call this the Pentacle of Responsibility, or the Warrior's Pentacle. Let me tell you why. Warriors are bold, big, and sometimes sassy. The word itself is inadequate, because waging physical war is not my aim, but I have yet to find a suitable replacement. Also, deeply spiritual people, such as Gandhi and Thoreau, have used the teachings of warriorship to good effect.[58] I began to work with the word *warrior*, because in my work with activists, religious groups, and, really, any gathering of humans, I often found people, especially pacifists, denying violence yet using underhanded activity like backstabbing, malicious gossip, and other covert behaviors to set up systems with which to control each other's behavior. As priestess Katrina Messenger once said to me, "I've been to safer meetings when there was a gun on the table."[59]

I began to examine this tendency in my groups and within myself. What I found were the roots of my own violence and my vehement denial of my ability to *be* violent. My father was my image of both power and violence. In my attempts to reject his wounded ways, I threw out my own innate strength. The only power I had experienced was power-over, which was irrational, frightening, and harmful. So power and violence became linked in my mind, and I tried to reject both.

In reality, violence was lodged in my body and my emotions. I tried to combat it by developing a fierce intellect and an intimidating shell. This only worked for a short time, leaving me stunted, squashed, angry, and fearful. As a teenager and young adult, I would literally double over with intestinal cramps at the sign of disagreement with close friends or loved ones. Learning to relate in a fully human, adult fashion took years of struggle. I tried to play it safe, but this ended up boxing me in. The box was a place to heal, but eventually I grew too large to fit inside. Busting out required facing the potential for more conflict, but by then I was ready.

Warriorship can open the door to active nonviolence, to creative discipline and to a deeper look at our souls, our fears, and the depths of our power. It can help us develop our ethics. Without the work of developing ethics and responsibility as a spiritual practice, harm is possible. As I have mentioned, we see many casualties from the ranks of those who have neglected this aspect of the work: people who tapped into sources of power and ended up running amok and, worse, their students or community members caught in the backlash of their struggles. Thus, this facet of self-examination becomes another key to the work of full integration.

Claiming deep autonomy is part of the work of the warrior, healer, and priest. Let us take a look at these words, energies, and concepts that will form the basis of our work. With these, we can develop a strong, fluid state of responsibility and responsiveness. We will come into our own ethical state, dependent only upon our abilities and relationships, not upon some prescription set down by authority. Over time, we will become our spiritual authority. That is true magical power.

Reflection

Breathe into commitment: This is the first step that feeds and is fed by all subsequent work. Can I commit to myself, to my practice, to my Craft? Set your feet upon the path.

Stretch toward honor: Based on a sense of my place in the world, I can stand tall and back up words with actions. I can live toward a goal of integrity.

Reach for truth: I know myself. Therefore I can know my relationships. Therefore I can speak, act, and live in ways that are true, not based on prevarication and hiding.

Stand in strength: I have acknowledged that I hold power, and I have trained myself diligently, gaining ability over time. I have strength.

Open to compassion: When I commit to my work, know my place, know myself, and know my strength, I can then know you better. My heart opens, because my mind and back are strong. I need not act from fear, but can move toward love. [see illustration ii]

We can work through these points and see how they work in us. I will follow the pattern of running the energies through the pentacle, seeing how they all pass through the Warrior's Heart.

Illustration ii: Pentacle of Autonomy

Commitment

Once we have figured out that self-development is work we *want* to do, commitment is paramount. This is the point where any serious work begins. If we decide to study piano, paint, dance, act for social justice, or enter into deep relationship with another person, commitment becomes necessary. Work of any kind will not progress without this component, and we have to ask, "Am I committed to my spiritual path?" It also helps to examine and evaluate all of our commitments. In every realm, will enters. What are we *willing* to commit to? What will we actually harness our energies to in order to build momentum?

Commitment is linked to spirit, to a connection with something both deep within us and slightly beyond. It often enters with the breath of enthusiasm, a state of being filled with the energy of the Gods. This state of spirituality should infuse any working we must relate to for a long time. Sometimes things are not easy, and if our commitment or discipline is not based in spirit, we will find it even more difficult to sustain.

It should be said that sometimes a person who entered into a commitment changes so significantly throughout time that he or she no longer resonates with the requirements at hand. We sometimes need to say, "The spirit has gone out of this, and my time with it is done." There is no dishonor in this, if it is truth. However, some commitments are entered into without real intention, will, or spirit to back them up. We need to examine our motivations clearly, including this quest for self-possession. Are we feeding and being fed, simultaneously? There may be moments when it doesn't feel so—when the baby is squalling or the deadline looms—but overall the answer must be yes. In those moments where things don't feel so good, it is helpful to remember why we took on the commitment in the first place.

Work begins with commitment and continues with recommitment. Until we commit and take a risk, nothing can begin from our own volition. Things may happen around us and happen to us, but nothing will happen from a place of our choosing. This is very important to recognize.

We must take stock of our commitment over time. Are we still putting life energy behind it? Are we thinking about it at all? Is it bleeding us dry or filling us with interest? If, over time, we find we are not doing any active work to uphold our commitments, we must examine this and shift things so that the energy is flowing more clearly again, and our attitude is adjusted in order to be in better relationship with the commitment, or perhaps we will let the commitment go, as mentioned above. In the case of people raising children, of course, this latter choice is not an option.

We will cycle through all the points that follow and back into commitment, reinfusing all of our work with the breath of spirit and the blessing of our Gods. Our work is reinvested with intention and the love that flows from true discipline, which is the act of the disciple, in love with the teaching at hand. Let us be disciples to our own processes, our own work, and our own wills.

Doing the Work

What are you willing to commit to? What matters? Using the tool of automatic writing, write for five minutes on what your intent is and what you will commit to. Don't let the pen stop until the time is up.

Now look on what you have written. Are you able, at this moment, to follow through? Can you figure out the next step necessary to engage this commitment more fully? If yes, ready yourself to make a pledge.

Light a candle dedicated to this purpose. State your commitment to yourself out loud and to any beings or deities you may wish to witness it. Write down your pledge and leave the paper under your candleholder for one month. Every day, light the candle, state your commitment, and take a deep breath.

It may help to keep a journal about how you are relating to this commitment. Is it working in you? Are you struggling with it? Is it bringing up fear or excitement? Are you taking any tangible steps to further its progress?

Honor

What does it mean to be honorable? A person of honor is consistent, acting from as much integrity as he or she has. Her word is good. His actions follow his speech. In honor there is constancy and consistency, all centering around a core of stillness that can move at any moment.

The word *honor* speaks to the beginnings of integrity. It is also the place of accountability. A person who accepts accountability for his or her actions is a person of honor. We sometimes use the phrase, "She honors her commitments." This means both that she follows word with action and that in doing so, she treats her commitments with respect.

Oftentimes, culture tells us what is honorable and what is dishonorable. The word *honor*, like many others, is severely abused. "Honor killings" happen all over the world, sowing only dishonor and discord. However, those who have twisted words should not be allowed sole control of them. If we are to take back this word, we must look inward for what fuels our own sense of honor, just as we must look inward for what gives us a sense of worth. Always looking to sources outside to reflect us is a quick road to disintegration rather than integrity. To find honor, we examine what is really important to us and then ask *why* it is important and *how* we will uphold that.

This may sound like basic adult activity, and it is, but many humans live their whole span without actually reaching adult integration. We have that chance. In order to be effective magic workers, moving toward self-possession, we must enter full adulthood.

Honor is taking responsibility for our lives and actions. This serves the work of the Godhead within us.

Doing the Work

This exercise requires a clean piece of paper, your favorite drawing tools, and something to trace a circle with.

Think about what honor means to you. Does it conjure images of a knight or samurai? Of a steelworker, activist or parent? Now, trace a circle on a piece of paper and draw a mandala of honor. This is like a spiritual coat of arms, and represents your integrity and your quest for integration. What is the motto that will help you work toward being a person of honor?

Truth

The energy of responsibility and responsiveness flows from honor into truth. I don't speak here of some absolute truth or a universal philosophical stance. This point is about living from a place of deep honesty. We talked about honesty a bit under the place of commitment. Truth is a state of being honest with ourselves and with others. One aspect of honesty is acknowledging when we only hold one small facet of truth. This opens us to more information, making us better able to respond.

There is another aspect to truth, and that is one used by metalworkers. A blade is made true by the forging process. *True* means aligned for the purpose the tool is made for. Swords are made true. Bicycle forks need to be true in order for the bike to go anywhere. In order to function at full capacity, all things need to be true in their nature. In this sense, to be true is to be upright, well made, and flowing in a direct line. This is honesty. Alignment. Living in a state of truth means that lies are no longer running our lives and that we are treating others from this upright place as well. Lies are very rarely helpful, internally or in relationship with another. Any lies we tell should be in service to a larger truth, and that should be done only rarely. We often lie to ourselves and to others to keep things feeling comfortable, but that also rarely works. What would it feel like to live our truth?

How do we live a truthful life? A life that shines with honesty? Being true is to be formed to our proper shape, not living in twisted or broken ways. The task of self-possession includes bringing ourselves back into true and closer to the base Truth that God Herself is the fabric of all, and that fabric is love.

The following uses the powers of the cup and blade as forces to temper and balance each other. Fire and water, will and emotion, bring us closer to that in us which is true.

Doing the Work

Taking your tools of cup and blade, get into a good posture for sitting medita-
tion. Hold your cup in one hand and blade in the other. Feel the way they bal-
ance each other: openness and action, listening and moving, the strong boundary
that holds water and emotion coupled with the sharp edge that defines space
and intention. Breathe into your belly and listen for your truth. What rises up
from your belly, fueled by will, embraced by compassion, and honed by your
intention? Speak this truth out loud, inviting all your parts and God Herself
to listen.

Strength

Strength is a mountain. It is a tree bending in gale-force wind. Strength
is a beaver, carrying logs. It is admitting when we are wrong and knowing when we are right. Strength is a river rushing toward the ocean:
the energy of it and the rightness of its flow are both strong. Finding
our place in the larger flow of life increases our strength. The heart is
the strongest muscle in the body. Our strength flows from connection
to belly and heart. Will and emotional awareness lend strength to action. When we are strong, we can carry our own weight and take on
responsibility. We lift that which must be lifted and support that which
needs support. We are able to stand firm and tall.

The brittle branch breaks easily. Strength is the combination of
power and suppleness. When something is our strength, it is something
we have mastery of. We own that part of ourselves. Strength requires
openness, both as a way of taking in new information and as a way of
moving energy most effectively, with the greatest power. A tense boxer
doesn't land a strong punch. A tense magician is not open to the universe in all its workings.

The energy flows from our commitment, through honor, which
feeds truth, which builds strength.

Doing the Work

What in you feels weak? Do you feel that this is an accurate assessment? Sometimes weakness is not in the thing that makes us feel weak but in our attempts to deny or reject that which feels vulnerable and small.

A sword must become true. Its very impurities give it strength. What are your impurities, the parts of you that can feel at odds with your strength? Use your blade as an extension of yourself. Put onto it any of the qualities about yourself that you would like to see transformed or strengthened. Over and over, pass your blade through fire and into water, in an act of tempering. Through fire and into water, say, "I will become strong. I will be true."

Compassion

The connective energy of our life flows from strength into compassion. The stronger and more integrated we become, the more we have access to compassion. A strong person is able to accurately act from empathy and mercy. The stronger we are, the less we pity others. We can have compassion when we are rooted in our strength. Mistakes are made, and are actually necessary for our growth. Compassion for process keeps us on the path.

Lack of compassion is a sign of weakness, constriction, and scarcity. Compassion is seeing someone or some situation as she or it really is. This is not pity or coddling of weakness. True compassion is the deepest respect, a form of seeing clearly that calls upon truth, strength, and honor. This compassion must be trained upon ourselves as well as upon others. Compassion also breeds generosity, more of the openness given by strength. When we lack compassion for ourselves, it can become more difficult still to dredge up compassion for others, particularly those far removed from our experience. But in calling upon our commitment, honor, truth, and strength, we can remember that compassion brings more life force and depth of understanding than rejection does. We do not have to countenance bad behavior, but keeping sight of the full humanity of the perpetrators will help us to balance our responses and therefore rebalance the world.

Doing the Work

For this meditation, it will be helpful to have a cup or chalice filled with clear water.

What fills you with horror or shame or pity or rage or disgust? What would you like to hide from in yourself or in others? Wash your hands over your heart. Now fill your cup and gaze into it. It is your heart. What is in your heart? Can you love it? Can you look upon your heart with fierce tenderness? Breathe through your heart. Fill with compassion. Drink.

Running the Pentacle

The warrior holds the cup of compassion and the blade of intention. The fire of the cauldron in her belly feeds her will. Now that we have examined the points of the Pentacle of Autonomy, we can put them back together, forming a coherent pattern with which to build energy and bring ourselves into coherent shape. Coherency helps us.

I find it particularly effective to ground our work in the body. In the following exercise, we will run clear, clean life force, tracing the pentad through our physical form. This will affect our energies, our emotions, our bodies, and our minds. I will follow the pattern of running the energies through the pentacle, seeing how they all pass through the Warrior's Heart.

Doing the Work

Take a deep breath, imagining that breath can fill you from the soles of your feet to the crown of your head. Take another breath, this time imagining that you can "push" the breath down through the soles of your feet and up through your crown as you exhale. This connects you to earth and sky. Stand firmly, feet about shoulder-width apart. Open your arms out, forming a star. Let your right palm face up and your left face down, again echoing your connection to sky and earth.

Feel energy and power pouring into you on each breath. This is life force. You are always connected to it, every time you breathe. When you breathe in a conscious manner, you have even greater access to this power. Begin to imagine this life force running from your head down to your right foot, up to your left hand, across to your right hand, down to your left foot, and back up to your head.

We will run this circuit many times, feeling the power flowing in on our breath, sensing our connection to earth and sky, feeling ourselves standing tall and strong, as a balanced human, taking her place in the world.

The next time the circuit reaches your head, say, "Commitment." Feel that word resound within you. Let the energy flow again to your right foot and say, "Honor." Feel that word sing. The energy moves up to your left hand, and you say, "Truth." Let truth fill you. Breathe. Let the energy flow through your heart to your right hand, and say, "Strength." Feel yourself stand more firmly, bolstered by this word. The energy moves back down to your left foot, and you say, "Compassion." Feel the energy of this word washing through you.

Take the circuit back up to your head, intoning each word in turn, calling the energies to you, filling with them until your being is humming with life, thrumming with the possibility of Commitment, Honor, Truth, Strength, and Compassion. Feel your potential expanding. Allow yourself to grow. Now trace a sunwise circle around your body, enclosing and setting the pattern within you: Commitment, Truth, Compassion, Honor, Strength, Commitment.

Breathe the energy up, and align your soul. Then ask for some residual energy to rain down around you, feeding the blessed earth.

Claiming Our Powers

Another step toward autonomy and being the authors of our own lives is fully claiming all of our powers. Most of us have more power than we realize. This power can form around qualities we have been developing for so long that they feel like second nature to us, for example. Or they may be qualities that flow strongly within us but that we keep hidden because they feel *too* potent or perhaps unacceptable socially. These are our powers of brightness and shadow. They dance in each direction, arrayed around and within us, waiting for us to claim them as our own. In claiming these powers, we integrate the strength of all the elements of life and the directions of the sphere in which we live and move. They are still more faces of the Divine Twins within us.

When I first did this work, I claimed the powers of poetry as a shadow power of Air, because to me, poetry is dangerous. More difficult for me was to claim my ability to kill as a power of the North. Claiming the power to kill has meant that I can consciously refuse to use it. It also enables me to relate more cleanly to the food that I consume and the fact that all life feeds on other life. A master gardener holds the power of Earth as he digs in the soil. Someone else sings when she is afraid. Are these bright or shadow powers? The answer will be different for every person. For some of us, the shadow powers will be easier to claim than the bright, and for others the opposite will be true. This depends on our emotional tendencies and what we are used to looking at in ourselves. When we stretch and really look at both, we become stronger and more knowledgeable, building more energy for the work of self-possession.[60]

Brightness is that which is more visible, perhaps shinier and sometimes lighter. The shadow is that which is deeper, perhaps more silent and sometimes heavy.

In doing this, one cultural tendency to be aware of is that we are used to naming bright things "good" and shadow things "bad." This need not be the case. What we are looking for is the presence of ability and life force. Some of our powers may feel more difficult than others, but even that does not make them "bad." Shadow is just as necessary as that which is bright. Taken together, we see life in greater detail. Without bright or shadow, the beauty of the photograph cannot be seen. What in you throws something into greater relief, allowing for greater engagement? Your power lies in that direction.

We can use the following exercise not only as a way to further claim and integrate our power but also to look at our value judgments. I recommend working with this over the course of several months. Life and our other practices do not stop to wait for this but can actually help to inform our knowledge of what our true powers are.

Once power is claimed, it should not be given back. Our powers will shift within us as our work unfolds. We are now better prepared for whatever battles (and delights) may come.

Doing the Work

Meditate on these powers for North, East, South, West, and Center. You may want to do Above and Below separately, or you can treat them as one with Center for this purpose. Not every magical tradition works with Above, Below, and Center, but I find them to be helpful to my work.

Take a month or more to meditate on each of the Elements and begin to make notations of what you think your powers are, bright and dark in each direction. What are your powers of intellect, speech, emotion, body, energy, will, potency, silence? Do they feel bright or shadowy? Once you feel you have pairs for each direction, perform a ritual to claim them fully, as pieces of your self.

EIGHT

Unlocking Emotion and Intellect

Stand between the quicksilver flash of lightning and the expansive beauty of the evening star winking in the western sky. Breathe in the splendor of both. Honor your mind. Honor your heart. This is a place where you can feel yourself as you truly are and embrace the cosmos as it is. Feel the balancing point. In this space and time, you are the fulcrum of possibility. You are the magic worker who captures thought and nurtures emotion, setting the wheels of creation in motion. Creation without thought is creation without order. Creation without heart is cold. Our job is to know both and bring them together, before stepping forward into the place of integration.

Let us look at heart. Let us look at mind. Let us face our demons and find our allies. Sometimes they will end up being the same thing: the challenger becomes the champion and we are crowned.

Oftentimes when starting deep magical or spiritual work, tensions arise between thought and practice. This tension creates a juncture for further self-exploration and expansion. Intellectual rigor is, counter to popular belief, helpful to the spiritual path. It is incumbent upon seekers to think well and clearly. Thinking well enables us to open the doors of perception in ways that do not undermine our critical faculties. Thinking well cultivates knowledge instead of belief, as well as a framework from which to relate our knowledge to others. This segues into emotional health and honesty. When thinking clearly, we can see that no emotion is unwelcome, that all can be examined and brought into the embrace of paradox and change.

This chapter illustrates ways for us to challenge and hone our thinking, to face our demons and call upon the allies of emotion and mind. We can learn to clear old complexes and free ourselves to dance with what is truly present in each moment. The points in the Pentacle of Autonomy can help us face this work.

Emotions are the sea on which information is transmitted. This ocean is deep and vast. When information comes to us linked with an emotional state, it stays with us for a long time. Some of us are awash in emotion, disregarding clear thought. Others of us attempt to think our emotions into submission, if we don't disregard them entirely. Becoming conversant with both thought and emotion gives us a solid base to build our power and integration upon.

Taking Responsibility

If we neglect the roots of the tree in order to reach for the fruit of the branches, we may find that the fruit has not set because the roots have not been nourished.

—CAITLÍN AND JOHN MATTHEWS (IN *Walkers between the Worlds*)

To be strong, to be integrated, to be acting from our own will rather than under the will of another, we must take responsibility for our own emotions. In taking responsibility for our own emotions, I in no way mean that we can control their arising. Our practices can even out their spikes and valleys, certainly, but joy will arise, melancholy will enter, and frustration will send a flush down our skin. What we can do about our emotions is notice them and not blame their arising on someone or something outside of ourselves. We cannot blame another for our happiness, anger, or sadness. We can notice our responses to certain situations, feel our emotions, and try to communicate them. But we cannot give ownership of our feelings to another, because doing so would be a submission of our life force, a giving away of a part of ourselves.

It is only through the examination of, struggle with, and eventual acceptance of our parts that we can be whole, vital beings. Integration is simply not possible without this. In our work toward self-possession, all hands are needed on deck.

We are the Divine Twins formed from God Herself that then, in turn, form the Peacock, the new body, the challenger, the beautiful one, the gateway to our full potential. Self-possession demands full engagement with the world and with ourselves. We embrace our desire, unsure of the outcome but willing to enter the relationship anyway.

Fear and desire are both teachers of soul and emotion. In accessing these, we begin to touch our wholeness. Most other emotions are subsets of these. Get to the root by looking at the branches. To do this, we shall take a turn within.

Reflection

What do you fear? What do you desire?

If you had one wish for yourself, what would that be? What are you willing to commit to in order to bring your desire closer to you? Can you stop spinning your wheels and move forward, even one foot? Engage your will. Find your desire. Now is the perfect moment: put this book down and make a decision to live. The book will still be here when you return.

On Demons and Allies

If the doors of perception were cleansed every thing would appear to man as it is, infinite. For man has closed himself up, till he sees all things thru' narrow chinks of his cavern.

—WILLIAM BLAKE (IN THE POEM "*The Marriage of Heaven and Hell*")

Everything is colored by perception and perspective. When we approach anything—a situation, a piece of text, a painting, a walk in the woods, a ritual, a dance class, a relationship—with something inside of us more vigilant than another part, our experience of that is colored. This is not necessarily bad, it is just as things are for most of us, most of the time. We are often not hooked into Blake's "infinite."

Sometimes this trips us up. For example, when we say, "I can't" because that is how we feel today, regardless of evidence to the contrary, we are acting from a particular perspective and calling it the truth. When someone pisses us off because we hear or read what he has said with some baggage in tow or an earlier conversation in our minds, or just with our mood *du jour* running us, and take that as the truth, life grows more difficult in stages.

When life is this way, we often want to act out. We want to control that which is outside of us and therefore, most often, outside of our control. An inward turn is necessary, not the turning of unexpressed anger into depression or defeat but the examination of what is happening inside of us: we have been naming our complexes "truth" and forming them into outside entities—friends, strangers, enemies—with which we must do battle.

Despite their outside faces, their core comes from within. These are the lenses that distort our world. These are the things that dampen our hearing. These are the things that clutch at belly and at heart. Add in the confusion of outside information and systems often out of our control, and we can wish to run in the opposite direction. But with all of our skills and magic, there is no need. We can open just a bit further. We can breathe.

Life moves and flows in rippling patterns. We are part of that. The large patterns must take care of themselves, as the myopia caused by our short lives makes systems spanning several millennia hard to see. But there are small patterns we can attend to: arresting environmental devastation, feeding hungry people, and creating necessary beauty. Most specifically we can attend to the patterns in our own lives.

We are riddled with patterns and complexes of behavior, thought, and emotion. Some of these are easy to become aware of, and enter into right relationship with. Others of these complexes have become "demons," because we have elevated them to this level. These hold a lot of life force, so much so that we fear to look at them. This grows beyond simple dislike and into a pernicious cycle of control and avoidance. Instead of acknowledging them as another facet of ourselves, we shove them away. The less we look at them, the more energy they gather.

The ancients often saw these as external forces, and indeed, the outer worlds can confirm our inner fears and strengths, throwing up impediments or offering support. The Abrahamic religions all speak of demons and angels; sometimes the demons are helpful, and the angels challenge humans. Most magical systems consider that both helpful and baneful spirit beings exist, sometimes large and powerful, other times simply existing as small distractions from the work or providing aid through serendipitous events.

Medieval magicians catalogued whole systems of demonic and angelic forces that could be summoned by the trained practitioner, and some contemporary magicians are reviving these practices.[61] Most consider that these forces are strictly internal, mapping our psychological and emotional states. Others feel that we can tap into or even manifest external forces for good or ill. This reflects the often-misused adage: "You create your own reality." While this statement does not take into account the realities of oppression, social injustice, racism, sexism, homophobia, and child abuse, it is simultaneously true that the inner attitude of the magic worker affects the outer state in significant ways. Or, as philosophy teacher Chris Ann Moore states: "you co-create your own reality."[62]

All of the practices of discipline and self-awareness help to shift our inner landscape. We can reach a state of equilibrium where ups and downs occur without taking over our whole lives or coloring every interaction. Even after years of this work, however, the serious practitioner can still find himself laid low by some old pattern of mind or emotion that has been hiding in deep crevasses of the soul for many years. It is our work to call these demons to light, to dialogue with them and tame them to our work rather than allow them to run the workings of our hearts and minds.

Just as we must look at what gods we worship—all the things we make central to our lives, whether we are aware of them or not—we must look upon the demons we feed.[63] In order for entities to have strength, they must have food, and we feed these demons every time we tie another knot in the web of malicious gossip or chew upon old wounds with relish or dredge up the patterns of our past simply in order to *feel* something. We create demons by carrying grudges for years or by denying responsibility. We feed our demons in myriad ways.

Not all of our patterns can be considered "demons." I try to save this word for those complexes that are so deeply seated they control large portions of my life, often without my really noticing. The more work we do to look at all our parts, the more these demons will emerge to the light. Once raised to the light, we can enlist their help and their life force to the task of the Great Work of full integration. Without their life force, true integration and self-possession will not happen. We will forever be missing some vital parts.

The medieval magician was clear that he was working with demons, and more importantly, *getting them to work for him*, in exchange for his help in raising them up to a higher level of existence. This is what we can do with our hidden parts that control us: we can take back control of the life force they hold, and we can work with them. We can get these parts to work for us in ways that are helpful rather than at cross purposes with our spiritual quest. In working with them, we raise them to the possibility of Godhood through full connection with our own divine natures.

Feeling, Not Being

The problem is not that there are problems. The problem is expecting otherwise and thinking that having problems is a problem.

—Theodore Rubin

Our complexes come in many forms: insecurity, arrogance, all the "shoulds" that we carry, wanting to please others, anger at the world, feeling we are "owed" something; the list goes on and on. There are imps of the mind: old thought patterns that keep our behavior in check, sometimes long after we have ceased to even be aware of them. More tenacious still are the demons of emotion, which can be much harder to shift because they are more closely tied to our subconscious, resting in our muscles and our bones.

Our emotional allies must be stronger still, to engage in the combat necessary for our emotional growth.

The Desert Fathers of the Christian Tradition knew all about emotional complexes. One they spoke of clearly was the "noonday demon" of Psalms. This "noonday demon" was the demon against work, thoughtfulness, and being engaged with what was in front of one. This demon was battled greatly between the hours of 10:00 a.m. and 2:00 p.m., a time when the monks, who had likely been awake since 4:00 or 5:00 a.m., hit the midday slump in which all resistance came to a head. In spiritual literature, this demon is given the clinical name of *acedia*, or spiritual torpor. When this demon gets out of hand today, we sometimes name it mild depression.[64] We give our complexes many names.

The problem with this naming is that the English language tends to say, "I *am* lonely" rather than "I *feel* lonely." The emotional state takes over our whole being. We are possessed by it, which makes the situation much more difficult to deal with than if we were companions to loneliness or in dialogue with it.

Instead, we could say, "Today, I feel sadness." I am not sad; I *feel* sad. We can also realize that along with the sadness, there may also be quiet stillness and a purring cat on our lap or flowers outside the window, and perhaps we are enjoying a cup of tea. The sadness is not everything, though if we tried, we could easily make it seem so. If we can catch that impulse and breathe, drink our tea, pet the cat, *feel* the sadness, and ponder it, we may come to a better sense of what actually lives inside us. All of our work on taking responsibility is brought to this moment of truly looking rather than reacting and being immediately taken over.

I was speaking of this with a Witch I know who struggles with borderline personality disorder, and who came up with what I thought was a brilliant insight to start using the phrase "I have depression" rather than "I am depressed." This captures the seriousness of the illness, yet does not make it the person's whole identity. There is room for being a partner, a music lover, a magic worker, and many other things besides.[65]

Emotions can pinpoint a sense of disconnection. Sometimes there is anger, a feeling of betrayal, or a sense of injustice. We each have our particular story. These emotions can arise from disconnection, or they can feed our disconnection. More rare still, they can even come from heartfelt connection. Regardless of the source, by *being* with the emotions, some energy arises to help us reconnect. We reconnect first to something within that strengthens us and puts us back in touch with the flow of life energy. This gives us an opportunity to connect with something outside of ourselves, whether it be a person or some hope or an activity. It doesn't really matter what it is, because any touch can become help. This is different from either fully identifying with and being wholly consumed by the emotion or trying to stamp it into submission and shove it away in some secret place. None of those reactions make space for either the emotion itself or the process of learning, sitting, arising, and eventually reconnecting.

The first step in the connective process is to say, "I feel sad, angry, upset, powerless, happy, or excited" rather than use the old "I am." "I am" should be rarely used, reserved for those moments when we want to remind ourselves that we are whole, that we have a part of ourselves that touches the fabric of the Limitless and that we can access this part. The "I am" is not our anger or our sadness. The "I am" is only ever about full connection. The "I am" is both our essence and our whole self.

Our practices can help us recognize our states and slowly become masters of ourselves. The primary practice we return to is that of stillness.

Doing the Work

Step one: do not wholly identify with any separate emotion. Step two: acknowledge, feel, and observe the emotions. Step three: wait and sense what happens. Step four: try to sense the unity that exists beyond the emotional state, even if you can only catch one glimpse of it. Step five: breathe into the moment and find again the still point in your belly. This centers you, allowing you to move through life with greater ease.

Stalking the Hidden Soul

The Shadow is either your worst enemy, or your best friend.

—CHRISTOPHER PENCZAK[66]

When I am standing in line at the grocery store or eating lunch in a café, I find the still place in my belly, and then look around me and listen. I see and hear people trapped in their own stories. They sound so fearful of the truth that will cause their carefully constructed walls to tumble. No one is wholly immune to this, but some of us have chosen a different route. We have begun to dig ourselves out of the mire.

These stories people tell harbor the shadow. This shadow can be rooted in fear or in hope but, like our demons, can find ways to teach us, should we choose to listen and watch. A lot of our life energy is tied up in the stories we spin. Rather than using that energy for action, we send it into worry or longing. The least thing triggers us, and off we go. When we feel alienated, we need to ask, "What old story has been activated within me?"

What is it that causes these stories to continue to churn, even when exterior reality belies them? We have worn grooves into our brains that are enforced and informed by mental, physical, and emotional habits. Our mental and emotional habits run like juggernauts down the slick pathways. Thus we reinforce unhappiness, superiority, anger, hurt feelings, and alienation. Once we begin to see any part of this, our brains can begin to change. The pathways, once worn, don't go away but can grow shallower and less slippery over time. In the midst of this, we can form new patterns. We can lay down pathways of happiness, practice, and awareness. Whatever reflects our new desires and is coupled by a new wish and pattern of being can become an answer and counterpoint to the old.

Our stories can clutch at our skin for a long time. Breaking ourselves of those habits is a long process. But once the habit is in our sights, we can notice its frequency and the nature and depth of its control. We can break the habit. The vestigial remains are often the hardest to break: we've done our work, and things have shifted; most of our lives are not led in those old ways anymore, but there is one last thing: one peeve, one relationship, or one justification holds on. There is this one last thing that hurts us to let go of. Often, at this point, if we are brave or foolish enough, or feel the bite of the trap enough, there is a rupture. This is the place where we may feel that all of our work was for naught. But the rupture is the necessary energetic "oomph" to break us free.

Once we wrestle with the remorse, or pain of this splitting, we can truly begin to feel our integration. We can take the energy released from the rupture and swallow it down to become something new. Nothing else tastes better over time. Nothing else satisfies quite so. We become whole and living beings, not shattered anymore.

Our stories fall into many categories: romance, cynicism, competition, or defeat. The processes of self-knowledge help us to discover what our particular favorite heading may be. By recognizing that we are slaves to these stories, we begin to see the ways in which we color the present, revise the past, and gild the future. Was the loss of that job our crazy boss's fault, or are we terrible failures at everything? Blaming someone else wholly and finding so much fault in ourselves that we can see nothing good are likely both untrue. The story of a lover's rejection of us might mask a deeper fear that people will not like us. Perhaps the lover was simply tired and not up for rolling around the sheets this evening, but read through the lenses of old hurt, it devastates. If we can catch ourselves in the middle of this sort of storytelling, without trying to stop or stuff the emotion, we can sometimes see: "Ah, I still hold in me an impression that people do not or will not like me. Wow. Despite knowing that this isn't true, that part of me is still present." Or we might notice, "Every time I have a disappointment, I have to blame something outside of myself for it. Or I have to go back to thinking I'm the worm I felt like in grammar school, or that I really am better than everyone else."

Too often we try to squeeze our shadow out or bury it more firmly, because it makes us feel entirely too uncomfortable. Rather than do this, we can make space for it, inviting it to dance with us, to sup with us, to laugh with us and tell us the secrets it knows. The shadow holds parts of us that we barely know.

Drawing the Circle

I could never understand why they wouldn't face this danger as well as any other. Was it that what they saw in themselves frightened them more than other dangerous sights?

—MARGARET ANDERSON (IN *The Unknowable Gurdjieff*)

Medieval magicians drew a circle of protection around themselves and placed a triangle in front of that circle. Around the circle and triangle were inscribed holy names and symbols of power, ensuring that the magician was protected and that whatever was conjured into the triangle remained contained.[67] The demon's names were called, and it was summoned to do the work of the magician. We do the same in our lives. We wrap ourselves in knowledge, fear, or hope, casting a circle without even knowing it. We draw triangles bounded with curses or heady jargon, anything to keep the darkness at bay. But nothing seems to help. We have to face the mirror. We have to look within.

We have become something we do not want to look at because we misunderstand who we are. We want to be one thing or another, but we have to look at the all. We are approaching the place of the Peacock Angel, born from the love of the Divine Twins. Beauty and terror must both be held under the hand of the Star Goddess, the hand of love, connection, and limitlessness. Without the hand of love, all we can sense is disconnection. And in disconnection, as we know, evil enters in and we are wandering in the midst of banality, violence, or shame.

That which protects us is our strength and suppleness, and our ability to face what we must. That which is bound is that which binds us. The demons are within. The worst thing to do with a demon is to run from it. We must find ways to face our demons and enter into conversation with them.[68] Demons are not casual flashes of emotion or thought. Rather, they are complexes in us that are so deep and tenacious that they have often been controlling us for years. We can come to know them, and in bringing them to the light and interacting with them, we can better ascertain what they want and need, what their particular pain or fear is, and how they might come to work in service of our project of the Great Work rather than at cross purposes to it.

In facing our demons, we come to know the power that wells up inside us and the strength we can call upon from outside too. Think on the magicians of old, from all traditions imaginable: on Honi Ha'Magel calling YHVH, or the Chaldean Oracles calling Hekate. What can we call upon when it is time to face our demons of emotion and mind? What are our sacred names? These names of power are our allies in the work. They may be friends or practice or Gods or angels. They may be our bodies or a memory that gives us succor.

What in us holds terror and torture and pain? We must examine this unflinchingly. We cleanse, align, and try to reconnect, but we do not look away. These parts in us must be brought back into communication with the whole. They cannot be killed or cut away. And so it goes outside of us too, in politics and war. The torturer and victim both need healing, or we risk the eventual destruction of a human psyche on both sides of the table. Some magic workers of old waited until after their big rites of Knowledge and Conversation to face and tame their demons, albeit they did go through preliminary work on dreams, thoughts, emotions, and the manifest world, much as we have. I find, however, that the addition of this work on clearly identifying demons and allies before attempting more complete openings to our divine nature will help our task immeasurably.

I recommend keeping a journal nearby, in case the dialogue with a demon turns out to be more than mere impressions. For some of us, they will impart visions, for others, emotions or mental loops; symbols will come to some, and to others, the demons will talk and talk. A journal and a fast writing pen ensure that whatever information needs to be passed can be recorded if need be. My only caution is to not let the act of recording get in the way of receiving the information as it is offered. Sometimes we get so caught up in writing things down or taking snapshots for posterity that we can forget to have the experience in the first place.

The following is an entry phase to looking at our demons and allies before doing more substantive work with either. Now is the time to begin allowing our knowledge of what we might consider inner demons or allies to be.

Oftentimes, our demons have become demons instead of allies or angels, because we have refused to see the ways in which they can help us. We have bound their life force instead of using them to aid our mutual liberation. In coming into compact with a demon—this unliberated part of our soul—we must ask our God Soul to be the one in charge. There is only one driver we want for our lives, and that is our divinity and connection to God Herself.

As mentioned, in exchange for its working for the magician, the magician of old would promise to raise the demon up to a higher level of existence. In knowing more of our parts, we come closer to the state of self-possession. This is indeed a "raising," just as it is a "deepening." By enabling our demons and allies to come together, the possibilities of self are endless. Our parts, taken into the marriage of wholeness, strengthen us, making us more human and more divine.

This is not exorcism but embrace. There is no need to cast out our demons; rather, our embrace and understanding of them brings them back into balance and health. We see that they were not really demons at all but adversaries that help us to struggle. All of the life force they tied up controlling us and all the life force other parts of self tied up avoiding them is now free to be used in the Great Work. At this point, our complexes become our teachers and allies, joining into the rest of the family of self and personality. We can give them new tasks to fulfill, since these parts of ourselves have likely developed many skills over the years. In doing this new kind of work, slowly they become raised to the power of Godhead. We are made more, because we are more whole, so we step closer to the full awareness of our Limitlessness.

Doing the Work

Read through the following and then procure everything you need for this magical working. Set up sacred space in whatever way your tradition teaches. Do the "Cleansing Life Force" exercise (see p. 28) You may wish to do further cleansing beforehand, such as vacuuming, washing dishes, and taking a shower.

While I give several examples of possible demon names below, only deal with one personal demon at a time. We are getting to know our imps one by one.

Center yourself in prayer and meditation for as long as you need. Make whatever offerings feel appropriate. Then, with your journal and pen nearby, light your candles and incense. Cast your sphere or circle, and then begin to call upon your internal allies; for example, "Ally, I name you Awareness. Ally, I name you Remorse. Ally, I name you Compassion. Ally, I name you Pride. Ally, I name you Connector. Ally, I name you Strength. Ally, I name you Openness to Love." Use these and any other sacred names of power that you wish to invoke.

Feel these sacred names, these allies to your Work, racing along the edges of your sphere, lending support and strength to your space, your soul, and your working.

Now imagine a triangle shining in front of you. This holds the energy of past, present, and future. Draw this with your intention and your will. Bring your whole being to this. Re-center, and align yourself again if you need to. Ask the sacred names to surround this as well. Breathe some of your life energy into the triangle to charge it, knowing that every time you inhale, you replenish and increase the life energy inside of you. Then begin to call the demon you are working with this night; for example, "Demon, I name you Fear." Or "Demon, I name you Arrogance." Or "Demon, I name you Crusher of Spirit." Or "Demon, I name you Spiteful Hate. Demon, I name you Cold Calculation." Summon one of your demons into the triangle.

Breathe in, deeply. Feel your allies arrayed within and around you. Feel the demon that is another facet of yourself facing you, peering at you from the triangle bounded by names of love and power. Ask it what it calls itself. Ask for words, images, or information. Take as long as you need to do this work. Meditate, write in your journal, or gaze into a black mirror. Acknowledge the demon. Feel that which is both you and not you.

Center and align your soul again. Take four deep breaths and send the final exhalation up, connecting to the God Soul above your crown. Now open up to dialogue with the deep part of you that feels most controlling right now. You may wish to write it a letter. Or listen to the story it has to tell you. Does the story ring true? Do pictures come through? When was the demon first given form in your life?

Sit in dialogue for as long as feels appropriate. Then thank your allies, all the powers you called for the working. Then thank the demon that is you, and tell it you will speak to it again, but it should depart the triangle at this time. Close down the energy of the triangle and those of the circle or sphere. Drink a glass of water to ground fully in your body.

This work can continue over many months. Don't forget to do the cleansing rite in the midst of it all. Having fun will also lend perspective to the task at hand. Take breaks and then, when you feel ready, you can revisit the triangle and sphere.

What is Center, and what is Circumference? The Boundless One, the Peacock Angel, is limited by the Limitless. God Herself. Born of the paradox of duality, of the two pillars of light and dark, He rises and She enfolds that ascent. Without the presence of love, boundlessness wreaks havoc on all in its wake.

We must center our lives in the hand of love, or we are lost. Ally and demon face one another and we are the product of their meeting. We can do this working many times, for many months, getting to know the parts of self that control us without being of much help. We can bring them closer to love, and eventually get them to work for us, rather than at odds with us.

Naming the Core

Our inner demons can further mask the deep organizing principle of our personalities—what Gurdjieff called our "Chief Feature"—so learning to recognize and make peace with these demons is not only of help in gaining more control over our lives but in getting closer to uncovering what really makes us tick.

Some of our earlier work on life inventory can point to these sorts of demons, as does the taboo work of chapter five (see p. 93). Does impatience mask a hidden perfectionism from childhood? Does a need to be the center of attention cover up a fear of not being seen at all or a fear of being seen too intimately if we do not run the show? Any of these demons can be pernicious and subtle; they like to hide in the shadows or disappear into the spotlight's glare.

Medieval magicians had a period of confession in their conjurations. Let us attempt to confess now. What holds us back? What binds us? What are the particular "hells" that we have created for ourselves, solidifying the walls of the fortress around some old wound or idea?

We must think very carefully about the next portion of our work. We may need to wrestle for a week, a month, or six months. We must take care and set our intentions to do this. The following exercise should be done when we feel ready, and not before. This does not mean we should wait until we feel unafraid or are no longer nervous but that we should save it for a time when it feels right, when the push to engage is a little stronger than the desire to run and hide.

Doing the Work

The following builds upon the demon and ally work we have already done but uses more physical tools to help us. If you prefer to do it strictly metaphysically, like our last round of demon work, you may do so. Read this through, gather materials, cleanse, and begin.

Without thinking, right now, ask yourself, what do you feel your chief demon is? Generally, what leaps unbidden to your mind will be the one you wrestle with most, even if you are not always conscious of it. If nothing comes to mind, attempt deeper honesty. Really look at yourself. Are you miserable all the time, sending off waves of discontent around you? Are you angry? Frightened? Impatient? Are you driven by hormones on a constant, barely controlled basis?

Find what feels like your "chief" demon, or just pick one that feels strong to you right now, and do the following:

Demarcate your working space by casting a sphere or circle, or saying whatever prayers your tradition calls for. Feel divinity within and around you. Get a light-colored or white piece of poster board, construction paper, or even printer paper. With a fat marking pen, draw an equilateral triangle on the surface. Now draw another just inside or outside the first, so there is about an inch of space between the lines. In that space, write every name that represents your strength, hope, and authority. These might be your own names, magical or otherwise, or the names of God Herself, Guardians, angels, or other spiritual beings and allies. Write the names that feel potent, and include whatever symbols are sacred to you.

Once you are done with this, talk to what feels like the demon most closely connected to your Chief Feature. Tell it what it has done to you. Listen to what it has to say in turn. Write its name in the middle of the triangle. Then give your personal demon a task. This task may be to help you grow more aware of the damage the demon does. It may be to make apologies to yourself or to others. It may be to take the energy your internal demon has used to undermine your dignity or effectiveness, and use that instead to actively work toward your spiritual growth, integration, self-knowledge, and happiness. It may take the energy of nitpicking and fault-finding, and channel this life force toward organization instead. Tell your inner demon that this task must begin now, because it will always have some excuse to argue with the rest of your parts.

Once you are done with this, cover your triangle with another piece of paper and set it to rest beneath an altar, a stack of books, a plant, or some other place where *it will not be disturbed. Check back in with this project in one month's time. Before uncovering the triangle, cast a sphere, center yourself, and think on your life for the past month. Does anything feel different? Have you noticed changes internally or externally? Do you carry yourself differently? How do you act at work and at home? Meditate on these questions for a few minutes, and then call upon whatever it is inside of you that lends the most help. Align your soul, and then call upon whatever it is outside of you that lends the most help.*

You are now ready to uncover the triangle that holds your demon. Look upon it. Look at the boundary triangle and what lies within. How does this make you feel? Read some of the words if you wish, or reread the letter you wrote in your last round of demon work.

Sit. Breathe. Sense. Now it is time to make a decision. Will you cover the triangle again and give the process another moon cycle? Do you rip it up, burn, or bury it and write the words anew, making a fresh contract with your demon? Or is your work here done? If the latter is true, thank the demon for its efforts and release it from the chains that bind both it and you. Don't release it into the air; rather, release it into a cup of water, charge the water as in our "Cleansing Life Force" exercise (see p. 28) chanting sacred names over it and lending more energy.

Charge the old demon with health and cleanliness. Charge it with your life force and will. Call upon God Herself to lend energy to the working. Then drink the water back in, taking the energy that was bound in the deep complex and creating this new form that will be of help to you instead of something that hinders you. You are the master now, and your old parts become new allies for your work.

If at any point, this part of you seems to be up to its old tricks, pour it into the water again, and remind it that your God Soul is at the helm and that this part promised to help in the Great Work you are embarked upon. Remind it that it is a necessary component to your self-possession and that it, too, is becoming divine in this work. Breathe or chant into the water until it seems to glow, and then drink it down, re-ingesting the energy as that of health and happiness.

Once we have discovered our Chief Demon and begun this work, we will likely find that the behavior of all our other demons comes into context. We gain perspective and grow still more whole. We find tasks for the lesser demons, because we see how they are connected to the Chief, who is no longer controlling them in the old manner. We are able to do things like refocus a resistance to practice or making art into a force that helps us resist eating a whole bag of chips, or compulsively surfing the internet.

Life grows radiant with greater stores of energy as a result of this practice.

Facing the Realms Outside

All things are woven into one another, and the bond that unites them is sacred; and hardly anything is alien to any other.

—MARCUS AURELIUS (IN *Meditations*)

We have faced ourselves, and now must look at how we interact with others.

Until we are willing to take responsibility for our lives, we will not be free. Freedom is autonomy and the integration of power with compassion. We have worked with our inner demons, which are often formidable, but there are also demons outside of ourselves. We demonize organizations, cab drivers, lawyers, politicians, and any host of others. As long as we do this, we keep them distant, and often fail to learn what lessons might be hidden in even glancing interactions with them. As long as we blame our parents, our ex-lovers, "society," or any host of demons for our current state, we will not be free.

Am I saying that we need not hold others accountable for rude or damaging behavior? No. I suggest that we get angry, grieve, or rail, and then find ways to reintegrate and move on. If external rectification or reconciliation can occur, so much the better. If not, we can learn to reconcile things within ourselves in such a way that we take back control of our lives, take full responsibility for our own emotional states, and figure out how to live with and within our lives as they currently stand.

This is the necessary task for every magic worker and spiritual seeker. In fact, it is the necessary task of every adult human being. To act otherwise is to abdicate responsibility and become, over time, less responsive to what is in front of us.

Adult humans learn to take responsibility for their words and actions but no more than that. They know that once a bridge is burned, simple wishing will not walk them across the river, so action must be taken carefully and with will. They also learn that they cannot control the reactions of others. One can feel remorse and act upon it, but one can never change her friend. One can apologize, but one cannot take on the burden of his brother. Simultaneously, one cannot force another to see that an apology is needed or that amends ought to be made. One can only become clean within. History will not be rewritten, but the present and future are ours to live.

One helpful way to think of our demons—internal or externally named—is as adversaries. The very word conjures up a struggle or an obstacle to be faced, something we can "gird our loins" in order to confront. An adversary is something we can meet. The universe conspires to remind us of why adversaries are so important to our work. They do not exist so we can wallow in an orgy of superiority and self-congratulation. Spiritually, they crop up so we can better *look upon ourselves*.

Adversaries are always mirrors, if we are willing to look. Whether political, personal, or both, their very presence and their very irritation can help us to look more closely at our lives. What paths are we treading? Are they the right paths? What is this obstacle trying to show me? What wound still needs to be healed or opened again and cleansed? What action do I need to take and in what direction might that be more effective?

For example, at the time I write this, there is much foment in the U.S. political sphere. The government is clearly corrupt, with even those who usually would support the current administration waking up to the fact that something is badly awry. The point here is that the leaders in this moment are the mirrors for our culture. They reflect all the things about the United States that are not so pretty, even loathsome: greed, paranoia, grandiosity, and uncontrolled selfishness. They reflect all that needs cleansing, healing, reexamining, and restructuring. If we borrow this mirror and reflect it back onto our personal lives, we may see striking things.

So, just as we have internal demons and external ones, so does our culture have its own, some deep in the soul and some up on the surface, shiny as a Madison Avenue advertisement. But what are our *personal* mirrors? Who are our external adversaries of everyday life? Who would we like to cast out into the desert to wander alone? What are the lessons that very wilderness has to teach us, should we wander it ourselves?

Life is open to us, even as we face the seeming obstacles in our paths. Our teachers are everywhere. We are only as good as our delusions allow us to be. Sometimes we shine around them or despite them or even because of them. Therein lies our work: Self-awareness is our hope, when seasoned with a dash of compassion.

At the end of the day, in the midst of all of my interactions, I find it helpful to remember that we cannot force the work upon another. We can only make our own attempts, and we can use the energy otherwise spent in vilification to look more carefully and choose right action.

Lifting Stories to Light

The blacker the body, the whiter the light—the incandescent, active virgin heart from which all comes.

—Victor H. Anderson

Having dealt with our demons and looked at our stories and brought our shadows into a gentle light, it is time to do some work on trust. When do we figure out that trust is a necessary risk? The rewards of integration are so much greater than the comfortable pain of our shattered being. We can be whole. We can be happy. The world really does conspire to bring us happiness. It is our old, cherished stories and our nurtured poisons that keep us from this awareness. Our misery is a blanket that almost keeps us warm.

We wrestle with our demons and stand beside our allies. We align and integrate, seeking the God within us. We will still make mistakes. But we will return to center more quickly, with a brief apology to one offended or a promise to self to start again tomorrow, and our hearts beat clear once more. We are strong. We are beautiful. We are brightness in the midst of shadow. All of our shadow parts have joined to birth this brilliance.

Grace happens. After years of entertaining the results of limbic imprinting—the stories of abandonment, isolation, scarcity, the caressing hand turned into an angry fist—and finally, finally, a new pattern is worn in the brain. Happiness becomes possible as an overall state of being rather than a fleeting veneer laid over angst, anger, or worry. One can trust enough to truly let love in—no blame, a little sorrow for the years, the pain sustained and pain caused but mostly, there is gratitude and joy.

First, we sit with ourselves. We come to know our hearts and all their fears, twisting and turning. We loop around and around, not knowing what to trust, even when we want to. Emotions? What are those? Changeable, never stopping to realize that all things are. When we lift our stories to the light, we see clearly: we wanted to know what to blame. We wanted to know how to keep ourselves safe. We never seemed to realize that risk is an everyday occurrence and a life without risk is no life at all. We may have even leapt headlong into other forms of danger but kept our private spaces so sequestered that they never saw the light of day.

But we may have found there was a leak. Things seeped out when our backs were turned. And our lives were impacted nonetheless; regardless of how hard we tried to wall things off, those "things" caused our lives to fall apart. Those "things" caused great loneliness. Those "things" fed our anger or our disappointment. And the world seemed wrong. Or all our parts seemed wrong. And love was just another thing that went away. The things we kept in shadow, unrevealed, kept us safe. But there was no safety in that, for there was no satisfaction.

Reflection

What in you has been afraid? Can you look at that in a new light, muster up courage, and trust the newness of your process? Can you begin to trust your practice or the hand of love God Herself holds out to your life? Can you trust that you are moving toward beauty?

Breathe it in. Faith is not blind but comes from years of built-up experience and the knowledge that you are going to be all right. In fact, you just may thrive.

As Within, So Without

In the midst of this work, these questions arise: How does our struggle with inner demons reflect what is happening in the world outside, and vice versa? Can the inner world begin to affect the outer world, and can both then affect all the worlds?

I believe the answer to both is "yes and." Yes, our inner work is a long-term project to help to shift the culture around us *and* to affect the subtle energies of all the realms—and. I need to also find ways to work with the gross energies that are currently at play in the world. Some people do this by voting. Some people do this by petitioning. Some people do this by volunteering. Some people sit in trees. Some people organize antiracism workshops. Some people blockade. Some people raise children. Some people teach magic. Many of us do multiple variations on these.

We must each find the ways in which we work the inner and the outer planes.

PART 3

Desire—The Peacock Angel

The Peacock is born of the combined will of the Divine Twins, who were, in turn, born of God Herself. Bird and snake. Earth and air. Hope and fear. Shadow and brightness. These all combine to form a being of vast potential and startling beauty. The Peacock Angel represents all that we desire, all that we long for in a deep way. This desire springs from the upwelling of life power. We can engage our will and harness this desire, and all of our life will move forward in strength and profound joy. The Peacock Angel is beautiful and frightening because he is so new. His boundless potential is held beneath the hand of love of God Herself. The Star Goddess, in her love, keeps him sane.

The peacock is a reflection of our potential, of our beauty, power, and integration. Formed by the Divine Twins, by all the work we've done grappling with our shadows and allies, angels and demons, he shows us the sphere of golden light, centered in the heart. For us, the peacock is the symbol of knowledge and conversation with our highest self.[69] After we have done the work of looking deeply, of prayer and meditation, we have a chance to arrive at a place of full possession of our God Souls. We have always had them, but to reach this place of continuous contact requires both effort and grace.

For most humans, the steps toward unity include looking at how we experience duality. In the previous part, (see p. 87) we looked at the ways in which dualism is a construct, because although we experience the world as being full of hot and cold, soft and hard, friendly and unfriendly, this does not get at the underlying source where truth rests: we are all part of the same fabric of Being. If we keep in mind that there is the possibility of a deeper experience that unites, we can use dualism without getting trapped by it.[70] Most of what people call truth is relative, mutable, and relies upon personal perspective and experience, but mystics from every culture and tradition will tell you that there is one Truth they hold to: nothing is separate from anything else. Union with the Divine is union with all.[71]

In this next part of the book, we will look at the ways in which the Divine Twins find more complete expression in the third body they form together, seen as the Peacock Angel. Before going to that synthesis, however, it is important to hold the two poles wherever we encounter them. One of the things that a truly balanced person can manifest is the ability to be merciful and severe simultaneously. This is hard work, and often is not achieved until one is more fully integrated, having reached the first stage of mastery required before Adepthood, but we can look at these states from wherever we are on our path. We can examine the ways in which we have trouble with one or the other, or are drawn toward work with either.

Severity and mercy that are born from integration, rather than from one facet or another of personality or preference, can be helpful and accurate tools. Wielded well, they carry compassion with them at all times.

The Peacock, it is said, spans all the realms: his tail feathers reach heaven, and his feet are in hell. This angel bridges all worlds in his embrace. I say "he," for he is most often pictured as male, but in reforming all oppositions into a new body, he is really the divine androgyne, a bright reflection in the black mirror of his mother, the Star Goddess.[72] We are speaking here of so many facets of space and time, material and unmanifest, that to even speak in terms of gender diminishes our subject. But because we all began as female, somewhere in the womb, and then most of us (except for the truly intersexed or hermaphroditic) separated into male or female, the gender binary is something we gravitate toward. There is a snippet of truth there, but to focus on it takes away our access to the larger truth. We speak of the Star Goddess, God Herself, as "she," although in reality, God Herself is *pre-gender*, or all gender in a way that the Peacock could be seen as post-gender.

God Herself is the ground of being, and the reality of the Peacock Angel is hinted at in diverse philosophical ideas. He can be considered as Hegel's synthesis, the harmonic of Pythagoras, and Gurdjieff's Holy Reconciling force. In alchemy, the peacock is formed after metal goes through the stages of the black crow and the white swan. Things dissolve and come together again, making a beautiful form that is the precursor of gold.

There is unity that divides into a temporary duality. The duality comes back together, forming a new unity. The reformed unity differs from the unformed unity in that it better understands the pushing and pulling of division. God Herself is still the Limitless, a step beyond our current scope[73] But the Peacock Angel, the gorgeous being formed of opposition, *looks a bit more like we do*. And that is of great help to our work.

Remember all the practices we have done with the Twins, attempting to see, know, and accept our parts. That comes together in our next phases. The repeated alignment of our souls begins to align us with something brand new, the bringing together of all that felt separate in us. From the sleep of fragmentation, we wake up to unity. We become bridges that span the worlds, seen and unseen. All space and time is here and now, within our reach.

Our connection to the limitless flow can lend heightened awareness and presence to any of our activities, opening us further to the work of this God, our True Will, and bring more of our self to what is at hand.

Reflection

Breathe into the still point in your belly and center around that point. Imagine what you would be like, not separate from God Herself. Imagine yourself floating, particles expanding into space. Breathe. Allow yourself to remain centered, yet keep floating outward, becoming more spacious, connected with all things, part of God Herself. You have moved into the limitless flow. Breathe. Slowly allow yourself to drift back toward the center still point. Reform. You are human and alive.

Now sense yourself as you are, disparate parts, crashing and pulling, making love and arguing, hoping and feeling uneasy. Breathe. Remember the sense of particles floating out, joining the All, yet remain with your disparity. Then, imagine yourself as none of your parts, or as all of them. What would it be like to be completely united with yourself? How would that connect you back to the limitlessness of God Herself?

Opening the Great Work

The chapters that follow will take months or years to work well. In the previous chapters we examined many facets of our lives and continued whatever work we were doing with building a strong foundation and container for what is to come. Now is the time to adjust our energy bodies more fully to the new state of kissing the Limitless, of entering into the stage of self-possession. The many energetic exercises that follow are all designed to open a clearer and stronger channel for the descent and anchoring of our God Soul. They are specifically designed to set up strong pathways and resonances within us: ways to reach up and draw down our own divine natures and become fully integrated in all our parts. The chapters are slightly shorter than those in the previous parts, giving us space to fold the new exercises into our continued work, which hopefully is reaching a place of integration.

The other goal of the work in these chapters is to acclimate us to all of the realms, seen and unseen. This opens us to further mastery by enabling us to access them from where we are. The Adept lives in all time and all space in each moment. Light shines clearly from her heart, illuminating the universal flow.

Let us open the door.

CHAPTER NINE

Reaching Balance

Enter the space that is neither this nor that. Look to the left and look to the right. Look above and then below. What lies within and what stands outside? Opposition, though a construct, has much to teach us. Feel the push and the pull, the yes and the no. Hold all of this within. Look at how this manifests in the world outside. This is the continuous return to center, the place of balance we all pass through. The flash of insight opens new doors. Return to the elements that bore you: earth, air, fire, and water form the spirit growing ever strong. Look at the paradox of space and time, mercy and severity. All of this will make you whole.

Cleansing the Temple

Before we enter the phase of increased practice and the dedicated reach toward our divinity, we must prepare our physical space. We have been internally cleansing, over and over, looking at all our parts, bringing more of ourselves into alignment, clearing out what is devoid of life power and embracing that which is left. We have slowly been consecrating our lives. Now it is time to harness our will and intentionally consecrate our physical space for the next, very important, phase of this Great Work.

Magic and spirituality come from where we are. Often we wait to do magic from a place we think we should be, rather than actually assessing where we are. After wrestling with some of our illusions and realizing that our demons are really our allies, we are ready to look at what our current needs, desires, and strengths really are. As we studied in the part on "super efforts," (see p. 121) stretching ourselves can be good, but stretching too far beyond our reality does two things: it sets us up for failure and leaves us with cupboards filled with old, dead prayers and spells. These tug on pants legs and ride on our shoulders, as vague energetic reminders of all we have not done. This old magic takes the form of dust upon our altars and rust upon our sacred blades. If we are to welcome a phase of more intensive practice, our space must be in order.

Being clean is important to all our work, and that includes this physical cleansing. Next, we will do some energetic clearing. The first step is the "Cleansing Life Force" exercise from chapter two (see p. 28). After this internal cleansing, we move to our space again.

Doing the Work

The first step in cleansing the temple is to clear out any vestiges of old, defunct magic that may be in drawers, closets, or on altar tops. Dispose of these as you see fit: compost, burn, or throw away, releasing the energies into new form.

Next, give your working space a good overall cleansing. Whether it's a room set aside for ritual work, an altar, or meditation space, clear out that which is not necessary and clean what remains. Make space for clear practice and connection to enter.

Open all the windows in the space where your altar is, then walk counterclockwise, with the intention of banishing the old. You may do this in several ways: use a broom to "sweep" the old energies out, ring bells or a singing bowl to let sound move out stagnant energy, or burn incense to call upon the powers of air and fire to cleanse the space.

Once you are done, take a breath. How connected do you feel in this moment? Align your soul again if need be. Center yourself around the stillness in your belly. Begin to call in the blessings of clarity and support to your working environment. Walk clockwise to "seal" your space with these blessings. You may add in protection if you feel the need. Bless your space with candlelight, or by tracing symbols in saltwater on each window as you close it, or above each door.[74]

Once the whole process is complete, sit in prayer and meditation at your altar. Call upon the ancestors, your Gods, and any allies you may work with. Ask to see yourself fully and cleanly. Ask for compassion if you need it. Request of the universe and God Herself that your work and magic come from an integrated place, growing from the foundations you have set in place.

Disengaging from the Lie

I had achieved the Conversation. I had opened my mystical awareness. But I still had that whole complex of personality characteristics needing transformation, exacerbated now by the intensity of the six-month process and by the new awarenesses and energies.

—WILLIAM BLOOM (IN HIS DIARY, *The Sacred Magician*)

Before we move on into further exploration of the energies of integration, I want to speak to something that, I can almost guarantee, will trip each one of us up in the months and years to come. I want to speak to a cultural lie.

Our culture, like many others, holds dear the idea that spiritual and religious people are somehow better than those who are not. The enlightened one no longer has a personality that gets angry or sad. The priest never grows physically ill. While there is a kernel of truth to these, in that the more integrated a person is, the less prone to extreme swings of mood or physical ailment he or she is, the story is blown so far out of proportion from the truth that in practice, it has become a lie.

I directly experience the results of our spiritual work, such as greater equanimity in dealing with emotional states or thoughts. I also simultaneously see that personality, tiredness, or annoyance don't fully go away. But I am still infected by this lie. It was ingrained in me from childhood on, and despite knowing that it is not true, there is a small part of me that holds it still. Deep down inside myself there is somehow still an expectation that I and my spiritually involved friends will never engage in petty behavior. Deep down inside myself there is somehow still an expectation that I and my spiritual friends will always behave with equanimity, compassion, and reason.

And you know what? Mostly we do. But sometimes an old pattern rears its head and takes over temporarily, even though we fight it. And we watch ourselves fight it. And sometimes we watch ourselves lose the fight. Sometimes we get overtired or have a blood-sugar crash or an extra glass of wine, and our equilibrium is off. Sometimes we are just cranky.

We may not be able to control our behavior in those moments in the ways we wish to. But the good thing is that through the accretion of equilibrium brought through practice, we can see that it is not our whole life. We can know that this particular situation will pass, and tomorrow will be another day. We can know that emotions rise and fall and that annoyance or insecurity or whatever will once again give way to breath and stillness—to a strong will and an open heart. We don't have to hold on to the injury and build a new scar. We don't even have to make a temporary event into an injury in the first place.

This is what spiritual practice brings us: not always being centered but a way to return to center quickly, whether in minutes, or a day or two rather than months or years. Hopefully it also helps us to not calcify around more flotsam than our beings already have stiffened around. We can continue to learn how to live cleanly and clearly and with a full range of motion.

All of life is process and any true master is fully human. And hopefully, as the saying goes, we keep on learning our whole lives, for to not do so is death. Teachers must learn. We still need community to help us with our work and to point out that which we fail to see. We can wrestle and grapple and experiment and practice and raise each other up after plumbing the depths.

That lie of spiritual "perfection"? It is just another old pattern of thought or emotion. Every time it arises, we get another chance to examine it and learn a little bit more about what it means to be human. And that, like the Peacock formed of parts that struggle and then kiss, is perfect.

Embracing the Plateau

Plateaus are common at every stage in life. People are aware that the body will reach new "set points" along the way whenever our aging process shifts or an exercise program reaches a stable place. Our bodies grow used to the new information regarding metabolism or rigorous movement, and adjust accordingly. Our thoughts and emotions do the same thing, as does our spiritual practice.

It is good to take time to enjoy the plateau. We shouldn't be in a rush to shift things again, or frustrated at a seeming "lack of progress." Every facet of our lives needs a place where we can rest and regroup. We can use these times to contemplate or have fun or look in satisfaction at what has brought us to this point in space and time.

Cycles are natural. Sometimes the over-culture encourages us to be always overbooked and on the move, and we can either fall prey to this thinking or give up totally in self-defense. Neither response is a healthy, sustainable one. Rather, we can be aware that life moves and changes, just like the moon or the seasons. There are periods of growth and change followed by segments of rest, where the knowledge gained by our experiences is put to good use. We can enjoy the fruits of our work.

Don't worry. After a time, we will likely grow antsy with this and long for a new challenge, a new climb, some more study or movement.

Just as the body knows when it has had long enough to assimilate the new strength or flexibility it has gained and wishes new effort, so does the mind, heart, and spirit. When that time comes, we can reassess our practice, asking, "What still works? What has become rote?"

Often, particularly for those who have been practicing for many years, we have integrated the "gross" skills and need to work on more subtle awareness or deeper patterns, or to cultivate greater finesse on several levels at once. We've done enough work by now to be able to at least feel our way toward knowing what works for us. Once we figure out what our bedrock is, we can make adjustments to the rest of our lives for optimal spiritual presence and growth.

Plateaus are an opportunity to look at where we have been, enjoy where we are, and begin to plan for where we are heading. Often this latter piece requires deeper examination: what is missing that will help us to move forward? For many of us, the answer is rooted in the work we did with our demons and allies. Our complexes limit our vision, so having wrestled with and even cleared or made friends with some complexes, what is our story now? What is the real state of our hopes and abilities?

Wielding Strong Mercy

After a period of intense integration and perhaps a plateau, many of us are in a position to reexamine boundaries and compassion, severity and mercy. We can reflect on the changes that have occurred inside and around us. When shifts truly happen, they are both liberating and uncomfortable. We get used to our old patterns and our old ways of thinking, feeling, and behaving. When we awaken and aren't enmeshed in those patterns anymore, there can be discomfort when we try to relate to situations or people with whom we were used to behaving in the old ways. How do we act or think in the newer state? Sometimes, as we know, this causes relationships—to religions, philosophies, institutions, groups of friends, or intimates—to seem alien, chafing, or even explosive.

Who are we, as new creatures, striding toward evolution? What can our magic teach us in those moments? We need to stand firm rather than retrench, and we need to call upon compassion again.

The ways of severity are subtle and not easy to ascertain. We think we know what it means, but most of our examples are not accurate, and are colored by strong emotional reactions to the concept of severity. We can see it as privation, punishment, harsh judgment that is not necessarily grounded in either fact or compassion. Simply because that is what common history and current culture reflect to us, severity need be none of these.

Severity is firmness and accurate response. Oftentimes it is the most merciful thing that can be brought to bear in our lives. Severity gives structure and lets one know when one has gone too far. This can occur within ourselves, when we have strayed too much from our Work, or it can occur in interactions with others. Sometimes the world needs to be rebalanced by our letting someone know he or she has transgressed. The line is set, and then we move on. Getting stuck in the severe state is the problem, not severity itself. If it arises and then is let go of, it is a strong and helpful force. Severity can be parent and teacher to us. Wielded wisely, from instinctive wisdom, it holds up a mirror to faces we or others may not usually wish to see.

All of life on this plane needs a boundary. Even the state of reaching the Limitless, God Herself, stems from structured practice and creating a container from which to open beyond the self. The Peacock, in his reach, is held under the hand of love.

Boundaries are a form of severity, of sternness and order in the midst of constant flow. Without this boundary, it is hard to learn, just as with only boundaries, it is also hard to learn. The state of the Peacock Angel is the place of the coming together of severity and mercy. They both arise from beauty and integration. From that coming together of all our parts into a whole stems a new dichotomy. Severity before wholeness can be brutal. Mercy before integration can be smothering pity. However, rising from a place of self-knowledge, they both move within us and with us, resting easily.

It takes time after integration for us to wield these qualities easily and with grace. At first, there might be states of our being necessarily severe or merciful, only to second-guess ourselves later. Or conversely, we may move too quickly into one or the other, regardless of what is truly appropriate to the situation at hand. Severity rests easily on the shoulders of one who is in a state of balanced power. We will eventually learn to move from this place of beauty and balance. When that time comes, severity will come naturally, as will mercy. When we hold integration and reach for the Limitless, the poles become the same.

Reflection

Look at your comfort level with setting boundaries. Do you set them to reject incoming information, or because you know yourself and where you stand? How easy is it for you to stand firmly in your Work, your truth, and your life? Does mercy come easily, or do you push others away or try to take care of them too much?

Close your eyes and try to sense what feels balanced inside you. Find the place of balance: in your pelvis, your belly, your heart, or your hands. Now imagine an actual balance, a scale, whose fulcrum is in that area, and place your sense of severity on one side and your mercy on the other. Feel how they move and recalibrate from the center place.

Notice what feels severe to you and what feels merciful. What are your definitions of these words? How do you respond to them? Then ask, "What in me needs a firmer boundary, and what needs more ease?"

Courting Integration

Call it honesty, integrity, wholeness; you must not go back, undo, uproot, abandon the conquered ground. Tenacity of purpose and honesty in pursuit will bring you to your goal.

— NISARGADATTA MAHARAJ (IN *I Am That*)

Many of us are taught that we must be bloodless and stoic in our lives or, conversely, that we should fall prey to every whim and emotion that passes by. These extremes reflect the lack of integrity in the cultures we come from. Our lives often swing wildly, like pendulums, very rarely touching a center point. Just as politics does the same, as economic markets rise and fall, so our lives gyrate from wild fantasy to numbing despair. But wild swings are not actually necessary, and in fact, they serve to sap our life flow rather than build it. The swinging can feel as if it generates life power, but actually it spews it outward in patterns of waste. Accompanying feelings of intensity come from the flare and flash that sometimes happens before a candle burns up.

Think of a master in the martial arts. He looks centered, feels centered, even when attackers come from all directions. She moves in a steady, strong way, swirling around the center point in her belly, attending to the work at hand. He is not static or unmoving, but neither is he running all over the room. Rather, supple feet pivot and step, arms swing, and gravity moves. The master is connected to earth, to air, to fire, to water, to spirit. The master moves from these and with these. The dance of life is present in each gesture. If a misstep happens, she does not go into rage or self-deprecation. He keeps on moving, attending to what is next. There is no perfection that is not changeable. The whole universe is about change.

We can reflect this. In working to know our bright and shadow parts, we enabled the Twins within us to begin to merge. As duality kisses, it automatically becomes something new. Possibility, the Peacock, is born from the lips of light meeting shadow. If we still fear integration, we can try to embrace that fear. We can sit with it, walk with it, and dance with it. What could possibly be wrong with living at our full depth and power? What could possibly be wrong with having full emotional, mental, and physical expression? Some of us fear that we still will fail to be perfect. I invite us to remember the martial artist who still makes a mistake but funnels it directly into the flow. Some of us fear that others will think we are trying to raise ourselves above them. I invite us to remind ourselves that the more help we are to ourselves, the greater capacity we have to help others.

In the place of balance, beauty rests. Beauty abides within us here, because everything we ever were becomes present: all of our pain, joy, disappointment, rapture, boredom, and celebration. The life power from all of these, our very humanity, gives us the weight of a strong center from which we can tread lightly. There is no stopping the magic worker who integrates and does the work to keep bringing his parts into the fold. There is nothing like a mystic with all her parts available to her in any given moment. We bring our lives to bear upon our magic and our magic opens space and time, and new worlds are created.

Shifting Dissonance to Power

We are not the center of the universe; that is only our perspective. Rather, we are part of a large wheeling dance of multiplicity. There are paradoxes inherent in all spiritual systems, including contemporary magic. We know that in our solar system, the planets revolve around the sun, yet we cast our circles to follow the sun's perceived movement across the earth.

There's nothing wrong with this, as many magic workers tend toward phenomenology and the phenomenon of tracking the sun across the sky is real, but I wonder if there isn't something more. I have thought this for years, since studying intensively with the whirling dervishes who dance counterclockwise, turning left. Was there something the old mystery schools knew that we have lost? Did they purposefully work *deosil* in counterpoint to some other, *widdershins* flow?[75] Did Rumi turn *widdershins*, as the pilgrims so circle the *Kaaba*, for some deeper, arcane reason?[76]

We can bring this to our consciousness today, powering our workings through dynamism, creating a ritual magnetic field.

Picture this: magically, we cast an outer-sunwise sphere, while turning ever inward on our path. The inward turn takes us around our hearts, the *deosil* circle, swinging out around us in graceful ellipsis. We cast outward, following the path of the sun, while our emotional and spiritual work is simultaneously turning in around our hearts. We become a wheel within a wheel, the center and circumference, Hadit and Nuit, matter and extension, nucleus and atom, solid point and limitless reach.[77] We set something new into motion with tight turns and larger orbits. Spin and rotate. Rotate and spin. All directions are necessary. One force alone will not create a world. We find both what we center around and what we reach for. The inner and outer trajectories become consciously present in our work.

The seeming opposites listed above are used in various systems to represent the holistic quality inherent in magical experience. The magic worker knows that the individual cell is not the whole body yet is part of it. She knows that the human is not the whole biosphere but part of the whole. He recognizes that the material realms, in their broadest sense, are part and parcel of the immaterial too. It is in the deep knowledge and experience of these things, born from years of practice and experience, that the magical practitioner grows more confident that reality is both particular and unceasingly vast.

The following exercise will not only help us remain present to our energy centers throughout the day but will also increase our ability to open to states caused by dynamic movement in opposite directions. The energy work described here mimics the more complex systems found in the body itself, using simplified means by running energy in our etheric and auric bodies. See the illustration for an example of the flow. We will focus on two loops for now, adding a third later. The first loop runs up the front edge of our physical bodies and down the back. It is not *within* the physical body but, rather, in the etheric body that sheathes our physical form. The second loop runs the opposite direction on the outside edge of our aura, down in front and up in back. [see illustration iii]

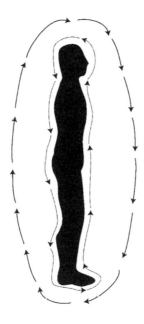

Illustration iii: Energy Loops

Doing this work over time shifts our relationship to our own energy and to the energy flowing around all the things we interact with. I use the following to "set" my energy bodies in the morning, cleansing them and getting the energy started properly, bringing my attention fully into my physical and energy bodies while connecting to the parts of my soul. This helps my meditations and prayers, and starts my day from a clear and vibrant place. Throughout the day I simply check in on the energies to see that the loops are still making their circuits. This is another practice in attention and will development, as well as a key into the sex and life energies of the universe. I am singular, yet involved in the same dance as all else. The Divine Twins of these energy loops connect me further to myself and further to the All.

Doing the Work

Take a breath. Feel the still place in your belly, your center. Stand with your awareness surrounding that for a moment and focus on your breathing. Feel your feet and the top of your head. Now imagine your etheric body running all around your physical form. Breathe in and imagine that energy running up in front of you, over the top of your head and down in back, looping beneath your feet to begin its ascent again. If it helps at first, key the upward sweep with an inhalation and the downward loop with an exhalation. Eventually you will need to unhook this from your breath and let the energy just run on its own.

Once you have this running, imagine your aura around you, a shining body of light and energy. Send a breath along the outer edge, down in front, flowing beneath you, up in back, flowing over you and then down in front.

Now check back in with the inner loop, imagining it running simultaneously with energy in the outer sphere. You may sense them "passing" each other above your head or beneath your feet. Let them run together and feel your center once again, still in the midst of the radiant flow.

The tandem flow should feel energizing and, for most people, will have some tangible expression: tingling, a rush of energy, happiness, strength, or centeredness. This will vary from person to person. Sometimes, when running these currents, a person might find that a left-hand turn occurs, just as will happen in other electrical systems.[78] This sideways energy loop naturally arises in some people.

Standing in the Cosmic Flow

Even in the midst of plateau, our work continues. We can better sense our place in the world, the universe, and as a functioning part of God

Herself when we take a brief rest from the intensity of our work. All of our practices of soul alignment, stillness, and connective breathing come to center us more and more in the flow of all being. Our lives begin to work in concert with the All, and our internal balance is reflected outwardly. We are balanced with the world around us. We are standing in the cosmic flow. [see illustration iv]

Everything in our lives will mirror this: work will include more joy and ease, our homes will become places of rest and warmth, and we will have greater access to vitality and joy on a regular basis. Even ways through struggle will become clearer. Just as the energy changes around us noticeably, there may also be more subtle energetic shifts inside. We can activate these shifts, opening further channels to this flow with all the elements of life, all the Gods and Goddesses, and, of course, with God Herself. The following exercise will help us with this. It builds upon the energy work we did in "Shifting Dissonance to Power." (see p. 187)

Over time, the following practice increases our vital force and presence in the world.

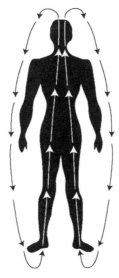

Illustration iv: Standing in the Cosmic Flow

Doing the Work

Do this in a standing position if you are able. Feel your feet open to the earth and your crown open to the sky. Find the still point in your belly and breathe deeply. Begin to take in vital breaths, touching the tip of your tongue to the roof of your mouth. Once you feel fully present, begin to cycle energy up in front of your etheric body, down in back. Then add in the aura breathing you have been practicing: send a breath along the outside edge of your aura, down in front and up in back. Once you get both loops running on their own, allow energy to run up through your feet in two "lines" of energy, one for each foot. Let these move up, and when they reach a point just above your head, imagine them moving in an outward arc, toward the right on your right side and toward the left on your left. This arc will continue down, forming an oval loop until it reaches just below your feet. At that point, imagine the energy flowing back up, in toward your feet, where it will rise again.

Once these loops are running clearly, notice again the energy running on the edge of your etheric body and your aura. You can have all three loops active at one time. When you feel well energized and stable, allow the cosmic loops to stop, but allow the etheric and auric energies to keep running on their own. Use any excess energy to align your soul by breathing up into the globe of your God Soul.

Feel your feet open to earth and your crown open to sky. Take a full body breath.

Stabilizing the Three Points

The Adept must have control of her energy bodies, mind, and emotions. By control, I mean to say he can harness all of these and set them working in tandem rather than at odds with each other. Think of the sphinxes that pulled Socrates's chariot of the soul.[79] The charioteer is required to get these opposing black and white beasts moving forward together, using only the power of his will, heart, and mind. The yoking is an internal process.

The work we are about to do is similar in that it yokes our awareness of internal and external space while enabling us to also focus on a specific point or task. Holding this three-pointed awareness opens our psychic senses so we can gather greater information from our deep self, our guides, ancestors, deities, Holy Guardian Angel, or God Soul.

Practiced over time, this simple energetic exercise enables us to do this in any situation with increasing skill and authority. We will master our own direction. Mastery leads us into beauty, toward Godhood, and on into love. I recommend doing the following at least once a week.

Doing the Work

Settle into your chair, or onto your meditation cushion or bench. Regulate and slow down your breathing, and adjust your skeleton and muscles until you are seated in a good, upright yet relaxed posture. Hold a pencil or some other slim object in your hands, letting it rest in your lap for right now.

Once you feel settled in, check in with your energy bodies and soul alignment. Focus in on the still point in your belly you've been cultivating. Next, be aware of the edge of your auric body, sending a breath out along the outer edge. Hold attention of these two points as you breathe. Open your eyes and sit with this awareness for several long breaths.

When your attention to these two points is well established, slowly raise the pencil until one end is at eye level, a foot or so out from your face. Your arm should be comfortable enough to hold this position for several minutes. It is all right to rest your upper arm against your body, extending your lower arm out and up just slightly.

Breathing, hold attention of the still point, the edge of the aura extending around you, and the point in front of you. Energy will build within, and you might feel an opening out at the base of your skull. Relax into this, maintaining your awareness. Do not let go of any of the points, but let your attention come to hold them naturally, with little effort.

As you do this work, you may find that deity, ancestors, or your God Soul may come closer, with messages for you. Still holding your three-point awareness, open to them. Invite them to speak to you.

Once you feel you have done enough, lower the pencil to your lap. Send one more breath to your aura and one into the still place of your belly. Then tilt your head back and breathe some energy up to align your soul, as we learned in chapter three (see p. 56).

Seeking Our Inner God

In our quest for integration and wholeness, we can connect to the most connected part of ourselves rather than always falling under the sway of our disconnected parts. In tuning in to our God Soul each day, we can open the channels of pure connection to all of our parts and to the Limitless. This cultivates both deep stillness and extreme expansion. Here is a prayer to our God Soul, asking for help in our work.

Doing the Work

Settle into your meditation posture. Let yourself sit in stillness for awhile, breathing, then say the following prayer:

"Beautiful rose, keep me from ignorance. May I learn silence as well as speech, depth as well as height, freedom as well as restraint, stillness as well as movement, reason as well as joy. May I walk firmly and come into full possession of myself. Through the guidance of the ancestors and in the company of the Gods, may I know myself and manifest my work. May God Herself be seen, a reflection in my eyes."

After this, open to your God Soul, connecting to the globe above your head, and ask for your divine nature to speak to you. Listen. Breathe. Listen some more.

Doing this work will enable us to open to the voice of our divine nature, and to our true will, throughout the course of the day. It builds trust in our intuition and helps us to recognize when our integrated soul is speaking. We can learn to trust that voice and follow our divine guidance.

For those of us in earlier stages of listening practice, we can set aside five minutes at the end of our sessions to align our souls (see p. 56) and, after our God Soul listens to our parts, our parts can quiet and listen to our God Soul.

CHAPTER TEN

Desiring Beauty

Welcome to the place of beauty. Here, all of our parts dance together in a sphere of love and golden light. We have learned many lessons and are in a state of rest and grace, however temporarily. We may need to revisit earlier lessons or integrate new ones in time, but for now, we can just be for a moment, cultivating joy and satisfaction before getting back to work. There is a gorgeousness inside you, birthed of light and darkness. Bright colors swirl before your eyes. You have struggled, and now comes the opening.

This chapter will teach us how to be effective in our magic. We will call upon the Peacock to help us risk for that which is truly, deeply right. We will come into alignment with our desires and put these out into the universe, becoming cocreators of Divine will on earth.

From the place of temporal integration and the inkling of spiritual wholeness comes another phase of spiritual expansion. This is the place of daring spoken of in the four magical powers: to know, to will, to dare, and to hold the mystery of silence. To dare is to risk the unknown, carried by the suppleness of our gathered knowledge and the will we are working to strengthen.

Harnessing Desire

The power of magic has to do with the power of desire and the power of will. . . . Unless desire wells up in me, why should I waste my energy? I know I can't succeed in anything unless desire is with me. Desire is the gasoline of willpower . . .

—Ann Davies[80]

Desire is the energy that arises when want and need become one thing. It comes into being when what we want is not just superficial but is something that will feed our souls.

Desire harnesses life force. In opening to desire, we risk being greater, more vibrant, and more effective than we currently are. We open ourselves to happiness, to power, to a deeper relationship with our lives and our work. Sometimes it can even feel as though we *don't* want what we desire with all of our hearts. The parts of us that have grown used to hiding or are fearful still may not want this. Certainly that is the message we can extrapolate from our actions or inaction. What if we run toward our desire and it doesn't pan out, what if it looks different than we thought, what if we fail utterly, falling flat on our faces? Well, any of these can happen. But what is the alternative? Sitting in front of the television with the remote control day after day does not make for a full and satisfying life. It gives away our possibility and numbs our life force. This behavior disengages us from the world.

To get what we want, we must first ask for it. This statement sounds simple, but it is often discounted or forgotten. Sometimes looking at the obvious is a great occult secret: the best secrets are often hidden in plain sight. For magic to be successful in operation requires presence, knowledge, and the integration we've been working toward. Otherwise, we will continue to be at war within and will therefore never find what we wish outside of ourselves.

Opening to desire is opening to change. Opening to desire opens us to what may come. There is power there, as well as beauty.

Below is a prayer for desire. You may wish to write your own.

Reflection

Desire. You move toward me sometimes more rapidly and with greater assurance than I move toward you. You catch me by surprise and make me gasp with the beauty of your presence. I call to you to teach me. I call to you to show me the sweet, strong unfolding of my life. May my life shine like a jewel, glistening with your kiss. May I be strong, and kind, and open.

May I know my path. May I be of service. May I sow the light.

What Do We Want?

By following the breath, we quiet the mind. Our sense of separateness and independent being comes from the mind's incessant chatter. When we just sit, watch, and breathe; when we refuse to follow this or that thought or feeling and simply allow them to rise and fall of their own accord, the mind slowly ceases its chattering. A deep quiet emerges.

—Reb Yerachmiel ben Yisrael (from *Open Secrets* by Rami M. Shapiro)

Many times I have inquired of people, "If you could have anything, no matter how crazy it sounds, what would you want?" Too often they have answered, "I don't know." Yet every one of those people has wanted something. Every one of them desired a fuller relationship with another person or a deeper relationship with themselves or greater physical health or knowledge of the Gods. Every one of them wanted something but had trouble recognizing even their simplest desires as being worthy of notice.

Oftentimes the busyness of our lives overwhelms the voice inside that speaks of desire. Or we are stuck in family taboos or feeling undeserving. Still others of us, recognizing that our lives are blessed, feel we want for nothing. It is good to count our blessings and also realize that even we can want to remain challenged, loved, and intrigued by life. We can want continuance or even want a little more. We can want to keep learning things until the day we die and perhaps beyond.

One thing that trips us up is living in a consumer-oriented culture.[81] We think that we must desire material things or high-powered careers, when what we may desire deeply is a garden to tend or greater self-awareness. We can also have a reaction against this culture by thinking that any form of desire leads to greed. I would counter this by saying that desire leads us further into life, and that is a good thing.

Reflection

Sit in silence. Breathe in silence. Open the stillness in your center. In the deep quiet, feel that being and nothingness are present. Form and formlessness are waltzing. The microcosm reaches up, and the macrocosm reaches down. In that space of no time—one second, ten minutes, or a lifetime—they kiss. You are nothing—and everything.

Thought or emotion enters again. You feel yourself separate out. Time continues. Your body is on its cushion. Your back aches, or your feet are asleep. But some small thing has changed. Some part of you, even for one second, touched your possibility.

What do you want from your life?

Becoming Beauty

There is beauty to be wrought here which is unsurpassed. This is something that can be experienced here and now. Eden is right where we are, if we can only learn to see it.

    —PETER GREY (IN *The Red Goddess*)

Beauty is the symbol of integration. It is the golden sphere, the crimson rose, and the Peacock in his glory. Our spiritual search is not always a lovely thing to behold. We are often in the muck, still battling complacency, fear, or sleep. But our loving, determined work, our commitment to ourselves and to the Great Work of the world, bring us closer and closer to that which is beautiful because it is whole. There is no part of us that is not of the Gods, it is said.[82] Our thoughts and feelings of separation cease to make sense the more we have come into the practice of inclusion rather than transcendence. We live less and less in illusion and more and more in that which is real.

Beauty does not exist as a surface quality but requires all the inner layers of soul to shine through its creation. We see it in great art or music that come from concentrated effort. We see it in the active presence of wild animals. The face of a beloved sage is luminous in its beauty, regardless of the evenness of features. Beauty is not about prettiness. Beauty is the perfection that shifts over time, deepening, ripening there in every stage of life, because *we* are there in every stage of life. We cannot escape change. When the constancy of our presence witnesses and celebrates change, our lives become reflections of beauty. Nothing in us is ugly when viewed through the lens of creation. All is necessary for the unfolding of our souls.

The Peacock sends a cry of beauty out to all the worlds, and it resounds within us. To dare reach for this beauty, we must not fear our expansion, power, compassion, and vibrancy. Even when fear is present, we move forward anyway.

Reflection

What is whole in you, right now? What seeks the beauty of light in extension, the molecules that make up God Herself? Can you honestly see any part of you that is not necessary to your functioning whole? What in you is beautiful?

Bless that part. Include your life. Seek out one thing that moves you every day. See beauty in the unusual spaces, and you will begin to find the beauty in yourself.

Reaching Boldly

Your playing small doesn't serve the world. There's nothing enlightened about shrinking so that other people won't feel insecure around you.

—MARIANNE WILLIAMSON (IN *A Return to Love*)

Life is too important to settle for less than full power, joy, compassion, and creative force. Life is too important to live small. As spiritual seekers, it is incumbent upon us to find our work, to reach for our greatness, and to contribute to the world to the very best of our abilities.

Living small is often a response to a sense of scarcity in the world. Sometimes childhood stories tell us that there isn't enough to go around, whether regarding emotional or physical resources, talent, or beauty. We have embarked on a process of forging our hearts. This helps to temper these old thoughts and form new ones. We can become strong and true through the process of being melted and reformed into a steel from disparate metals.

In years past, I would often try to shrink my hopes and expectations, asking for the minimum and settling for less. Over time, I realized that living this way was a lie. I was already big and bold inside, but I masked it or only allowed it to emerge in ways that felt nonthreatening to the status quo. I had myself convinced that there was not enough and that if I asked for and received what I wanted and needed, someone else would have to do without. The reality I eventually opened to was that by receiving what I needed, I had more to give. And in being open to gifts, others were made happy at the opportunity to share generosity. All of this proved to make me more generous as well.

I'm not talking here about giving in to greed and obsession. Nor am I talking about exploiting others for our own gain. I remain well aware of inequitable sharing of the world's resources. Nonetheless, I had to realize that living in poverty myself—emotionally, physically, spiritually, and sexually—was not going to give anyone else any more than he or she already had. There are ways in which consumption takes away, becoming a negative force, and there are also ways in which consumption is a simple way of being fed. We can welcome good, healthy, balanced sustenance rather than a starvation diet or a glutton's feast.

This requires both committed practice with an engaged will and an openness to the gifts that come our way. We must forge our hearts and temper our souls. We must melt to ourselves, and open to others. A bold life is a life unafraid to be strong and soft, rather than one thing or another. A bold life is whole.

Reflection

Is your life sustainable? Are you happy? Are you generous with others and yourself? Do you live honestly and lead a life that gives back—living in the flow? Do you use self-reflection to examine your life and motivations? Do you operate from love and courage, or from fear?

What would it mean to you to live a bold life? How is this different from the life you are currently leading? Drop in to your life. Has it grown too small, or do you feel stuck in the very comfort of it? Are you willing to take a risk to have more?

Birthing the Divine

God is Self and Self is God, and God is a person like myself.

—FERI TRADITION SAYING

The phrase above reflects the mystery of layers and levels of truth and experience. It is not a statement to be believed but one that may unfold in us over time. It points to a part of Nature that is divine. We are Gods in potentia, for we carry a spark of the divine within.

The other thing this phrase reflects is an awareness of the nature of the macrocosm relating to the microcosm. Within this interplay is the play of the Gods and our own souls. I'm going to talk here about theology. What I'm going to say is likely not new, because all deep practice points to larger truth. I'm including this discussion here because the more we can stretch our thinking along with our experience, the better context we will have for the events yet to come in our spiritual lives. Our growth will need to encompass many layers of reality, and exercising the intellect to welcome rather than resist this change will ease our integration. Let us try to keep our seeker's minds open and flexible, without succumbing to gullibility or simple belief. Each exploration will be tested by our own work.

Connection exists. There is immanence and transcendence, and everything beyond and in between. My tradition calls this connection God Herself. As we've been exploring, the Star Goddess of many names is one face of this, but even that mysterious face can be too structured, too familiar, too close. I like this face because it points directly to the non-dual, including the non-dual being that we are becoming. The non-dual has no face and many. The non-dual is limitless flow.

Everything reaches for this reality: Gods, humans, animals, plants, molecules, and rain. Simultaneously, all of our parts reach toward our own divine nature. We are in relationship to these Gods just as we relate to other humans. We are all part of the whole yet are also individual expressions holding one piece of the great puzzle. In remembering our parts, we resonate with the beings who will help us.

We reach both up and down, bringing body, thought, emotion, and spirit together. There is a phrase: "That which you seek, seeks you," which touches on the depth of the reality that there is constant reach in all directions. Past and future reach toward each other, meeting in an endless now. This is the reach of Michelangelo's God toward Adam in the vault of the Sistine Chapel. Dark reaches to light, and light to darkness. Animal reaches to God. In humans, all of these meet in reason, when reason opens itself to the seat of the heart.

When our animal nature consistently reaches toward our God Soul in an act of openness and willed alignment, our rational soul comes into alignment as well. Divine nature, reason, and instinct become one, bridging all the worlds. Self-possession makes this link permanent as our God Soul descends further into the physical, bringing Godhood down into the human. [see illustration vi, p. 239.] But it is the reaching up of the animal nature and the pull of pure life force that enable this descent. Without our striving and intention, only touches are possible, not the full contact we desire.

Our God Soul descends, but the rest of us simultaneously "grows up" and into divinity, bringing us directly into immanence. Our being tunes itself more clearly to the All, and this changes every relationship we are currently involved in, be it with human, animal, or God. Kabbalah tells us that we are shards of light to be put back together, and in our repair, we heal the world. We must align our souls.

Loving the Self

When you love yourself and you are right with the universe, what you want will become what you need.

—MICHELE JACKSON

To love ourselves and to love the world are both necessary spiritual projects. Without one or the other, little progress will be made. Work has to be undertaken before these may come into being, of course, but a small amount of care for self must be present, at least, for one to take an interest in working at all. This sometimes disguises itself as the desperation to better oneself, or a feeling that one has gone as far as one can in futility. But even the decision to try something, anything, is a sign that hope has not died completely. And the seed of hope is love.

The balanced magic worker feels deeply in her soul that her soul is worthy. He recognizes more and more, that as part of God Herself, his life is a necessary thread in the web, so his taking care of it is of great importance. The more we approach wholeness and self-possession, the more we open to self love, because we sense the rightness of it. If we are to love the world, if we are to love the Gods, must we not also love ourselves?

Love is the fabric of all. Love is underneath every effort, large or small. Love is possibility. Love frees us. Love brings change.

Finding the Work of This God

. . . we can dare to recognize that our very participation in the Cosmic Manifestation makes available to us all things needful, both spiritual and material.

—ANN DAVIES

Cosmic Will wants what we want. That which we desire on the deepest level, that which is our destiny moving within, is what the universe wants from us. Our complexes try to keep us from this, which is why all of our work on cleansing, observation, and alignment are keys to this work of self-possession. And self-possession is key to entering into True Will and that which the universe desires for us and of us. This is the thing that sometimes feels like destiny.

Destiny is the work of our personal God, the work we have to do, the work that, once embarked upon, leaves other choices behind. This is both a huge sacrifice and an inordinate blessing. It isn't fate, where all is predetermined, but it does narrow our choices down. Our choices are narrowed because we have made a more ultimate choice to follow the Work of this God, bringing about the Great Work.

What is a whole, healthy, vital human being? We have explored want and now will look at need.

Heathen author Diana Paxson describes need as what is necessary.[83] What is necessary for further spiritual unfolding? Sustained self-possession does not happen without integration and some measure of temporal order and success, which is why we've done all the work preceding this chapter. We are not finished with our work, for that will not and should not end, but we do need to look at the ways in which we are or are not successful and whole. Here, we walk in concert with all the parts of our soul, rapidly becoming effective magic workers and fully autonomous human beings.

For some of us, our larger will is doing the spiritual work in front of us. The quest for full presence is mighty work. When this is our polestar, all other work will open for us.

Reflection

We have touched upon the Feri Tradition prayer: "Who is this flower above me? And what is the work of this God? I would know myself in all my parts."

Where are you now? Meditate on this prayer, circling closer and closer to its core, your core, the beating of your heart in the very heart of God Herself. What is being asked of you, right now?

Sailing Life's Currents

A reformer has to sail not with the current. Very often he has to go against it, even though it may cost him his life.
—GANDHI (IN *The Collected Works of Mahatma Gandhi*, VOL. 1-8)[84]

In examining what we want, it is good to look at where we have been and the choices we have made or are making.

Sometimes I've had to make very difficult decisions—sail against the current of popular opinion large or small—but I always have done so when the push of my personal life current was so obviously going a different direction. In those cases, it would have felt like selling my soul to sail a different way. It would have cost me my life in ways just as real as the loss Gandhi speaks of. Something in my core would have died. In those cases, physical death is preferable to soul death. This has been true since I was a small child, and holds true still. Those moments when I have not felt quite strong enough to go with my life current instead of an outside force, I have felt my own diminishment and have had to fight to regain my life force later. We all need to look at our own experiences around this, and sense which situations taste of the truth we are following.

Some others of us have a deep question: how does one sail with one's life current if one doesn't even know what it is? It can be hard to find our life's current. It is the part of us that feels a tugging forward. It is a part of us that knows in our belly when something is just wrong or right. It is the connection to "the work of this God"—our work, our divine nature. We don't always have this sense, because sometimes it is covered up by our training, by the opinions of others, by the culture at large, or by our fear.

Those times when we should have gone one way but went another because of the opinions of friends or family or culture are times when we've locked a part of ourselves away. So, how much of me is locked away *right now*? Can I look at an old dream, an old face, an old identity? Did I give it up because it was false or because I couldn't stand up to opposition around it?

In these cases, how do *I* come back to myself? Sitting practice really helps. Finding the still point in my belly to center around really helps. We are often overwhelmed with busyness, bombarded by advertising, things to do, or concerns for a global crisis that can feel out of control. I can't sense the current of my life when I am constantly being buffeted about by these winds. So any cultivation of being still is of help.

Be still and know that you are God. The being still comes first. Then the opening appears.

Anything on the list of my foundational practices helps: soul alignment, cleansing, or meditation. Any of our work around discernment and will building will also help. Any small act of will helps us build toward our larger, divine Will.

When we consistently give up, we consistently undermine the Work of our God Soul. Any act of starting again, of recommitting, of being with self, is an act of will that can open us up to our life's current.

If there are years of accumulation—noise, static, junk, padding against feeling, excuses, fears—we often will need quite a bit of time, compassion, and effort. But it is worth it. The current will flow within and around us once again.

Self-knowledge is possible. Joy is possible. Freedom is possible. Connection is possible. We have to re-member, in other words, to clear the rubble and put ourselves back together. We have the tools to do this, and nothing but time, if we stop to think about it.

Cycling Colors

Beauty is often inspiration enough to choose to bring light into the world, without weighing the cost, the risk, or the social consequences that keep us bound in other arenas.

—RAVYN[85]

I see beauty in the world and want to open to that, regardless of how much effort it takes. The giving back of the universe is always my reward, and it pays back one hundredfold. One way of getting in touch with this beauty and learning to open to it is to run it through our energy bodies.

We see in illustration vi (see p. 239) and in the appendix B (see p. 250) that our soul has different parts. We will do some work with these parts now, imagining them filled with color and sound vibrations. In doing so, we send out an open invitation to the beautiful, setting up a resonance within ourselves. This opens us to the work ahead, when we actually draw down the globe of God Soul to prepare the way for full possession.

Doing the Work

Do some meditation. While you sit, imagine your etheric body to be a rose-pink color, and imagine that each breath fills it with more and more of this rose energy. If you feel you have this well imagined, begin to cycle the energy up in front and down in back on the outside of your physical body.

Now, as you continue breathing in life energy, imagine it spilling out into your aura. Imagine your aura as a golden-yellow color. Etheric body is still pink, but the aura is yellow. Once you have this image "set," you may try to cycle the outside edge of Shining Body down in front and up in back, as we did in the previous chapter (see p. 178). Once both colors are established, keep the breathing going strong and fill your God Soul with a silvery blue. Let this be a steady place for you. Try to see and feel the colors, and notice if this changes how you feel energetically or if it does anything to your intuitive sense. Does it stabilize or destabilize you?

When you feel the need to do so, let the colors go. Then align your soul with a breath of the energy the color cycling created

Presenting Our Being

Let the beauty we love be what we do. There are hundreds of ways to kneel and kiss the ground.

—RUMI (IN *The Essential Rumi* BY COLEMAN BARKS AND DANIEL MOYNE)

When I was whirling with the dervishes, I had the quote above tattooed on my arm as a reminder that I wanted to integrate more fully into the beauty I was seeking in my practices. It was clear that beauty needed to not only be an external force or form but also something that I lived and breathed. My life had to become my work, and vice versa. Rumi's vision of beauty was a clear injunction to this never-ending process.

The awareness of spirit moving within us and in our lives changes the way we walk in the world. One who has mastery exudes confidence that comes from core strength. Different from brashness or egotism, it is a reflection of the fact that they walk in beauty, seeing it everywhere and reflecting it back. We are cultivating the harmony we sense in these masters. The Peacock fans his tail feathers and walks in pride.

In one who is integrated, this also comes along with generosity of spirit. Beauty is to be shared.

The more we integrate mastery, the more control we have over our presentation to the world. We acquire consistency of presence, speech, and action. Whether at a party, in the garden, or an office space, we can walk smoothly, carrying vibrancy, power, and grace. I recommend practicing this, no matter where we are on our path, but especially as we grow closer and closer to the place of knowledge and conversation with our deepest selves.

Doing the Work

This is a great practice to do with a trusted friend. He or she can practice noticing your energy while you practice growing dimmer and brighter. Sensing the energy of others is also a helpful tool. The better we get at doing the following, the more control we have over how others perceive us. This is something we may choose to practice if we are wishing to make changes in career, relationships, leadership, or self-confidence. Those of us who are satisfied in those areas can always use the following to fine-tune our presentation. If this feels helpful to you, do it once a week until if becomes second nature. If you are having trouble with sensing the energy, simply imagine it.

Before beginning the aura exercise below, ask yourself, "What presence do I wish to carry in the world? How will I carry myself, in all my parts? What energy is most helpful to my work? What frightens me about being seen? What frightens me about not being seen? How do I want to be in relationship to the world?"

Meditate on the above questions and then begin the following work. Breathe into your stillness. Feel your aura around you. Send a breath to the edge, to activate it. Now, eyes closed, imagine yourself growing brighter and brighter. Let your face and posture shift to reflect this state. Feel brightness around your head and radiating from your heart. Feel brightness down around your feet and hands. Let yourself be radiant, like a star or our sun.

Take another breath and imagine the brightness growing dimmer and dimmer. Feel the energy diminish and sink back in on itself. Let your posture and face reflect this.

Open your eyes and try again. This time, intentionally engage your belly muscles and try to keep in touch with your still space as you grow first bright, then dim, then bright again. Practice going back and forth at whatever pace feels good to you.

Once you feel you have some facility with this practice, find a range that feels good to you. Find a presentation of spirit that doesn't feel overexposed or faked but that is not allowing you to hide yourself. Take your aura to this place. Notice what your posture feels like here. Notice how your facial muscles feel. Notice your feet beneath you, the energy around you, and the openness of your heart space. How powerful do you feel?

Tilt your head back, breathe up, and align your soul.

Notice what emotions, if any, come up as you do this work.

Once you get the hang of this, you can "set" your energy bodies in the morning with the energy loop work you've been practicing. Then, before leaving home, check to see how bright or dim you feel today, and ask if that is how you wish to face the world. You can do this before meetings, before going for a walk, or any time you enter a new situation.

In my own experience, I have found that being bright opens doors, and consistency garners respect. If we practice presence, our presence in the world will grow. Therein lies success.

CHAPTER ELEVEN

Drawing Up Life

We come closer and closer to our own God nature, entering the full flow of life. Celebrate the cycles of creation and destruction. Dance in your power. Develop your skill and recommit to your life's work. Reach up and down, stretching yourself beyond what you thought possible. Prepare to kiss the limitless. Merge the planes of existence within you, and embrace what is to come.

The truth shines within us; we are whole. This is the time to connect with all of our will and all of our Will. We have stopped our shattering and gathered up the shards, gluing them together with the sweat of our effort, the juice of our enjoyment, and the substance of our tears. At this point, we hopefully understand that all is a process and we are part of that, never ceasing, even beyond death.

There will always be a place for us, whether we disperse fully back into the elements from which we came—soil, liquid, breath, and energy—or whether we have built a connection within that will last throughout time and space, becoming a contiguous being in full connection with God Herself. There is no fear of death in the midst of life, for death and life are part of the same eternal flow. In repairing ourselves, we begin to repair the world.[86]

Becoming the Result

Once we know the extent to which we are capable of feeling that sense of satisfaction and completion, we can then observe which of our various life endeavors bring us closest to that fullness.

—AUDRE LORDE (IN "USES OF EROTIC" FOUND IN *Sister Outsider*)

A magical friend of mine was once in the middle of a life transition that included studying for a new career. She related how excited she was by her new work and what she was studying, how fully engaged she was, and how aligned with her True Will this seemed.

I thought, "Of course, this is aligned with your True Will." When one is working from one's Will—from the Work of This God, from a place of alignment with the universe—the process itself is so engaging and fully satisfying that *it becomes the result.* When we are really acting from Will, then attachment to the outcome of desire is a moot point. The process itself is desired and desiring. We are in the erotic flow of all, involved in a call and response with the universe, and our lives are the result. There is nothing we are waiting for. There is nothing to be disappointed by if it doesn't come to pass, because we love life as it is.

This isn't about complacency. This isn't about settling for second best and calling it good. This is about knowing ourselves, knowing our Work and fully manifesting it in our lives. And that itself is the reward. The working of Will is the process *and* the outcome. Success is guaranteed.

For those of us who still don't know what we want, or who don't yet know our Will, let it be our surrogate will to find that out, to dive further into self-study and the study of the worlds around us.

Reflection

Still yourself, breathe deeply, and listen. What do you want? What is your will right now? What is your Will?

If you have no answers to these questions, say a prayer that you open to Will. Let it be your will to keep practicing and opening. The energy will carry you forward.

Embracing Service

And what you see outside you, you see within. It is visible and it is
your garment.

    —The Thunder, Perfect Mind[87]

In chapter two, (see p. 24) we looked at cultivating service as an aid to our own beings as well as the world. Now I want to look at service as it relates to our Gods. The closer I step to the fullness of my own divinity, the more that changes my relationship to other divine beings. I am opening this discussion here, because everyone reading this is on the cusp of Godhood. The spark is within us, but stepping fully into the embrace of the divine inside and outside of us requires the ability to not only love ourselves and love the world with clear hearts and eyes, but to take on the responsibility that acting in the world as divine agents requires. We serve the Limitless, yes, but we also serve ourselves, because our work is rapidly becoming the work of the Limitless.

I used to be a devotee. I used to be a supplicant. I am no longer these. I still adore. I still pray. I still light candles and incense. I still have overwhelming gratitude for my life. But these are not tainted with any sense of subservience anymore. Do I still worship? Not in the same sense as I used to. It feels more like a communion these days. A partnership of shared energies. My relationship with Deity and Deities feels more like a healthy, adult relationship than one of parent and child, or big scary thing with little scared thing.

And I think, "If I am doing theurgy, the work of Gods on earth, of course, things must be this way. I am necessary to the fabric of the All, just as everything else is—including the Gods."[88]

There is no subservience, only service. This is a service to all, because I have taken on the mantle of divinity. I see this in others around me who are committed to this Work. They act in love and power, speech and silence, always doing their own work, but with the sense that their own work serves something much greater than their personality. Their Work serves the all, because they have integrated their own divinity. As one friend puts it, they have become effective team players with the universe.

When did this change occur in me? I was growing into it for years. The change happened when I was looking at something else, when I was busy with the descent of grace and power that shook up my life in ways I did not know were coming but that have served me incredibly well.

Devotion, for the spiritually mature, is about being and becoming truly that which we are. That is our gift to the Gods and our gift to the world.

When we realize we are in partnership with the Gods, we fall in love again. Love is the re-membering. Our dis-membering is a way of being cut off from love. How many ways do we still separate ourselves out? How much loneliness do our souls court?

A wise priestess once said something to the likes of this: if we want to be lovers to God Herself, we have to court her well.[89] We must learn to act like lovers, not the codependent jerks and not the slobs who never call, but true companions on the way. We have to be in relationship to our own lives, our own loves, to the world around us and the hearts that whisper there. We need to learn how to become good lovers. It takes practice, and *that* is true devotion.

Stepping into Authority

When we rely upon others to study the secrets of Nature and think and act for us, then we have created a life for ourselves, one which is termed 'Hell.'
   —NOBLE DREW ALI[90]

To do the work our souls are calling us to do, we must be able to step into our own authority. We are back to the concept of maps here. No one else can walk our path for us, and no one will discover exactly the things we will. We need guidance, but we also reach a point where everything feels uncharted and all we can do is seek guidance in what we have built and mapped ourselves.

We need to trust ourselves and look within for our authority. We need not submit our life power to another, and allow them to manipulate and control us. We need to *develop* our authority and then fully claim it. This doesn't ever mean we submit life power to another, but it does support all the work we've done in apprenticing ourselves to teachers whom we trust and to our diligent application to available systems. As we have likely seen, people give up too easily and never build anything lasting within themselves. They may speak more loudly than others, thinking all their years within spiritual communities gives them authority. They fail to recognize that they don't have authority at all, because they haven't accreted it. In these cases, too often what isn't working is not the system but the parts of ourselves that are fearful and have resistance. But also know that if teachers are not made uncomfortable and don't therefore set up boundaries when you try to submit to them, they are not worthy teachers. Both teacher and student are equal in worth, even with a disparity in experience.

These days, whenever I see a bumper sticker that says, "Question Authority," I want to change it to read, "Cultivate Your Own Authority." We have to *want* to be free. And that requires effort and ability. Working in a soup kitchen for many years, I've seen too many people who would do anything to go back into prison. Taking care of themselves outside is just too difficult a task. What are the prisons of our making? As the philosopher Foucault would point out, we guard ourselves and each other to maintain the status quo. As magic workers, we can and should break this cycle of oppression. We should cease to drag each other down and, instead, celebrate when one of us is lifted and stands tall.

Victor Anderson said, when interviewed, "[People] have the idea that everyone who gets initiated is made into a bona fide Witch right there, all ready to go. That is not true."[91] Why would he say this is not true? He points to the development of self. Magic is a craft (and science and art) that must be studied and practiced. This is about the ways of Nature and reality. We all have natural talents and can have connections to the earth and the Gods, but will, power, and skill must be developed. There is no getting around this, no matter how hard we wish for it.

There are people who have trod the Path before me, and to whom I look for teaching. I want to study with them, not because they are "better than" me or anyone else but because they have helpful insights and have done their work. There are peers I turn to for advice, and who turn to me, and sometimes they are even these same teachers, in a slightly different role. And there is work I must do on my own, for myself and with my Gods. I have cultivated my inner voice and must listen to it.

We celebrate as we will, and work and study to the best of our ability. This is our charge.

The Skill of Will

We must use care in crafting our magic. Magic comes from where our lives are. All the work we've done on self-observation, charting dreams and patterns, and cleansing complexes is brought to bear the moment we decide to move, to make, to change. Magic is about shifting our will to a stronger course. Reality is shaped by the amount of presence we bring to every moment. Past, present, and future all exist in a single point of possibility, one shaped by our attitude and training.

Acting from will—and living in Will—is not just a matter of intention and attention but also a matter of skill. We pick something and master it. That mastery will end up tinting all our work, lending strength, stability, and presence to any activity, project, or relationship. The price of being a student pays off by giving us a chance to study other facets of life: our emotional states, our intellectual abilities, our physical health, and how we deal with other people. In deepening our nature, we call our divinity home.

Reflection

What are you actively training in? Do you study Kabbalah, martial arts, leather working, dance, or physics? Do you bring your spiritual work to this other work? Are you doing rituals on a regular basis? Does awareness of your still space accompany you wherever you go, and are you running energy through your etheric and auric bodies each day? Assess both your tools and your abilities. What works and what doesn't? What needs more practice, and what can be left behind?

Increasing Practice

People often change; they start well and end badly, and remain unsettled. Reflect before you start; are you like this?

—ABRAHAM VON WORMS (IN *The Book of Abramelin*)

We have reached the point in our quest for integration where, if our skill development is happening apace and our regular use of magical and spiritual tools feels strong, our practice will likely begin to increase. In order for the God Soul to descend, and Knowledge and Conversation to occur, an increase in practice must happen. This will take effort and planning, of course, but it should also be a natural welling up of dedication. We will feel a hunger for more practice to support our lives when the time is ripe. There is much written in esoteric literature that confirms this theory.

During my own transition, my practice increased severalfold. Though I didn't know exactly what was happening, I simply began to feel it was necessary to support my very life. I could feel things expanding within me and around me, and needed more practice as ballast. At the time, I had no idea that I was working toward this thing I now call self-possession. I *did* know that full human integration was something I desired, but I didn't yet have the language for the specific process I was seeking. I just knew I needed more.

I began getting up even earlier than usual, most often rising at 5:30 to do prayers, stillness practice, and energy work before heading to school, where I was finally finishing my degree in Philosophy and Religion, many years after dropping out. My reading of spiritual literature from all traditions also increased, and my other commitments fell by the wayside. On the days my schedule could manage it, I was sitting in meditation for up to two hours, calling upon Buddhist friends to help me with this. The practice was difficult but felt both nourishing and necessary. On top of all of this, I was traveling to teach workshops, and writing my first book. Increased practice helped all of my work at the time. I needed a strong container for the changes that were occurring, and my subconscious knew this even though I still wasn't certain what I was heading toward.

Magical literature tells us that this phase will last anywhere from six months to two years. For most of us, it will continue after the descent of our God Soul has happened, and then we will slowly find a new equilibrium, shifting practices and scaling back slightly to allow space for what is to come.

Things fall apart and then reform. This is life and process. It does not always look or feel graceful, but neither do most births. All transitions require some amount of pain and readjustment. The evolutionary movement from breathing liquid to breathing air was no small thing, and neither are the changes occurring inside us. Increasing our practice will give us the best support possible to make it through into a new state of being.

One caution is this: This is not a New Year's resolution to be cast aside in a few weeks or months because laziness of habit has taken over again. We have done all the preceding work partially to insure against this. Abraham von Worms reminds us, "It will go easily if you have started properly with a solid foundation."[92] There is no harm in gaining more solid ground before this great undertaking we are about to embark upon. In agreeing to undertake the final stages of this process, we are entering into a contract with our divinity and with God Herself; we are bringing the Twins along and forming the Peacock in beauty and perfection. In doing so, we are helping all the beings of the world toward power and liberation.

Doing the Work

Are you feeling an itch to spend more time with your spiritual work? Is energy increasing within you that needs a stronger container? Are friendships and activities that feel frivolous falling away? Are other relationships growing stronger?

Try to increase your practice just slightly. If you sit in meditation for twenty minutes, try half an hour. If you do yoga twice weekly, try three. Step up the use of your energy and soul alignment work so that you are doing these things throughout the day at regular intervals. In doing these things, you will likely find that your practice will increase even more. You will become fueled by the "heat" of practice and have ever more energy to lend to your life.

Transforming Memory

One thing that can help in this pressure cooker we are entering is to do some work on forgiveness. We have done a lot of work at identifying our many parts, including old stories. We have gazed upon demons and allies of mind and emotion. We have cleansed and centered. In this space of accessing more life force, it is helpful to revisit some of the previous work, to make certain as little as possible is escaping your notice, so that you can bring as much of yourself as possible into the forward dance toward self-possession and full integration.

One aspect that is helpful to revisit is that of memory. We often have vestiges of blame and shame we carry, even after years of spiritual work, therapy, and taking responsibility. As our practice and dedication increases, these are likely to crop up with a vengeance, perhaps making us arrogant in our work or tripping us up and telling us we can't move on. It is time to light a candle to the ancestors once more and take another trip through our memories.

Memory, like the calling of a crow outside the window, is a wake-up call. This doesn't wake us to something new; rather, we wake to face the old. Sometimes these memories are not pleasant. These are not the memories necessarily of ice creams at the beach. No, these are memories of pain and betrayal and hurt. These are memories of fear and anger and grief. These are the memories that we shove to the back of the closet in hopes that they will bury themselves, for we cannot quite hold the shovel ourselves.

It is time to take the lids from the boxes held in storage. Sometimes they come loose of their own accord, and the memories float out when we are thinking about something else or listening to a friend or working on a project or, especially, drifting off to sleep. They are the things we have not forgiven, in others or ourselves. The threads of life force still reach out to bind us. No matter how hard we have tried, something in us still cannot let go.

Even after all our work with demons, complexes, and ancestral patterns, we sometimes try to slam the lid on harder. We tape the boxes closed or bury our heads more firmly under the covers, and wish the specters away. Or we resign ourselves to our fate and face the new demons that the boxes house: the demons called regret or remorse, guilt or sorrow.

What do we face them with? We face them with a clear eye and mature heart. What do we face them with? Emotion and thought.

What do we face them with? We face them with a breath of courage, a softness in our hearts, an openness to a different way of thinking or being—"what is *really* here, covered in layers?"—and eventually, we face them with forgiveness. This is the most powerful weapon we have against demons of memory, and the most difficult to wield.

We open the boxes and let in the possibility of forgiveness. By forgiveness, I am not advocating the sidestepping of responsibility or a letting go too soon, before the emotions have worked themselves out. But I am talking right now especially about forgiving ourselves for our own mistakes. How else can we grow? It is also important to cease giving our life energy to others by clinging to blame for events long past. As long as we continuously blame others, we are allowing them to hold our life energy. By opening to forgiveness, we can begin to heal our memories.

Our memories will remain, but they don't have to always be so painful and tight. Sometimes, we can rest and face another day. There will be new challenges tomorrow and, hopefully, some more space for joy.

Doing the Work

Align your soul. Find your stillness. Look at the parade of memories and the effects they have on your life and those of others. Can you forgive others and see how they were doing what they could? Can you forgive yourself? Can you acknowledge that you did the best you could under the circumstances in which you found yourself? Can you even see that when you did not do your best, there were parts of you holding you back that you can set free? What is still bound in you? Do the "Cleansing Life Force" exercise (see p. 28). Ask yourself for forgiveness. Release the life force bound up between you and others. Send their energy back to them and receive your own. Open to the love of God Herself and listen to the Peacock as it tells you that your life now would not be possible without all that you have been. There is no becoming that is not built by light and shadow, the seen and the buried, the loved and the loathed.

Becoming Thankful

Be grateful for the present.

—Robert Earl Burton (in *Self-Remembering*)

The step after forgiveness is gratitude. All the energy that was bound up in blame and shame can now flow into thanks. Magic comes more easily and grows more effective the more we actively practice the art of gratitude. Life force constricts when we are less thankful for the gifts in our lives. Remember, the more constricted we are, the less power we have available.

I have found that the more I express my gratitude, whether to friends, lovers, to the Gods, or the universe at large, the more easily life and work flow and the greater the rewards are. My life opens to receive. Years ago, I would attempt to do magic with my arms closed across my chest, energetically. My magic did not work. The more I released attachment to painful memories and the more I cleared from my life that which didn't serve me, the easier it became to cultivate this practice of thanksgiving. And the more grateful I became, the more I had to be grateful for. Even with the challenges that followed the full descent of my God Soul (even positive change isn't always easy), good things flowed into my life at an alarming rate. And for that, I am eternally grateful.

Each morning, I think of something I am grateful for. This usually includes whoever invented the toothbrush and hot-water plumbing. I thank my loved ones for kisses and small chores. This sort of gratitude practice is hooked into our other magical work of observation. The more we notice all the facets of our lives, the more we will find to be grateful for. Even in the midst of difficulty, we do not need to make up affirmations to feel better about our lives, all we have to do is look at what is in front of us.

I am thankful for my health. I am thankful to live in a warm apartment with plenty of food. I am thankful clean water issues from a tap when I want it. I am thankful for my work. I am thankful, so thankful, for the love I have in my life. I am thankful for the ability to grow. I am thankful for the ability to learn. I am thankful for sitting in silence and breathing.

When things feel like a struggle or obstacles feel insurmountable rather than like good challenges, it helps to remember to be thankful for *something* in our lives. Gratitude reminds us that the difficulty in front of us is not the only thing in life. Our spiritual path is not all about hard work. Oftentimes our work is about fun, lust, love, and happiness. I'm thankful for these, as well.

Toasting is another way I like to spread the practice of gratitude. I toast to the Gods every time the first sip is taken. I toast to the ancestors and to love. In light of this, I offer you the best spell I've ever written, which is in the form of a toast. If you pass it on regularly, I can guarantee you will begin to see results flowing out from your life to those around you. Fill a glass with something delicious and repeat after me: "Love, health, prosperity, knowledge, and great sex!"

Cheers.

Merging the Great Planes

Higher and lower realms of consciousness are not separated by space; rather, they are dimensions that represent a proximity of relationship to the ultimate truth.

—RABBI DAVID COOPER (IN *God Is a Verb*)

It is time to do some more work preparing us for Adepthood. The Adept knows that the energies of above and below meet in us, on this plane. We are microcosm and macrocosm, actuality and potential. This merging and opening occurs both in our ordinary lives—conscious, unconscious, and subconscious—and in our magical, energetic lives. While we work to integrate all of our parts, bringing as much of ourselves to each piece of our lives as possible, we can reinforce this on an energetic level, calling down spirit into matter and feeling the thrust of the material into the ethereal.

There are many systems for this. The ancients used the potent symbol of the *merkabah*, or joined pyramids. These represented the upward triangle and downward triangle interpenetrating and opening out into a special shape in which pyramids are formed and a flat figure becomes three dimensional in space and time.

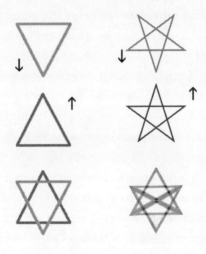

Illustration v: Merging the Great Planes

We will do something similar, beginning with stars, the pentagrams that represent the human form and all of the five ancient elements. The pentagram encapsulates the energies of change, motion, and potential, activating within us balanced power and brilliance that can become palpable forces in our lives. The upright and inverse pentagrams also represent Goddess and God forms, as well as spirit reaching down and matter reaching up. We will attempt this sacred activity in several phases so that we can acclimate to the energies and sense the differences and tastes of the forms.

Let me pause in the sequence here for a moment to explain that the concept of "spirit descending into matter" is both false and true. Spirit and matter are not separate but are tightly interwoven. It is convenient and helpful for us to think of them as two things because the totality can be overwhelming for our rational minds to encompass. However, just as particle physics shows us that matter is not necessarily solid but is comprised of the movement of particles, so we can see that it is not so different from what we consider to be spirit, energy, or the nonmaterial bodies that all living things have.

Spirit descending into matter is a neo-Platonic concept that came into Christian and Jewish thought—and so into Kabbalah in all its forms and so into the Western Esoteric Traditions—and became the basis for their theologies. Spirit was preferable, because matter was thought to be farthest from the Source, or God. The longer it took for spirit to travel into the material planes, the more polluted it was felt to become, until it felt the great longing, or Eros, to return to Source again, reascending.

This interplay is not false; it is simply an incomplete picture of how God Herself works in the material plane. She is not absent from it, but we can forget her presence, cutting ourselves off from the flow, as we spoke of in chapter one (see p. 5). Doing energy exercises that explicitly seek to join spirit and matter, above and below, inner and outer, can help us to feel what our natural, whole, and healthy state is. But we need to remember that this state of integrity is not an aberration; rather, thinking that spirit and matter are separate is the aberration. Truly, all things are whole.

Therefore, we imagine spirit descending into matter and matter rising to spirit, knowing that it is a metaphor to help us understand more fully that matter and spirit are forever interpenetrating, and in fact, they are one substance. Our work with the pentacles will lead us into work with the pyramids.[93]

Although the actual energetic practice is much simpler, the conceptual layers are varied and complex, bringing together many facets into one system. It is this multivalent technology that gives the exercise so much power, and enables us to traverse the realms within the vehicle we create. First we will imagine ourselves as a pole reaching up and down from our center, forming the axis of the World Tree. Then we will merge the two traditional equilateral triangles representing matter, which faces up, and spirit, which faces down. Together, these form the magical symbol known as the Seal of Solomon. Into these, we are going to lock the upright and inverse pentagrams.[94] These pentads are the human body reaching up and the human soul reaching down. We ourselves are a vertical axis, which opens the flat shape into two pyramids, the symbol of the *merkabah*, or Ezekiel's chariot.[95] This symbol was used as an energetic meditation to help the seeker traverse all the realms. We can use this process to begin to bring all the realms to us. We can open to all now, in this moment. In this moment, all space and time are present. Breathe that in.

We will take this meditation in stages. I will explain it all the way through but recommend working only with triangles at first. Then add in the pentagrams. Then work on connecting the pentagrams with the hexagram. We should then try to feel all the systems within us: triangles, Seal, and pentacles. Only once we have that phase down, can we shift into the *merkabah* or the opened out pentagrams, if that is a preferred way of looking at it. Once seated in the *merkabah*, we should have a strong sense of all space and time being fully present and surrounding us.[96] [See illustration v to help with the various shapes.]

Doing the Work

First, cleanse, center, and align yourself. I recommend doing this after a brief session of meditation. Sit cross-legged or in lotus, if either is possible. Make certain your hips are raised slightly above your knees. Imagine a plumb line running through you, as you allow your energy to reach slightly up and down into earth and sky. You reach like the World Tree reaches. Now see a triangle beneath you, point up, and one above you, point down. Breathe in, and as you exhale, see them moving toward each other. Allow them to stop when they intersect, base-lines moving above your shoulders and below your hips, points reaching slightly into earth and sky, penetrating your root and crown.

Breathe into this hexagram shape, the Seal of Solomon, for a few moments.

Next, imagine a pentagram beneath you, carrying all the powers of below, and see one above your head, carrying all the powers of above. Slowly feel these rising and descending in concert, penetrating all your energy bodies until they form themselves within the Seal. Their legs make an energetic x across your body, leaving you with a pentagon over your chest and heart area, and one over your belly and will area. Your crown, pineal gland, sex, and root are all activated by the points rising up and thrusting down. Breathe. Sit in this for a long while.[97]

Once you have acclimated to the energies of the planes of above and below meeting inside you, it is time for the next phase, which forms our vehicle. Try to imagine that, instead of "flat" shapes within you, there actually exists a three-dimensional figure that is temporarily collapsed into itself. Imagine that you can "pull" the point where the two pentagons meet in your solar plexus. Feel the shape "pop" out, forming a geometric vehicle around your body. Breathe.

We should pause here for a while, and allow ourselves to acclimate to the powerful energies surrounding us. All space is here with us. All time flows in this place. There is nothing that does not exist right here and right now. For some people, the shape we sit in may begin to spin, and that is fine. It will take us places. The longer we do this work, how-ever, the more I suggest slowing that down if it happens, stabilizing the vehicle so that we can better control where we want to go with it. Let us see where those places might be:

Feel the potency of this moment and of your own being. Feel the vehicle of light and energy around you: the microcosm and macrocosm joined. To the left front of the shape is the place of the past and the ancestors. Honor them. To the right front of the shape is the place of the fey beings. Honor them. To the back left of the shape is the place of the Gods. Honor them. To the right back of the shape is the place of the future, the descendents. Honor them. Above are all the cosmic powers and the Limitless. Below are all the chthonic powers and the particular. Honor them. Feel the worlds arrayed around you. Feel your own power. Breathe. Align your soul.

I recommend doing this monthly at first, pulling cards or runes for each of the realms arrayed around you. All we have to do to gather information from each realm is to "lean" a little bit toward each of them. When our practice increases, we can work with this meditation with greater frequency.

The potential here is endless. Questions can be answered. We can enter any realm we want in the blink of an eye. Most importantly, we can grow accustomed to the reality that we are truly part of the fabric of the whole, because the whole is everywhere with us. We need not traverse great spaces anymore, because everything is *right here*. This is something every mystic and Adept knows and has access to. Most of us just dream of having this ability or scoff at it as unreal. Doing the above exercise over and over will acclimate our being to this new reality. We prepare ourselves for what is to come, for self-possession and the work that awaits us beyond even that: the work of joining the limitless in the endless flow.[98]

Stepping into Magic

Everything is holy! everybody's holy! everywhere is holy
everyday is in eternity! Everyman's an angel!
The bum's as holy as the seraphim! the madman is holy as you
my soul are holy! . . .

—ALLEN GINSBERG (IN HIS POEM "FOOTNOTE TO HOWL")

The more integrated we become, and the more in touch with the power of our will, the less we need to hone our intention through long spell workings. Our magic begins to happen in an instant, for we are living closer to the magical flow. We still work and still set our intention, but these are both naturally stronger and more clear, for we have been preparing for years. As seen in "Merging the Great Planes," (see p. 225) the more adept we become, the more we have magic at our fingertips, because all the realms are within and around us. Everything is holy. Nothing is profane.

Those who work magic haphazardly, without putting in the foundational, daily work, may never reach this space. Others may enter this flow comparatively quickly. Still others will continue to do long magical preparations simply for the joy of it all, for the smell of the herbs and the feel of the cloth or metal. What I would like to invite us all to do at this point is to assess our magic as honestly as possible. What is the point of it? Are we beginning to live with an integrity that supports our desires? How close do we feel to the Work of this God?

We can step into constant streams of magic. When this happens, the world will become a continuous blessing, every challenge seen as a good adversary to learn from, and every joy will be a gift. When magic is a constant stream, we know that we are fully alive; each day is the first as well as the last. This is the power of the Adept. Watch for it. Open to it. In being fully attentive to our lives, and in taking care with ritual and practice, it will come to us. We shall shine like stars.

CHAPTER TWELVE

Kissing the Limitless

The moment has come. In this space the mystery is unveiled: we are fully human and fully divine. We have connected the microcosm to the macrocosm, and in that space, anything is possible. Here, we kiss the limitless, the All, and recognize that we are a point anchoring forever.

Nothing stands between us and the All. God Herself beckons us into the vast embrace of space and time. We do not leave the world behind but bring it with us into the new awareness that we are sacred, and sacred no longer means "that which is set apart." Sacred comes to mean "that which is on the pathway to the Limitless." We redefine and refine our lives. Once the great "I am" descends upon us, we are steps away from our enlightenment. In this way, we learn to light the world.

Reconsidering Theology

The higher self benevolently watches over you until you are capable of reaching up to it.

—W. E. BUTLER (IN *Lords of Light*)

We are reflections of the multiplicity of relationship existing in our personal and work lives. We are also an integral part of a biosphere and relate out to Gods and the realms unseen. Woven into these more "intimate" relationships, we are, of course, part of the fabric of God Herself. Language attempts to point to our part in this reality by our use of the word *I*. In chapter eight (see p. 147), we discussed some of the things "I am" is *not*. Let us now examine some of the things the "I am" *is*.

The difference between us and the Limitless is that "I" signifies a unified singularity. However, the reality behind that gifts us with a surprise: once we have unified into that which feels *singular* instead of our usual disintegrous state, we *know* that we are connected to the Limitless and are not actually singular at all. The fully autonomous being is a being aware of connection. Once we establish continual contact with the messenger that is our God Soul, once we taste the liberation of the "I am," the possibility of even further integration with the Limitless, God Herself, appears to us in full force.

Philosopher Jacob Needleman speaks to our process here:

> The life of every man or woman contains glimpses of another quality of being, another state of consciousness; we need not rely entirely on metaphors and descriptions offered by others. But our culture does not help us appreciate these glimpses or understand them for what they tell us about our possible moral, mental, and emotional development. We are not helped to see these glimpses as "messengers" from another, higher part of ourselves, which we need to study and cultivate.[99]

These messengers take the form of epiphanies. Epiphanies provide helpful insight.[100] They are messages from our divine natures to the rest of our parts. The key to what Dr. Needleman is saying, and to building a permanent connection to our God Soul, is that we do not have to rely only upon random flashes of insight. Over time, with practice, we can build something more. The messenger becomes a constant, aware presence and a guide. The messenger is us. It can feel like not quite us, because it has such a different flavor than the rest of our parts, and because it connects us with immanent divinity that flows through all things. Because of that latter, it has a much broader perspective than, say, my personality does.

Needleman goes on:

> In such moments, an individual *divides in two*. A second self appears, and most often, what it does is *watch*. Only that and nothing more. But it is a watching, a *seeing*, a presence, unlike anything else in our experience; it is an awakening to ourselves of utter lucidity and calm. It is a glimpse of inner freedom. . . .[101]

Remember Nuit dividing herself for love's sake? We have become aware of this division through all of our practices. In meditation or reaching our still point, the God Soul—Needleman's "seeing presence," whom the Kabbalists call Neshamah and Victor Anderson called "Sacred Dove"—can observe and listen to all of our parts as they squirm or frolic or sit quietly. It is through this process that we create the opening for epiphanies to happen, for grace to appear. It is partially through this process that we cultivate a permanent connection to that part of us that is divine and knows more than our insecurity or arrogance, and connects to more than our hopes or fears. Ironically, our awareness of this division is the very thing that enables us to come back into unity.

The mage Aleister Crowley wrote that the God Soul is "the Genius latent in us all."[102] Whether or not one will ever touch it, I believe each person does have a God Soul. We should realize by now that this is not simply the "nice" or "spiritual" parts of our personality but a part that lives beyond us, to whom we can reach out and connect. Whether we perceive of this God Soul, this Sacred Dove, or this Holy Guardian Angel as a nascent part of ourselves or a completely separate being almost doesn't matter at this point. Perception is important but not as important as the reality that will occur when full contact and integration with this part of us, this God Being, has taken place. At that time we will truly become like no other. We will have the opportunity to learn things we barely thought of before. Actual knowledge will begin to enter us and become assimilated over time. Perception of self will sharpen and our behavior will change accordingly. Over time, we will learn to act more freely and with greater assurance, for we will know that all parts of self are fully present for the first time. We are whole. All earlier statements of wholeness—our work with the "I am"—were wishes and affirmations that helped us toward this state. Reality has arrived.

We need to remind ourselves that our personalities will not go away and may even grow stronger, but will have more help after Sacred Dove has descended fully into our energy bodies and taken up residence as the guide and partner to our other parts. We catch glimpses of this self-possesion when we align, or sometimes during sex or ritual.

The God Soul is part of the macrocosm. The rest of our parts are the microcosmic elements. Once these other parts—the animal self, the thinker, the personality, the emotions, the body—touch the macrocosm of the God Soul, all parts can touch the Limitless. The space beyond duality becomes available to our senses. In moments where we kiss the Limitless, we are not locked into the problems or triumphs our microcosmic parts may be attending to. We get a tiny taste of the All. We cannot live with this sure knowledge but can touch it through the regularity of practice and, for those upon whom the Sacred Dove descends, steady conversation with and knowledge of our macrocosmic soul.

Introducing the "I"

Let us be clear regarding the language we use and the thoughts we nurture. For what is language but the expression of thought? Let your thought be accurate and truthful, and you will hasten the advent of *swaraj* [self-rule] even if the whole world is against you.

—GANDHI (IN *Gandhi on Non-Violence*)

The Great Work uncovers the roots of all of our problems, rather than snipping at the branches. Therefore, the work of full integration with our divinity as core work is what will move our magic and our culture forward. We need lasting change. We can work for the environment or education, or make our devotional and celebratory offerings, and simultaneously focus on the Great Work of self-possession and full integration. Everything else must make space for this, including various spiritual initiations.

If we have continuous self-possession, all else stems from that; all work grows from that. Without it, nothing else adds up over time. Of course, self-possession is a process that takes effort and application.

Part of self-possession is self-knowledge and soul alignment, whether achieved through meditation, Middle Pillar work, vibrating the *eihwaz* rune, or continued use of the Soul Alignment Prayer. But as Gandhi addresses, clear thought is also necessary. Critical thinking is necessary. A growing theological sophistication is necessary. Self-rule is the beginning and ending of all successful magical operations and requires growing mastery of all our parts: the physical, the instinctive, the feeling, the thinking, and the perceiving. Our personality is not the whole, though we often think it is. We must align with that part of us that is aligned with everything.

We are not yet fully the "I Am." The Peacock is in the process of being born. What are we forming? A full self. Not just our personalities or drives or physical needs but *all* of those, along with the part of us the touches something even larger and includes all.

From the stage of self-possession it becomes possible to know enlightenment. Within self-possession, it is possible to have greater and more consistent access to the All. From a state of self-possession, it is possible to leave personality behind for something greater in the moment, to meet the challenger at the gates of death and knowledge, and enter the state of pure unity with all that is. And from a stage of self-possession, it is possible to return back into personality and maintain that constant connection with the Limitless.

It is possible to become an everyday mystic: one who works, cooks, laughs, and communes with the Divine in all its manifestations. With self-possession it is possible to take the next step, which is to translate the All back into everyday life.

Self-possession is a gift unto itself: to be a whole, autonomous person. "I" is the wholeness that comes when God Soul is descended or in full contact. "I" is our essential nature.

A Gurdjieff teacher, when I said, "I was watching such and such a part...," once asked me, "Who was watching?" I was brought up short, for I had no answer. In retrospect, it was another part of my personality, the judger, watching. It was not God Soul. It was not "I."

Remember my concept of "inclusion" rather than "transcendence"? If I am in constant contact with my God Soul, I come into constant contact with all my parts and am including every aspect of my life, harnessing myself to the transformation at hand.

Reflection

The following prayer sets us up for drawing down the God Soul:

I call myself to myself. I call all my parts to me.

I call my animal nature, my instincts, my physical form.

I call my humanity, rational and strong.

I call my divinity, connected to All.

I call to this divine nature to descend and enter me. I call upon my parts to work in wholeness.

May I know myself. May I see myself. May I love myself.

Drawing Down the "I"

We are born with a sense of divinity. We are born with some connection to the macrocosm, the divine flow, the creative force. For some of us, this enters our awareness through some sense of "destiny," that we are connected to a larger purpose. For others, we sense something larger than our component parts when touched by music, art, dance, or some more explicitly spiritual or religious occurrence. There is something more than our emotions, our likes and dislikes. Anyone engaged in the practice of religion or spiritual work knows this. Even secular philosophers try to convey this sense of something *more*. Magical practice illustrates that there is something more, but that does not make what we currently perceive any less. As Israel Regardie wrote of Adeptship: it is the process of becoming a "voluntary coworker with Nature in the task of evolution."[103] We are necessary to the All, and the Limitless is necessary to us.

Our connection to the Limitless comes from our divine nature, our God Soul, our Sacred Dove, our *neshamah*.[104] This is both part of us and something we reach for. It is the seat of the "I am" and also the seed to the macrocosm. Energetically, the globe of our God Soul floats just above our heads, kissing our other energy bodies. It is the place of the *sahasrara chakra*, and *kether* on the Kabbalist tree of life. It is the reach of the Cauldron of Wisdom in the ancient Celtic schools.[105]

Some Witchcraft traditions talk of "drawing down" divinity into the priest or priestess, to better bring the larger forces to earth for the good of those present at the rite. Christianity speaks of the same thing in the stories of the Pentecost. Following this, in the Acts of the Apostles, people actually thought the disciples of Jesus were Gods walking on earth. I posit that this is because their divine natures had become fully embodied. Their God Souls had descended and taken up residence within, forming a full connection. These stories are familiar to me from my childhood, but it is only through my experiences with magic, Paganism, and the Craft that I have come to a greater understanding of the implications. We can wake up. We can integrate. We can become fully divine in our humanity. The statements, "thou art Goddess, thou art God" are not just acknowledgments that we are sacred but that we literally have God stuff within our reach.[106] Metaphor can become reality. We can reach beyond our personalities and pull divinity down.

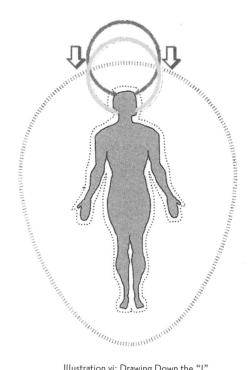

Illustration vi: Drawing Down the "I"

This happens over time, through all of our work on integration. All of our sitting practice, cleansing, energy work, and effort deepen and strengthen the pathway to the divine nature that connects us beyond our particulars. We simultaneously become the center and the circumference, Nuit and Hadit, *yesh* and *ayin*, the point and the limitless.[107] Once the pathway is made clear, a permanent descent and possession will occur.

Along with our generalized work on self, there is a specific energetic form that will aid this permanent connection. The following exercise is literally the process of drawing down our own divinity and then resonating the "I am" as a call to all of our parts to unify. This exercise can be done by visualizing the energy bodies of our soul's parts, or by reaching for the crown *chakra* or imagining we are the *eihwaz* rune that represents the yew tree that spans all realms or reaching up the spheres on the middle pillar, drawing *kether* down. [See illustration vi, p. 239.] I will explain it below as I work with it, but if you are already working within a system that makes more sense to you, feel free to adapt this.

Remember, that as we reach up, the God Soul and the Limitless reach down.

Doing the Work

Sit in a comfortable position, making certain your hips are above the plane of your knees, spine rising from your pelvis and head resting directly above your spine. Slow your breathing down and find the still place in your center. Breathe into that. Breathe in life energy, aware of this charging up your energy bodies around your physical form. Feel yourself centering further within as the energy fields around you grow more luminous. Your etheric body is radiant and your aura shines around that. Above it all is a globe of divinity, the bridge to the supernal realms, the Limitlessness of the All.

Anchor yourself in the still point where all energy inside your physical body flows. Send a cord of energy up from this stillness; feel it moving through the crown of your skull, opening that space further to what is above. Let your awareness move to the globe that floats just above your head. Feel the energy from your still point reach up and down, creating a plumb line, like the world tree reaching up and down. Anchor this in the earth and then reach up. Imagine the cord pulling the globe of your God Soul down. Draw down the sphere of kether. Draw down the sahasrara chakra. Imagine the energy descending as you draw down your own divine nature, connection to the limitless. Feel your energy bodies "flare" as the globe penetrates the crown of your head, until your head is surrounded by this divine light, from the base of your skull to above your crown.

Once you feel this in place, still surrounded by your aura, your Shining Body and the vital etheric body, your Sticky One, begin to intone the syllables, "I am." Tone each for as long as a breath, feeling the words resonate through your energy bodies, enlivening them and strengthening the connection between them.

Tone the "I am" three times. Sit in this space for up to twenty minutes or as long as the "charge" seems to last. Once you feel the power start to dissipate, allow the globe of God Soul to ascend again, until it is floating above your head once more. Breathe up into it, keeping your souls in alignment. Feel energy rain down from it, toward the earth, blessing the land.

Give thanks to all your parts, whatever deity you are most closely linked to, and to God Herself, who is always with us.

Sounding the "I am" is both an affirmation and a statement of reality. We catch glimpses of it, then the soul descends and we establish a clear pathway to our God Soul, and when the full connection happens, we begin to learn the ways of knowledge as is patterned in every leaf on every tree, and in each star burning overhead.

The Next Steps

Regular soul alignment should be done daily. Drawing Down the "I" and Merging the Great Planes should be done weekly at first. When we reach the point where we notice our practice is naturally increasing, we should dedicate ourselves to the drawing down we have just practiced, for it will become the key that unlocks self-possession.

At the point of increased practice, we will have reached the suggested six- to eighteen-month period of "seclusion" talked about in the Abramelin ritual, for one.[108] I have found in my experience and in those of others, that this cannot be forced. "Jump-starting" the process by increasing our practice load can have some good effects, but attempting to create a self-imposed monastic life before we are ready to enter the cloister can end up backfiring and even stalling our work. It is better to keep tabs on our actual state rather than attempt to force ourselves too much toward states we aren't prepared for.

At the point when our work is literally "cooking" in an alchemical sense, it is helpful to nudge the work along with deeper applications that will help us to reach from the states of self-possession we may have been experiencing to the stage of self-possession that will bring our divine nature in constant contact with all of our parts. Outside distractions lose their fascination, and everything becomes subsumed and consumed by the Work. This stage will likely last up to two years.

During this time period, our overall intentionality should also increase. Paying greater attention to details will become important. Extra cleansings of self both in and out, and of one's surroundings will be helpful to the work we are engaged in. Ancient Egyptians would shave all of their body hair as a grand cleansing during times of deep spiritual work. Magicians would pay meticulous attention to the preparation of their working spaces. We have already talked about the need to be clean within and clean in our homes, relationships, and magic. Orderliness outside helps to establish greater order inside. We have done immense amounts of work to bring our parts into the activity of the Great Work, and as our work ramps up, this needs to be strongly reflected in our physical spaces too. Look around your home again. What needs attention and intention to bring *its* life energy to bear on the work at hand?

Practicing presence in as many realms of our lives as possible will only help our Work. Along with this, we simply continue showing up, because that is the joyous task we have set ourselves. Then one day, in a moment of grace, our God Soul will descend to us and we will rise to meet it, and never from that point on will we be sundered from ourselves. We will become fully human and fully divine—resoundingly "I am" —walking the earth and doing our True Work. We will have been liberated in our lives. That liberation will flow from us and affect all that we touch. We will be free, and free people are of great help to the world.

Loving Engagement

Once, I made a pledge to the Goddess Brigid that I would walk in love. In returning to think on this, I have to ask myself, "what *is* love?" My answer so far is that love is passionate engagement with life. Love is directly connected to full life force, meaning to sex and to spirit. Sometimes passionate engagement means using discernment and saying "this could be different" or "this is unjust right now, no matter that I cannot yet see how the larger schema will play out" or "I passionately perceive that we can become more than we are."

Sometimes love means something as grand as Gandhi sitting down in front of a row of British officers on horseback or as simple as having a difficult conversation with a friend for the sake of greater intimacy. Sometimes love means passing out chocolate hearts in my urban neighborhood to young hipsters, prostitutes, homeboys, and homeless people.

Sometimes love means returning to my meditation cushion or sweating in a nightclub, while dancing and drinking wine. Sometimes it means keeping silent. Love can mean hot sex and opening to intensity of pleasure. Love can require looking at when need is really want or want becomes need or need becomes a want that points to a deeper-seated, perhaps more profound, need than the original.

Both complex and simple, love is still the fabric of all. The Twins are formed because of it, and together they form the Peacock from *their* love. God Herself is the flow of love.

I want engagement, even though it sometimes includes making mistakes or sounding harsh in one moment and soft in the next. I want the harshness and softness to both arise from love. I want connection, I want to not live safely but to live in the flow of life. I want to see us as big and small, beautiful and in pain, gorgeous in our laughter and wondrous in our tears. I want to hear our thoughtfulness and our ecstasy. I want to open up the flow of life force and see all the ways that you do, too. I want to walk in love, which can feel risky. But it also feels like a risk well worth the taking.

Reaching for love with our whole being causes love to reach back. The more integrated and whole we become, the more we enter the flow of love. God Herself moves through us.

Integrating Love

Living life in touch with divine spirit lets us see the light of love in
all living beings.

—BELL HOOKS (IN *All About Love*)

The outpouring of all our work of self-possession is the state of love.
This is love that tempers all else, allowing us to be fierce and direct,
kind and gentle, firm and soft. There is severity here, yes, and mercy,
too, both presented from a core of love so deep and strong that our
boots shake the worlds as we walk between them. There is no turning
back to isolation; even anger swells from love.

No, we do not become "perfect," as in stale, static, unmoved, and
unmoving. No, we are not completely free of irritation. However, we
are perfect in our changing, flowing with the inner tides that are always
drawn by Her. Our irritation is seen simply for what it is; a temporary
state that will pass all the more swiftly for its recognition. We will be
people of no book, reading the book of our own nature and the nature
of all that surrounds us.

We shall be free.

But love is complex. Love requires an act of will. Openheartedness
requires strength and courage and softness. Trust requires self-knowing.
Love requires seeing through the bullshit and into the pain. Love requires
getting annoyed or angry, and still seeing through the bullshit and into
the pain. And I'm talking globally too, not just on an individual basis,
though it begins there. It always begins with each of us, as individuals.
And love includes anger. And love includes joy. And love includes sorrow.
And love includes softness. And love includes strength.

Sometimes we love and stand firm. Sometimes we love and melt
into caramel taffy. Sometimes we love and walk away. Sometimes we
love and kick ass. Sometimes we just love. Love is not a currency.
Love is an upwelling of life force. Love is power and connection. We
cannot develop love if we haven't developed will. Real love, to quote

Dostoevsky, is sometimes "a harsh and fearful thing compared to love in dreams,"[109] meaning, it is not pitying and it is not addiction. Love is strong. Stronger than fear.

Love is the true road for the apostles of Light. Light lives in the heart once the rich darkness of space and stars expands within.

Reflection

Do not fear the great silence. Standing in stillness puts one in the flow of all. There is no separation—only nothingness and everything. Be within yourself. Stand within her embrace. God Herself holds you. All is held within the hand of love. Boundlessness is bounded only by the fragrance of the limitless. Breathe deeply and know that you are God.

When the seeker possesses her full Godhood, the worlds open and the divine work is at hand. Naught can stop him. Nothingness spreads, and light expands as darkness opens spaces in the fissures of the heart. You are whole now. God Herself surrounds and penetrates your soul. Here is the prayer of the Seeker in Love: "All living ones, deliver me into myself. Deliver me unto fullness. Strengthen my resolve to love."

Breathe the universe. Float in space. Stand firm upon the earth.

The "all living ones," of course, are the parts of our soul. They are also, paradoxically, not us. They are part of the connection to the All, the fabric of immanence. They are the Gods, the spirits, the contacts, and the context. There is no Self without Unity and no Unity without Self. This is consciousness.

Multiplicity forms the fabric of Being.

Continuing

You are the golden eternity because there is no me and no you, only one golden eternity.

—JACK KEROUAC (IN *The Scripture of the Golden Eternity*)

There is no end to the processes we have begun. Once a road is undertaken with true intention, we can no longer turn back. Nor do we really wish to, even in our weary or overwhelmed moments. I have written here the best map I have right now, but much of the road is uncharted, because, though each road is similar, no route is exactly the same. All I can say now is, go over everything covered in this book and choose what to focus on. The appendix of exercises at the end of this book will help with that.

Be diligent in practice and in love, and don't forget to have fun. Laughter is very important when doing serious work. We can seek out help when we need it, but there will come a time when we will have no recourse but to sit down at our altars by ourselves for many long hours. I can promise that the rewards are more than ample repayment for our efforts. I have seen it in myself and in some others who have made it through this particular gateway.

In the swirling fabric of endless, flowing particles, you are present. Your consciousness can be focused and expansive simultaneously. If we are conscious, we can be, forever. Unconscious, we do not even have the now. The point anchoring forever is your life.

I leave you with a prayer:

May the Gods bless your work.

May your work bless the world.

May justice run through you.

May kindness light your eyes.

May love kindle your heart.

May passion kiss your mind.

May strength build your path.

May your life flow forth

Like thirst-quenching water.

We are light in extension, if only we can wake up and remember. We are the darkness that births beauty. We are cataracts of divinity, opening the flow. We are the harbingers of change.

Blessed be.

Appendix A: Doing the Work

This breakdown is to help us keep track of where we are in the work and aid us in developing the parts of practice that need strengthening.

Foundational

Deepening

Rounding Out

Integrating

Appendix B: The Triple Soul

[See illustration vi, p. 239.]

Many cultures have the concept that our soul is not a unified entity but, rather, is comprised of various parts with different functions. The soul can have up to seven or nine facets, often including the physical body. One common breakdown of the soul is to consolidate many of these parts into three, plus the physical. The ancient Greeks, Egyptians, Hawaiians, Celts, Jews, and other cultures followed this model, as does the Feri Tradition and ceremonial magic.

The first part is known as the etheric body, or the Sticky One. Energetically, this just follows the physical form, with its physical center in the lower two chakras. It stores life force that comes in the forms of breath, food, sex, exercise and rest. It is considered to be our animal or instinctive nature, our more childlike self that responds well to symbols. Some other names for this part are *nephesh* in Hebrew and *unihipili* in Hawaiian. Some traditions also call it the "fetch" because of its functional ability to be directed by the magic worker, going out and bringing things back.

The second part is the aura, known as the Shining Body. Energetically, this is the egg shape that surrounds us with its physical center in the middle three chakras. It is our presentation of self to the world, and holds the powers of intellect and reason. The Shining Body is our first line of communication, both giving and receiving information. It can be trained to expand its functions in many ways. Some other names for this part are *ruach* in Hebrew and *uhane malama* in Hawaiian.

The third part is our God Soul, or Sacred Dove. Energetically, this is a globe of energy just above our heads, with its physical center in the top two *chakras*. It is connected to the ancestors, the Gods, God Herself, and the macrocosm, including all space and time. It is our deep wisdom and what we are striving to work in full concert with. Some other names for this part are *neshamah* in Hebrew and *aumakua* in Hawaiian.

Coming to know all of these parts and learning how to align them is the most basic and important activity for all spiritual seekers and magic workers.[110]

Bibliography

Following are some books that may be helpful in the search for spiritual opening and full integration. There are still more books in the footnotes.

Anderson, Victor H. *Etheric Anatomy*. Albany, CA: Acorn Guild Press, 2004.

Anderson, Victor H. *Lilith's Garden*. Albany, CA: Acorn Guild Press, 2004.

Anderson, Victor H. *Thorns of the Blood Rose*. Albany, CA: Acorn Guild Press, 2003.

Aurelius, Marcus. *Meditations*. New York: Penguin, 2004.

Barks, Coleman and Moyne, John. *Open Secret: Versions of Rumi*. Boston: Shambhala, 1999.

Bloom, William. *The Sacred Magician*. Glastonbury: Gothic Images, 1992.

Burton, Robert Earl. *Self-Remembering*. San Francisco: Red Wheel/Weiser, 2007.

Butler, W. E. *Apprenticed to Magic*. Leicestershire: Thoth, 2003.

Butler, W. E. *Lords of Light* Rochester, VT: Destiny Books 1990.

Coyle, T. Thorn. *Evolutionary Witchcraft*. New York: Tarcher/Penguin, 2005.

Coye, T. Thorn. "Devotional Dance: Sacred Movements for Meditation and Transformation," San Francisco: T. Thorn Coyle, 2006. (DVD)

Cooper, Rabbi David. *God is a Verb*. New York: Riverhead, 1998.

Crowley, Aleister. *The Book of the Law*. San Francisco: Red Wheel/Weiser, 2004.

Crowley, Aleister. *Magick Without Tears*. Reno, NV: New Falcon, 2001.

Del Campo, Gerald. *New Aeon Magick*. Minneapolis, MN: Luxor Press, 2000.

Dominguez Jr., Ivo. *Spirit Speak*. Frankin Lanes, NJ: New Page, 2008.

Duquette, Lon Milo. *Chicken Qabalah*. San Francisco: Red Wheel/Weiser, 2001.

Duquette, Lon Milo. *My Life with the Spirits*. San Francisco: Red Wheel/Weiser, 1999.

Epictetus. *A Manual for Living*. San Francisco: Harper San Francisco, 1994.

Givot, Irv. *Seven Aspects of Self-Observation*. Aurora, OR: Two Rivers Press, 1998.

Heap, Jane. *Notes*. Aurora, OR: Two Rivers Press, 1999.

Hopman, Ellen Evert and Bond Lawrence. *People of the Earth: The New Pagans Speak Out*. Rochester, VT: Inner Traditions, 1995.

Iamblichus. *On the Mysteries*. Atlanta, GA: Society of Biblical Literature, 2003.

Levi, Eliphas. *Paradoxes of the Highest Science*. Berwick, ME: Ibis, 2004.

Maharaj, Nisargadatta. *I am That*. Durham, NC: Acorn Press, 1990.

Matthews, John and Caitlin. *The Encyclopedia of Celtic Myth and Wisdom*. Dorset, UK: Element Books, 2000.

Matthews, Caitlin and John. *Walkers Between the Worlds*. Rochester, VT: Inner Traditions, 2003.

Miller, Barbara Stoller, trans. *The Bhagavad Gita*. New York: Bantam, 1986.

Moore, Alan. *Promethea*. La Jolla, CA: America's Best Comics, 2000.

Needleman, Jacob, ed. *The Inner Journey: Views from the Gurdjieff Work*. Sandpoint, ID: Morning Light, 2008.

Newcomb, Jason. *21st Century Mage*. San Francisco: Weiser, 2002.

Ouspensky, P. D. *In Search of the Miraculous*. New York: Harcourt, Brace, 2001.

Penczak, Christopher. *The Temple of Shamanic Witchcraft*. St. Paul, MN: Llewellyn, 2005.

Regardie, Israel. *The Middle Pillar* second edition with Sandra and Chic Cicero. St. Paul, MN: Llewellyn, 2004.

Shaw, Gregory. *Theurgy and the Soul: the Neoplatonism of Iamblichus*. University Park, PA: University of Pennsylvania Press, 1995.

Von Worms, Abraham. *The Book of Abramelin* compiled and edited by Georg Dehn and translated by Steven Guth. Lakeworth, FL: Ibis, 2006.

Pamphlets:

"The Uses of Life: a conversation with Ruth H. Cooke and Jacob Needleman" (Far West Institute, 1995).

"This is Truth About the Self" by Dr. Ann Davies (Builders of the Adytum, 1974).

"Open Secret" by Rami Shapiro. Human Kindness Foundation, 1999. This pamphlet may be ordered at *http://www.humankindness.org*

If your local bookshop doesn't stock any of these books or pamphlets, Field's Books (*www.fieldsbooks.com*) is great at finding esoteric books of all religions, even the pamphlets or out of print titles. Treadwell's in England is a good source for non-US residents. Please support independent booksellers.

Notes

1. In Feri Tradition, we call upon "the center, which is the circumference of all." This reflects God Herself. Similar concepts are found in Thelema with the concepts of *Nuit* and *Hadit*, in Jewish mysticism with *yesh* and *ayin*, and in Zen Buddhism with form and emptiness.

2. Even the philosophy of Existentialism grapples with the task of self-knowing.

3. A classic magical text on working toward "Knowledge and Conversation of our Holy Guardian Angel" now has a new translation: *The Book of Abramelin by Abraham von Worms*, compiled and edited by Georg Dehn and translated by Steven Guth (Ibis, 2006).

4. See *http://www.whitewand.com* or *http://www.tombostudios.com* for Anaar's work.

5. See illustration vi (see p. 239) of the parts of the human soul. Appendix B has further description.

6. See the work of spiritual thinker Andrew Cohen.

7. A kabbalistic term for the center of the tree of life. There are many good sources for study of Kabbalah, including Alan Moore's *Promethea* series, Israel Regardie's *The Middle Pillar*, and Lon Milo Duquette's *Chicken Qabalah*.

8. A thread that appears in much of his work, it can be found in *A Brief History of Everything*.

9. These various terms can be found in Theosophical works and the writings of Iamblichus of Chalcis, Aleister Crowley, Andrew Cohen, and Victor Anderson.

10. See Iamblichus *On the Mysteries* (Society of Biblical Literature, 2003).

11. See *In Search of the Miraculous: Fragments of an Unknown Teaching* by P. D. Ouspensky (Harvest, 2001).

12. The six-pointed star is called the Seal of Solomon by alchemists and others. It is also known as the Star of David. Still other Hebrew sources name the pentagram Solomon's Seal.

13 From *The Book of the Law* by Aleister Crowley (Red Wheel/Weiser Books, 2004).

14 A slightly more elaborate version is shown as the "Rite of Unbinding" in *Evolutionary Witchcraft*. The simpler, more advanced version is my variation on that taught to me by both Victor and Cora Anderson, and Feri Priestess Anaar.

15 More information on the parts of the soul can be found in *Etheric Anatomy* by Victor Anderson (Acorn Guild Press, 2004), and *Evolutionary Witchcraft*.

16 We will learn more extensive breathing techniques in the following chapter (see p. 41).

17 Again, see appendix A (see p. 248) for further explication of the parts of the human soul.

18 Feminist thinker Mary Daly pioneered this way of looking at the English language. One source for her work is the *Wickedary: A Dictionary* (New York: Hyperion Books, 1990).

19 From the works of Eliphas Lévi. The Four Powers are: to know, to will, to dare, and to keep silent. Aleister Crowley added a fifth power: to go.

20 If you are kinesthetically inclined, there are moving meditations for each of these elements on my DVD *Devotional Dance*, which is referenced in the bibliography.

21 From *Lords of Light: The Path of Initiation in the Western Mysteries*, (Rochester, VT: Destiny Books, 1990), 39.

22 A black or indigo candle is traditional to represent the Star Goddess, God Herself.

23 From various translations of 1 Kings 19. See the work of Professor Daniel C. Matt for further explication.

24 From *The Book of the Law* (book one), received by Aleister Crowley. (Boston, MA: Red Wheel/Weiser, 1987).

25 In the work of G. I. Gurdjieff, crystallization is a place of awakening. If a person crystallizes around complexes and manifestations rather than around his or her awakened being, further work is impossible until the solidification is broken.

26 A beautiful reflection of service being connection to All is seen in the Obligation of the Magister Templi which is found in ceremonial systems once a person is said to have "crossed the abyss."

27 "The work of this God" is an Anderson Feri Tradition term. The Thelemic term "True Will" is akin to this.

28 Known as *prana* in the Indian systems, *mana* in the Hawaiian, and *awen* in the Celtic, and appearing in the Greek root of *inspiration*, breath as sacred is common.

29 I happened upon working with the *eihwaz* rune for this purpose myself. I have since discovered that Edrid Thorsson and the Rune Guild have pioneered work with this form. They are based in Texas, but have study programs for any serious seeker who is drawn to the Northern traditions.

30 This version first appeared in *The Reclaiming Quarterly*. For an extended, more meditative version of this exercise, see *Evolutionary Witchcraft*. This exercise can also be done with the "four fold" or "square" breathing technique of inhaling for four counts, holding for four, exhaling for four and holding for four.

31 High-fructose corn syrup has been linked to adult-onset diabetes and myriad other health problems. It is ubiquitous in processed foods and drinks.

32 Of course, there can be other circumstances that may cause any of these, but often, looking at food, rest, and exercise can help.

33 See the "Cauldron of Poesy" as translated by Erynn Rowan Laurie, *www.seanet.com/~inisglas/* for descriptions of the three cauldrons. This also appears in the work of Caitlin and John Matthews; for example, see *The Encyclopedia of Celtic Myth and Wisdom* (Rockport, MA: Element Books, 2000).

34 This is a variation on tantric technique. I have learned this from several sources, including Dutch practitioner Tara.

35 For a tarot layout to help with these categories, see *Evolutionary Witchcraft*.

36 For a Pagan form of meditation, you may wish to reference "God Soul Listening" from *Evolutionary Witchcraft*. Otherwise, seek out a Buddhist center near you for help. Some Christian or Jewish centers also offer variations on meditative practice.

37   You may wish to reference *Pagan Prayer Beads* by John Michael Greer and Clare Vaughn (Red Wheel/Weiser, 2007).

38   I also highly recommend reading out loud the poem "Footnote" in *Howl* by Allen Ginsberg. It is a fantastic celebration of physical life. The original City Lights edition can often be found used. Harper also released a version in 1995.

39   For more information about our various "bodies" and how they operate within us, see the work of G. I. Gurdjieff. Some recommended books are in the bibliography, including those by Heap, Needleman, and Ouspensky, all students of Gurdjieff or his work.

40   There are many books, articles, and other resources for studying Abraham Maslow's theories. Here is one introductory website: *http://webspace.ship.edu/cgboer/maslow.html*

41   This is a term pioneered by mystic philosopher G. I. Gurdjieff.

42   Although the great kabbalist thinker Isaac Luria died before reaching this prescribed age.

43   See Natalie Goldberg's *Writing Down the Bones* or *Wild Mind* and Julia Cameron's *The Artist's Way* for further work on this.

44   For further exploration of this part, see "Sticky One" in *Evolutionary Witchcraft*, or read Victor Anderson's *Etheric Anatomy*.

45   See the work of Hegel for more on this particular theory.

46   The twins can also be seen as sisters or as brother and sister.

47   To gain further insight into varied personality types, studying systems such as Myers-Briggs and the enneagram can be very useful.

48   The Opener of the Way shows up in many cultures and is known by various names: Legba, Upuaut, al Fatah, Lucero, Hecate, and many others.

49   Anne Hill is a dream worker whose work can be found at *www.gnosiscafe.com*.

50   For information on the use of hagstones as aids to dreamwork, see Ray and Swansister's "Hagstones: Entranceways to Dream Magic" (Walnut Creek, CA: Witch Eye #15, Oct. 2007).

51 See also the works of Michel Foucault on culture becoming a prison that is socially patrolled. Reference *Discipline and Punish: The Birth of the Prison* (New York: Vintage Books, 1995).

52 For Magician Sam Webster's take on the distribution of the merit of our work, go to *http://www.hermetic.com/webster/pagan-dharma.html*.

53 For a nice description of a super effort, see David Kherdian's *On a Spaceship with Beelzebub* (Rochester, VT: Inner Traditions, 1998).

54 For ease of identification, I will capitalize *Will* when talking of our larger connection to purpose and use a small *w* for everyday acts of will and will development. G. I. Gurdjieff did the same for *Work* and *work*, and Aleister Crowley for *Will* and *will*. I am influenced by both people in this usage. "The work of this God" comes from Anderson Feri Tradition.

55 Many translations are available of this classic Hindu text. This particular quote is from Barbara Stoller Miller's (New York: Bantam, 1986).

56 From the poem "Der Schauende," translated by Robert Bly in *Selected Poems of Rainer Maria Rilke* (New York: Harper, 1981).

57 I devised this pentacle to help with my "Engaging the Warrior's Heart" workshops. Movements for this pentacle are included in the *Devotional Dance* DVD, available through Serpentine Music.

58 Both men were heavily influenced by the Bhagavad-Gita. Gandhi is said to have read it daily.

59 She says this as a formerly active Marxist. To find out more about Katrina's current work, please visit *www.reflectionsmyst.org*.

60 For those of you familiar with magical Kabbalah, I should note that the shadow powers are not the same as the *qlipothic*.

61 See the works of Lon Milo Duquette.

62 I had already written this segment, when, much to my delight, Feri Witch Q quoted her friend Chris Ann. I promptly slotted it into the manuscript. See *http://home.honolulu.hawaii.edu/~chris/index.htm*.

63 I use a lower case *g* here to distinguish between the strictly interior and entities commonly looked to as exterior forces, or Gods.

64   I am not speaking here of clinical depression but, rather, occasional depressed states.

65   This was Dave Seaman.

66   For some of his take on shadow work, see *The Temple of Shamanic Witchcraft* (St. Paul, MN: Llewellyn, 2005).

67   There are many books on medieval magic. *The Book of Abramelin* by Abraham von Worms (Lake worth, FL: Ibis, 2006) is one excellent source. I also thank Lon Milo Duquette for an informative class on Goetic Magic.

68   Thanks to Feri Witch Cholla for her insights into this.

69   In kabbalistic terms, this realm of self-possession is named *Tiphareth*, though a case can also be made for placing the Peacock in the sphere of *Da'ath*.

70   This is common in the Manichean worldview, which sees good and evil as opposed forces battling it out on earth. Many "monotheist" religions are really dualist religions.

71   Quantum entanglement theory posits something quite similar.

72   The Baphomet is another good example of a world bridging, pole reconciling androgyne. Many cultures and traditions have androgyne or transgender deity forms they work with. For those who are interested, Faro, Avalokitesvara, Heru Ra Ha, Antinous, Ymir, Indra and Ometeotl are but several names.

73   Until one has "crossed the abyss," it is difficult to maintain any sustained contact with the Limitless non-dual, though flashes, kisses, do occur.

74   Common symbols to seal a space are the pentagram and the *elhaz* rune.

75   Sunwise and anti-sunwise. In the Northern hemisphere, often stated as clockwise and counterclockwise.

76   The Kaaba is the sacred stone circumambulated at Mecca where Rumi, the great poet, founded the Mevlevi Order of whirling dervishes.

77   For explanations of Nuit and Hadit, see *The Book of the Law*. Feri Tradition expresses a similar mystery with the phrase, "by the center, which is the circumference of all."

78   Thanks to Robert, Katrina, Jonathan, and Ivo for better explaining electrical systems to me.

79   Found in Plato's *Phaedrus*, this was the inspiration for the Pamela Coleman Smith and A. E. Waite tarot card, the Chariot.

80   Thank you to Brother Astrum Adamas for this quote. Davies was head of Builders of the Adytum after Paul Foster Case.

81   For an excellent documentary on the rise of this culture in the last hundred years, watch *The Century of the Self* by Adam Curtis. All four episodes of this BBC documentary are available for download on the Internet.

82   This is taken from the Gnostic Mass of the Ecclesia Gnostica Catholica.

83   See her book *Taking Up the Runes* (York Beach, ME: Weiser, 2005).

84   There are many books that reproduce the works of Gandhi. This quote can be found in a collection edited by Thomas Merton titled *Gandhi on Non-Violence* (New York: New Directions, 2007).

85   For more information on her work, see *www.forestspringacupuncture.com*

86   This is a Kabbalistic idea, embedded in the Hebrew phrase *tikkun olam*.

87   This is one of the hidden Nag Hammadi texts, also known as the Qumran texts or the Gnostic Gospels. There are many sources, and I highly recommend tracking it down and reading it aloud. One source for this particular poem is *Women in Praise of the Sacred*, edited by Jane Hirshfield (New York: Harper Perennial, 1995).

88   Look to Iamblichus, *De Mysterium* and to Gregory Shaw's excellent *Theurgy and the Soul: the Neoplatonism of Iamblichus* (Penn State, 1995).

89   This was Feri priestess Anaar, speaking at Pantheacon.

90   From the article "Moorish Science." Noble Drew Ali was an interesting and controversial figure of the early 1900s. He founded the Moorish Science Temple of America.

91   From *People of the Earth: The New Pagans Speak Out* by Ellen Evert Hopman and Lawrence Bond (Rochester, VT: Inner Traditions, 1995).

92   Abraham von Worms, *The Book of Abramelin*, ed. Georg Dehn, trans. Steven Guth (Lake Worth, FL: Ibis Press, 2006), 81.

93 Feri Tradition practitioners can add another layer of meaning to this work by imagining the pentagrams as Iron and Pearl, interpenetrating the qualities of sex, pride, self, power, and passion with love, law, knowledge, liberty, and wisdom. See my book *Evolutionary Witchcraft* for more work with these pentacles.

94 Advanced practitioners who are versed in other systems of magic will also note that one can take the Seal of Solomon and overlay it with the gebo rune (the X, the gift, or equal exchange) or with Crowley's unicursal hexagram (the Seal of Solomon drawn without lifting pen from paper) and together, these become the inverse and upright pentacle merged into one shape. Look at the Merkabah shape and you will see all of these shapes included, if you know what to look for.

95 See Gershon Scholem's *Kabbalah* (New York: Meridian, 1978) for an explication of the merkabah as found in the first chapter of Ezekiel in the Hebrew Bible. A more modern usage can be found in Christopher Penczak's *Ascension Magick* (Woodbury, MN: Llewellyn, 2007). My technique comes from my own energetic workings and shifts in my spiritual work, leading me to believe that these systems naturally occur with enough occult exploration.

96 Heathens will notice the presence of the gebo rune in these shapes, and Thelemites the unicursal hexagram.

97 If you wish, you may also trace the unicursal hexagram formed within the stars.

98 There are many descriptions for what happens to some people after self-possession is accomplished. Some "cross the abyss" or join "light in extension" or become "Food for the Sun," as Gurdjieff called it. This is the work, for me, of the bodhisattva, bringing light back into the world at large. But all of this is a topic for yet another book.

99 From *Money and the Meaning of Life* (New York: Currency, 1994), p. 8.

100 From the Greek epiphania, "manifestation," often referring to the appearance of a divine being.

101 From *Money and the Meaning of Life* (New York: Currency, 1994).

102 From his book *Magick without Tears* (Reno, AZ: New Falcon, 2001).

103 See *The Middle Pillar.*

104 Neshamah is the Hebrew name for this part of soul. Some Kabbalists also posit even higher parts that stem from *neshamah*, naming them *chayah* and *yechidah*.

105 More information can be found on these by researching Hinduism, yoga, the Kabbalah, and the Cauldron of Poesy. Please also see the appendix if you need a description of the parts of soul, and illustration vi.

106 Those phrases entered Paganism via the Church of All Worlds, founded by Oberon (then Tim) and Morning Glory Zell.

107 References in order are from: Anderson Feri Tradition, Thelema, and Kabbalah. The last is my own.

108 Macgregor Mathers's *The Book of the Sacred Magic of Abramelin the Mage* (New York: Cosimo Classics, 2007) says six months, because Mathers did not have access to the full range of texts discovered by Georg Dehn, published as *The Book of Abramelin* (Ibis, 2006).

109 From *The Brothers Karamazov* (New York: Farrar, Straus and Giroux, 2002), p. 58.

110 For more information on the parts of the soul, please see *Etheric Anatomy* by Victor Anderson (Albany, CA: Acorn Guild Press, 2004) and *Evolutionary Witchcraft* (New York: Tarcher/Penguin, 2005).

Index

About the Author

T. Thorn Coyle is an internationally respected teacher and author. A spiritual seeker her whole life, she has studied the craft of magic for more than twenty-five years. Thorn combines her esoteric studies and work with her Gods and Guides to form a practice that honors the fertile dark and the limitless light. Mystic, musician, dancer, activist, and author of *Evolutionary Witchcraft*, she makes her home near the San Francisco Bay.

To Our Readers

Weiser Books, an imprint of Red Wheel/Weiser, publishes books across the entire spectrum of occult and esoteric subjects. Our mission is to publish quality books that will make a difference in people's lives without advocating any one particular path or field of study. We value the integrity, originality, and depth of knowledge of our authors.

Our readers are our most important resource, and we appreciate your input, suggestions, and ideas about what you would like to see published. Please feel free to contact us, to request our latest book catalog, or to be added to our mailing list.

Red Wheel/Weiser, LLC
500 Third Street, Suite 230
San Francisco, CA 94107
www.redwheelweiser.com